が ga	ぎ gi	ぐ gu	げ ge	ご go
ざ za	じ ji	ず zu	ぜ ze	ぞ zo
だ da	(ぢ) ji	(づ) zu	で de	ど do

ぎゃ gya	ぎゅ gyu	ぎょ gyo
じゃ ja	じゅ ju	じょ jo

ば ba	び bi	ぶ bu	べ be	ぼ bo
ぱ pa	ぴ pi	ぷ pu	ぺ pe	ぽ po

びゃ bya	びゅ byu	びょ byo
ぴゃ pya	ぴゅ pyu	ぴょ pyo

Basic Japanese for Expats

A Practical Course in Business Japanese

Otemachi Language Group
大手町ランゲージグループ

まるごとビジネス日本語初級

[Book 1]

The Japan Times

First edition: December 2009

Illustrations: Toshihiro Miyairi
Layout design and typesetting: guild
Jacket design: Hiroki Yamaoka

Published by The Japan Times, Ltd.
5-4, Shibaura 4-chome, Minato-ku, Tokyo 108-0023, Japan
Tel: 03-3453-2013
http://bookclub.japantimes.co.jp/

ISBN978-4-7890-1334-5

Printed in Japan

Preface

This book is designed for English-speaking business people whose language at work is English but who are interested in developing a basic language competence that is necessary to communicate in Japanese in day to day situations. It has been written by four experienced teachers from Otemachi Language Group, Ltd. (OLG), whose members have been teaching Japanese to business people and their families for decades, in some cases for more than thirty years.

Unlike fulltime students, business people have limited amounts of time for study, which makes them particular and demanding as to what they want to learn and achieve in the short amounts of time that they do have.

Also, the business world has changed since some of us started teaching Japanese at an in-company program in Otemachi more than thirty years ago. There is increasing mobility among our clients and our target learners have become more diverse.

Thus, we have always been seeking more effective ways of teaching the language to our students and have accumulated useful ideas and valuable experiences over the years. The result is this new textbook. Based on the learner-centered teaching method, this book enables students to learn what they really need and want.

The publication of this book would not have been possible without the countless suggestions from and the editing of Ms. Chiaki Sekido of The Japan Times. We are also very grateful to Mr. Toshihiro Miyairi for his illustrations, which have added greatly to the book's appeal. Special thanks go to Ms. Reiko Nakajima for her proofreading, comments and suggestions. And we wish to express special thanks to our former boss, Mr. James Moore, for his continuous support, encouragement, and assistance in the English portions of the text.

Finally, to our students: We wish you much success and enjoyment in using this textbook.

November 2009
Otemachi Language Group, Ltd.

Contents

About This Book

Features

Target learners

This book is basically designed for learners who study with instructors, but it can also be used with little difficulty by those who study on their own. Students will find the English translations for the dialogues and new words, instructions for drills, and explanations of grammar to be very helpful, as they will the attached CD.

Syllabus

The syllabus for this book has been organized according to the functions/notions of communication rather than grammar. The authors have carefully selected these functions/notions, incorporating them into equally carefully selected topics which illustrate typical situations that learners are likely to encounter. Sentence structures and vocabulary have been chosen according to frequency of use in social situations and their usefulness in communication, not in the order of easier to more difficult to learn.

Language teaching typically starts out with dots (words) and lines (structures), and then moves on to a situational syllabus, which focuses on how the language is used in specific situations. This approach is certainly effective when students only need to use a few fixed phrases that have limited application, but it is not very helpful for business people who need to communicate flexibly in more complicated situations.

Thus we have adopted what might be called a "three- or multi-dimensional" syllabus, in which more than two factors (language and situation) are considered. As an example, our approach incorporates the cultural backgrounds or psychological states of the people engaged in the communication, and deals with relationships between people who bring different cultural assumptions or moods to the conversation.

Language variations

The language used in the conversations varies depending on such factors as the person to whom one is speaking, the situation in which the conversation is taking place, and the reason that the people are talking; it also reflects the mood or psychological burdens of the speakers. The dialogues in this book thus put the focus on communication between people with different roles, such as superiors and subordinates, non-Japanese and Japanese, women and men, in both working and non-working situations.

We also use the informal speaking style as well as the formal style right from the beginning of the text to reflect everyday interactions in which both speech styles are used as in a mosaic.

Structure of This Book

This book consists of ten lessons, each divided into three parts: 1) Dialogues, 2) Grammar Notes, and 3) Drills.

1) Dialogues

There are three dialogues in every lesson:

Dialogue 1, which is presented in the formal speaking style, represents the pedagogical goal for the learners. They are expected to reproduce this dialogue.

Dialogue 2 mixes formal and informal speech styles. In this dialogue, the Japanese speak in a rather informal speech style, while non-Japanese speak in a formal speech style.

Comprehension Drill(s) follow immediately after Dialogues 1 and 2. They include true/false questions and questions requiring the learner to put sentences in the correct order (only in relation to Dialogue 1).

Each lesson concludes with a **Closing Dialogue**. To the extent possible, these dialogues have been designed to approximate conversations from the real world. In order for students to develop language recognition ability, they have not been modified greatly from language that is used in actual situations.

Dialogue 2 and the Closing Dialogue are designed for the purpose of language perception rather than reproduction. Woven through each of the dialogues is a story line that continues through all of the ten lessons.

2) Grammar Notes

Grammar Notes explain how the Japanese language works rather than focus on grammatical rules. That is, they explain what structure should be used to express a certain function or notion in a given context. The structures are carefully selected to be appropriate for the target learners of this textbook. The explanation is practical and sometimes based on the mistakes that the learners are likely to make. Many diagrams and tables are used to help busy and pragmatic business people quickly grasp the picture of communication rules.

3) Drills

Four different drills are presented in this section: A. Conversation Drills, B. Grammar & Vocabulary Building Drills, C. Listening Tasks, and D. Review Drills.

A. Conversation Drills are practices whose aim is to reproduce the target dialogue. Students fill in the blanks according to the English instructions (not translations) and complete the dialogues.

B. Grammar & Vocabulary Building Drills provide such practices as substitution drills, fill-in-the-blank drills, and questions and answers. They enable learners to master the grammar points explained in Grammar Notes and to expand the vocabulary related to the function/notion for each lesson. Many illustrations are used as cues here for the sake of efficient practice.

C. There are three types of **Listening Tasks**: catching the keyword, choosing the appropriate answers for the questions asked, and choosing the correct pictures/words/phrases that match the content.

D. Review Drills basically consist of three types of drills: creating sentences according to the English instructions; matching questions with responses; and arranging sentences into their correct order.

4) Other sections

Culture Notes: Notes on Japanese culture are provided at the end of Lessons 1, 3, 5, 7 and 10. Learners can take a break from their lessons and enjoy reading them.

Appendixes, etc.: At back of this book, there are fourteen appendixes, in addition to scripts for Listening Tasks, answers for drills, and an index. You will also find a CD attached, which includes all the dialogues as well as the drills marked with the CD icon ⬛.

Characters in This Book

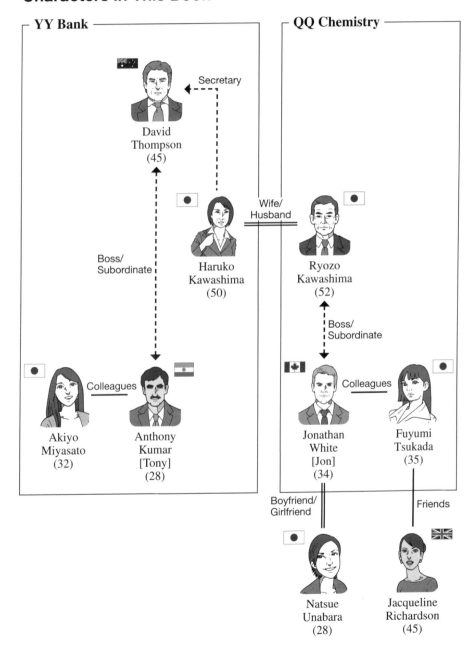

YY Bank

David Thompson (45)

← Secretary

Haruko Kawashima (50) — Wife/Husband — Ryozo Kawashima (52)

Boss/Subordinate

Boss/Subordinate

Akiyo Miyasato (32) — Colleagues — Anthony Kumar [Tony] (28)

QQ Chemistry

Jonathan White [Jon] (34) — Colleagues — Fuyumi Tsukada (35)

Boyfriend/Girlfriend

Friends

Natsue Unabara (28)

Jacqueline Richardson (45)

このテキストをお使いになる先生方へ

　本教材は、ビジネスピープルを主な対象にした日本語初級テキストシリーズの Book 1 として作成されました。全10課構成で、初級の入門レベルをカバーしています。時間に制約のあるビジネスピープルの学習環境やニーズをふまえ、文型や語彙の難易度を重視する積み上げ式ではなく、頻度や有用性を重視したファンクショナルなシラバスを採用しました。

1. テキストの構成

Dialogues

　各課には3つのダイアログがあります。

　Dialogue 1 はフォーマルスタイル（です・ます体）の会話で、その課のゴールとして学習者が運用できるよう目標とするものです。意味、文法等を確認し、練習をして定着を図ります。

　Dialogue 2 は、登場人物の人間関係によってフォーマル（です・ます体）・インフォーマル（普通体）の両スタイルが入り混じった会話であることに注目してください。Dialogue 1・2 それぞれのすぐ後には、意味・内容確認のため **正誤ドリル** があります。

　各課の終わりには、**Closing Dialogue** が提示されています。これは、できるだけ現実の会話に近い自然な表現を残しているので、聞いて、あるいは、読んで意味が分かればいいと思います。このレベルでは難しいだろうと思われる文型は、そのまま一つの表現として理解するよう指導します。

　なお、これらのダイアログは、主要登場人物を中心に、全編を通してストーリー性を持って展開していきます。

Grammar Notes

　Grammar Notes は、学習者に事前に読んできてもらい、質問があればクラスで取り上げる程度にします。ただし、ドリルをするときに Grammar Notes の関連事項に戻ってルールを確認するのも効果的な使い方です。

　文型の構造は一覧できるように表にしましたが、このテキストの文法説明は、構造より「その文型が実際のコミュニケーションの中でどのように機能するのか」に焦点を当てて書かれていますので、常にファンクションに注目して指導してください。

　なお、上記 Dialogue の説明でも触れたように、このテキストでは Dialogue 2 や Closing Dialogue で早くからインフォーマルスタイル（普通体）を導入します。Grammar Notes では4課でインフォーマルスタイル（普通体）及びフォーマル（で

す・ます体）を「Speech Level 1」及び「Speech Level 2」として説明し、8課で両スタイルの動詞の活用が提示されます。これは、教室の外での日本人同士の会話などを早くから理解できるようにするためです。インフォーマルスタイルの運用を学習者に強制する必要はありません。

さらに、学習者に、紋切り型の発話ではなくより自然な会話を覚えてもらうために「会話ストラテジー」も随所に提示しました。

Drills

このセクションには4つのタイプのドリルがあります。

- **Ⓐ Conversation Drills** （会話ドリル）
- **Ⓑ Grammar & Vocabulary Building Drills** （文法・語彙ドリル）
- **Ⓒ Listening Tasks** （聴解タスク）
- **Ⓓ Review Drills** （復習ドリル）

Ⓐ Conversation Drills は、会話の下線部について、（　　　）に英語で書かれている指示にあう発話を考えるドリルです。（　　　）内の英語は訳ではなく、どのような発話をするかについての指示書きであることに注意してください。

Ⓑ Grammar & Vocabulary Building Drills は、機械的な代入、変換、穴埋め、質問等で、文法・文型の定着と同時に、語彙の拡大を図ります。

Ⓒ Listening Tasks は、添付のCDを聞いて解答します。

Ⓓ Review Drills は、英語の指示に従って質問文を作るもの（学習者がよく聞く質問です）、質問と答えや発話と受け答えの正しいペアを結びつけるもの、バラバラになった文を並べ替えて正しい会話にするもの、などがあります。

その他

CULTURE NOTE として日本文化についてのコラムを5つ設けました。1課・3課・5課・7課・10課の後に掲載されています。

巻末には、助数詞や活用形などの文法項目をより詳しい14の表にまとめた **Appendixes** のほか、聴解タスクのスクリプト、ドリルの解答、さくいんを収録しています。

また、添付のCDには、全ダイアログと、CDマーク🎵の付いているドリルが収録されています。

2. テキストの使い方

授業時数

1対1の授業でこのテキスト（Book 1）を修了するのに、1課4時間、総計で50時間程度を想定しています。例えば、1週間に60分授業を2回受ける学習者の

場合、25週間＝約6カ月で修了することを目標にします。1課4時間とすると、計算上は40時間で修了できると考えられますが、キャンセルがあると次のレッスンは復習をしてから進まなければなりません。そのようなことも考慮して、個人差はありますが、約50時間で10課を修了することを目安に使ってみてください。

課・セクションの使用順序

　次にこのテキストは、1課から始めて10課まで、と順序よく使う必要はありません。本書のシラバスは、文型や語彙の難易度を重視する積み上げ式ではなく、頻度と有用性を第一に考えたものですから、学習者のニーズや希望に合わせて、どの課からでも始めることができます。学習者は、どこで、誰に、どんなことを言いたいのか、そのためにはどんな語彙・文型を必要としているのか、こんな場面に遭遇するだろうか・しないだろうかなど、教師は常に自問自答しながら、適切な情報が提供できるインフォーマントとしてクラスに臨むことが大切です。

　また、各課内での導入の順序も、学習者の個性、希望、ニーズによって異なります。トップダウン式では、まずダイアログを聞いたり、読んだり、復唱したりしながら、英訳やイラストを見て状況・内容を把握した後に、正誤ドリルをします。文法は予習として読んできてもらいますが、質問があればクラスで説明をします。そして、ドリルへと進みます。会話ドリルでは、学習者が遭遇するであろう状況を考えて、新出語彙なども躊躇せずに与えて十分な運用の練習をし、その後提示されている順にドリルを終えて、再度ダイアログに戻って定着度を確認します。

　逆にボトムアップ式として、単語を確認し、文法を説明し、その関係項目のドリルをした後に、まとめとしてダイアログへと進む、という方法も可能です。

　なお、ビジネスピープルの場合、ルールを最初に把握する演繹法（deductive way）を好み、例文等からルールを類推する帰納法（inductive way）は時間の無駄と考える学習者も少なくありません。同じ理由で入門レベルでは、時間のかかる直説法よりも的確な英語を適宜使用して、説明に要する時間を最小限に抑えるような教え方が好まれます。例文をたくさん挙げて日本語だけで分かってもらおうとすると意図しない方向に発展し、説明の核心に至らないうちに授業が終わってしまう場合も出てきます。事前の綿密な教材研究や教案作りも欠かせませんが、クラスでの学習者のニーズや希望に敏感かつ即座に対応できるエネルギーを温存しておくことが大切です。そのためには、英会話ではなく文法機能や意味を的確な英語で与えることができる教師を目指して研鑽を積み、学習者が満足するような教え方を工夫することが重要です。

　最後に、OLGではブログを開設しています。本教材について、皆様のフィードバックを得ることができれば幸いです。

　OLG オンライン：http://olg-online.cocolog-nifty.com/blog/

Basic Japanese for Expats

A Practical Course in Business Japanese

[Book 1]

LESSON 1: INTRODUCING AND GREETING

—Hajimemashite. 'How do you do?'

Dialogue 1   Introducing oneself and others · · · · · · · ·

(Ryozo Kawashima and David Thompson introduce themselves to each other. They work for different companies.)

Kawashima (R): QQ *kagaku no Kawashima desu.*

Tonpuson: *Hajimemashite,* YY *ginkō no Dēbiddo Tonpuson desu.*
    Dōzo yoroshiku. Dēbiddo to yonde kudasai.

Kawashima: *Hajimemashite, kochira koso yoroshiku onegaishimasu.*

(Then Fuyumi Tsukada comes in. Mr. Kawashima introduces her, a member of his staff, to Mr. Thompson from YY Bank.)

Kawashima: *Goshōkai shimasu. Tsukada Fuyumi desu.*
    (To Ms. Tsukada) *Kochira wa,* YY *ginkō no Dēbiddo Tonpuson-san desu.*

Tsukada: *Tsukada to mōshimasu.*
    Dōzo yoroshiku onegaishimasu.

Tonpuson: *Dēbiddo Tonpuson desu.*

Tsukada: *Tonpuson-san . . . desu ka.*

Tonpuson: *Hai. Dēbiddo to yonde kudasai.*
    Dōzo yoroshiku.

> Mr. Ryozo Kawashima: (I'm) Kawashima from QQ Chemistry.
> Mr. Thompson: How do you do? (lit., For the first time.)
>   (I'm) David Thompson of YY Bank. Glad to meet you. Please call me David.
> Mr. Kawashima: How do you do? Glad to meet you, too.
> ******

Vocabulary

kagaku: chemistry
no: of
desu: am; are; is
Hajimemashite.: How do you do?
ginkō: bank
dōzo: please

yoroshiku: it is a pleasure to meet you
~ to yonde kudasai.: Please call me ~.
kochira koso: me, too
onegaishimasu: please [requesting]
shōkai suru (shimasu): to introduce
kochira: this (person)

wa: [topic marker]
~ to mōshimasu.: I'm called ~.; My name is ~.
ka: [question marker]
-san: [addressing people]
hai: yes; right

Mr. Kawashima:	Let me introduce (my assistant) to you. (This is) Ms. Fuyumi Tsukada. This is Mr. David Thompson of YY Bank.
Ms. Tsukada:	I'm Tsukada (lit., I'm called Tsukada). Pleased to meet you.
Mr. Thompson:	I'm David Thompson.
Ms. Tsukada:	Mr. Thompson (is my pronunciation all right)?
Mr. Thompson:	Yes (fine). Call me David. Pleased to meet you, too.

川島良三：　　QQ化学の川島です。

トンプソン：　はじめまして、YY銀行のデービッド・トンプソンです。

　　　　　　　どうぞ　よろしく。デービッドと　よんでください。

川島：　　　　はじめまして、こちらこそ　よろしく　おねがいします。

******

川島：　　　　ごしょうかいします。塚田冬美です。

　　　　　　　こちらは、YY銀行のデービッド・トンプソンさんです。

塚田：　　　　塚田と　もうします。どうぞ　よろしく　おねがいします。

トンプソン：　デービッド・トンプソンです。

塚田：　　　　トンプソンさん……ですか。

トンプソン：　はい。デービッドと　よんでください。どうぞ　よろしく。

● Comprehension Drill

1. Listen to or read Dialogue 1 and decide if the following statements are true, false or you don't know as not enough information has been given.

1. Mr. Thompson works for YY Bank.	(T / F / DK)
2. Mr. Thompson is a customer of QQ Chemistry.	(T / F / DK)
3. Mr. Kawashima and Mr. Thompson have met before.	(T / F / DK)
4. Ms. Tsukada is Mr. Thompson's colleague.	(T / F / DK)
5. Mr. Thompson wants to be called David.	(T / F / DK)

2. Put these sentences in the correct order to make a conversation.

(a) → (d) → (c) → (b) → (e)

a. QQ *kagaku no Kawashima desu.*

b. *Goshōkai shimasu. Tsukada Fuyumi desu. Kochira wa,* YY *ginkō no Dēbiddo Tonpuson-san desu.*

c. *Hajimemashite, kochira koso yoroshiku onegaishimasu.*

d. *Hajimemashite,* YY *ginkō no Dēbiddo Tonpuson desu. Dōzo yoroshiku.*

e. *Tsukada to mōshimasu. Dōzo yoroshiku onegaishimasu.*

Dialogue 2 Greetings ···················· Formal Informal

a. Daily greeting `03`

(On the way to the office in the morning.)

Tonpuson: *Ohayō gozaimasu. Ii tenki desu ne.*

Kinjo no hito: *Hontō ni ii tenki desu ne. Itte rasshai.*

> Mr. Thompson: Good morning. It's fine weather, isn't it?
> Neighbor: Yes, it really is. Have a nice day! (lit., Hurry back.)

b. Leave taking `04`

(Jonathan White, Ms.Tsukada's colleague, is still working hard at around 8 p.m. Ms. Tsukada is ready to leave.)

Tsukada: *Osaki ni.*

Howaito: *Otsukaresama deshita.*

Tsukada: *Ja, mata ashita.*

> Ms. Tsukada: Bye! (lit., I'm leaving before you.)
> Mr. White: OK. See you. (lit., You should be tired.)
> Ms. Tsukada: See you tomorrow.

c. Expressing gratitude `05`

(Jacqueline Richardson and Fuyumi Tsukada have just run into each other.)

Richādoson: *Fuyumi-san, senjitsu wa iroiro arigatō gozaimashita.*

Tsukada: *Iie, kochira koso.*
 Korekara mo yoroshiku.

Richādoson: *Hai.*

Vocabulary

Ohayō gozaimasu.: Good morning.	*Osaki ni.*: lit., I'm leaving before you.	*senjitsu*: the other day
ii: good		*iroiro*: a lot; various
tenki: weather	*Otsukaresama deshita.*: lit., You should be tired.	*arigatō gozaimashita*: thank you very much (for what you have done)
ne: isn't it?; right?		
kinjo no hito: neighbor	*ja*: well then	*iie.*: Don't mention it.
hontō ni: really	*mata*: again	*korekara*: from now on
Itte rasshai.: Have a good day.	*ashita*: tomorrow	*mo*: also

4

> Ms. Richardson: Thank you for everything (lit., for what you have done) the other day, Fuyumi.
>
> Ms. Tsukada: Don't mention it. Same to you. I'd be happy to be of help to you anytime. (lit., I hope we will support each other in the future, too.)
>
> Ms. Richardson: Sure.

a.

トンプソン： おはようございます。いいてんきですね。

近所の人： ほんとうに　いいてんきですね。いってらっしゃい。

b.

塚田： おさきに。

ホワイト： おつかれさまでした。

塚田： じゃ、また　あした。

c.

リチャードソン： 冬美さん、せんじつは　いろいろ　ありがとうございました。

塚田： いいえ、こちらこそ。これからも　よろしく。

リチャードソン： はい。

● **Comprehension Drill**

Listen to or read Dialogue 2 and decide if the following statements are true, false or you don't know as not enough information has been given.

1. Mr. Thompson goes out on a clear morning. (T / F / DK)
2. It is cold when Mr. Thompson goes out. (T / F / DK)
3. Mr. White leaves the office before Ms. Tsukada. (T / F / DK)
4. Mr. White and Ms. Tsukada work at the same company. (T / F / DK)
5. Ms. Richardson hasn't met Ms. Tsukada before. (T / F / DK)

◆　　◆　　◆

Grammar Note 1 Introducing oneself（自己紹介）

a. [Person's Name] *desu.*

Family Name	
Kawashima	*desu.*
'(I'm) Kawashima.'	

This is used when introducing yourself to someone else. Japanese people usually use their family names in business situations as well as in non-business situations. Occasionally full names are used before *desu* 'am/is/are' in business situations in the order of family name and first name, as shown in the first box below. In non-business/informal situations, only the speaker's first name may sometimes be used. Also note that the first name and family name order is usually used when a non-Japanese person introduces him/herself. See the second box below:

Family Name	First Name	
Tsukada	*Fuyumi*	*desu.*
'(I'm) Fuyumi Tsukada.' (D-1)		

First Name	Family Name	
David	Thompson	*desu.*
'(I'm) David Thompson.' (D-1)		

b. [Company Name] *no* [Person's Name] *desu.*   '(I'm) ~ of ~.'

Company Name		Person's Name	
YY *ginkō*	*no*	David Thompson	*desu.*
'(I'm) David Thompson of YY Bank.' (D-1)			

This pattern is used when you identify yourself and your company affiliation. When a Japanese business person introduces him/herself, it's important to mention which company or group s/he belongs to.

No is a particle which connects two nouns. It signifies that the first noun is giving more information about the noun that follows. In other words, "Noun + *no*" modifies the second noun. One of the fundamental rules in Japanese grammar is that the modifier always precedes the modified word or phrase, which is not always true in English.

c. [Person's Name] *to mōshimasu.*   'I'm called ~.'

Person's Name		Verb
Tsukada	*to*	*mōshimasu.*
'(I'm) called Tsukada.' (D-1)		

This pattern is often used instead of ~ *desu* in extremely formal situations both in business and non-business situations.

d. [Name] *to yonde kudasai.* 'Call me ~, please.'

Person's Name		Verb
David	*to*	*yonde kudasai.*
'Call me David(, please).' (D-1)		

Having introduced yourself with your full name, you can let your business associates know how you would like to be called in a friendly or shorter way. This can be important because in formal business situations, your name might be difficult for a Japanese person to catch or to repeat. It would be easier for you just to memorize and use the two sentences mentioned above as set-phrases because a structural discussion would be a bit complicated at this stage.

Grammar Note 2   Introducing others one by one (一人ずつ他者紹介)

a. Introducing someone from another company

Kochira wa [Name]-*san desu.*   'This is ~.'

	TM*	Person's Name	
Kochira	*wa*	David Thompson-*san*	*desu.*
'This is Mr. David Thompson.' (D-1)			

*TM: Topic Marker

You can use this pattern when introducing people from other companies or groups. *Kochira wa* literally means 'As for this way/person ~' and is necessary when introducing a group of people one after another.

b. Particle [*wa*]

Wa is a topic marker which denotes that you are speaking about one person as opposed to the rest of the people in a group, who are being introduced one by one.

c. -*san*

When you introduce yourself/your colleagues/family members, you should not use -*san*, but don't forget to add -*san* when introducing others. The -*san* follows the full name or the family name or even at times the first name. The -*san* is a gender-free and status-free suffix and it corresponds to 'Mr./Mrs./Ms.' in English. Also, remember that when you answer the phone and identify yourself, you should say "[Your Name] *desu*" not "[Your Name]-*san desu.*"
Caution: Do not add [-*san*] to your own name, or to the names of your colleagues or family members.

d. Sentence particle [*ka*]

Constructing a question can be accomplished by simply adding *ka* to the end of any sentence. Although a rising/falling intonation for *ka* denotes its specific mode in a sentence, in this usage *ka* functions as a question marker with rising intonation as when Ms. Tsukada says, "*Tonpuson-san desu ka.*" in Dialogue 1.

First/Family Name		SP*
Tompuson-san	*desu*	*ka.*
'Mr. Thompson?' (D-1)		

*SP: Sentence Particle

Grammar Note 3 Introducing colleagues or family members to others（同僚・家族を紹介する）

a. *Goshōkai shimasu.* [Person's Name/Family Term] *desu.*   'Let me introduce, ~.'

C.Starter*	Person's Name/Family Term	
Goshōkai shimasu.	*Tsukada Fuyumi*	*desu.*
	Tsuma	
'Let me introduce, (this is) Ms. Fuyumi Tsukada.' (D-1)		
'Let me introduce, (this is) my wife.'		

*C.Starter: Conversation Starter

b. [Position/Family Term] *no* [Name] *desu.*

Position/Family Term		Name	
Sutaffu	*no*	Jonathan White	*desu.*
Tsuma		Louise	
'(This is) a member of my staff, Jonathan White.'			
'(This is) my wife, Louise.'			

When introducing a colleague or a family member, to the manager or someone from another company, use pattern a. If you want to add their names or other specific information, use pattern b.

Grammar Note 4 Greetings（挨拶）

a. Three speech levels: informal, formal and very formal

Level 1	Informal	with family, colleagues, subordinates, close friends
Level 2	Formal	with managers, strangers, acquaintances, friends
Level 3	Very formal	with directors, managers, clients/customers

In Japanese, how one sees his/her relationship to others is reflected in the speech level s/he uses. Here, we will discuss the three speech levels shown above.

Level 1, the informal speech style, is used among family members, colleagues or close friends. Also when a boss says "Good morning" or "Goodbye" to his subordinates at the office, he uses Level 1.

In speaking with a stranger, an acquaintance, a senior friend or your boss, Level 2 is used. This level is considered to be neutral and polite enough for anybody or any situation.

Level 3, the very formal speaking style, is usually used when speaking to a boss at a senior level such as managers, or to clients/customers in any situation.

In business situations, business cards are usually exchanged to confirm one's social status and to determine what the appropriate speech level should be. When a higher status/position is recognized from the card, the speech level is sometimes changed from Level 2 to Level 3 to show one's respect and humbleness even if at an informal drinking place. However, the more often people meet, the closer they will become, consequently, the less formal the speech level will become.

b. Daily greetings

Speech Level	Japanese Expressions	English Equivalent
Level 1	*Ohayō.*	Good morning.
Level 2 & 3	*Ohayō gozaimasu.*	
Level 1 & 2	*Konnichiwa.*	Hello.
Level 3		Good afternoon.
Level 1 & 2	*Konbanwa.*	Hello.
Level 3		Good evening.
Level 1	*Oyasumi.**	Good night.
Level 2 & 3	*Oyasuminasai.**	

*Do not use this expression when you leave the office at around 5 p.m.

c. Commenting on the weather

[Today's weather] *desu ne.*

Weather		SP*
Ii tenki	*desu*	*ne.*
'It's fine weather, isn't it?' (D-2)		

*SP: Sentence Particle

After greetings such as *Ohayō gozaimasu* or *Konnichiwa*, Japanese people usually talk about the weather. They usually do not say *Ogenki desu ka* 'How are you?' except when they are genuinely enquiring after someone's health.

d. Sentence particle [*ne*]

In Dialogue 2, the sentence particle *ne* is used to ask for or to show agreement as in *Ii tenki desu ne.—Hontō ni ii tenki desu ne.* 'It is fine weather, isn't it?—Yes, it really is.' Both sentences are pronounced with a falling intonation.

e. Leave taking: *Osaki ni, otsukaresama.*   'Goodbye.'

Osaki ni, otsukaresama is often used around the office when someone leaves before his/her colleagues, as presented in Dialogue 2. Here are more expressions that can be used in leave taking:

Speech Level	Starters	Secondary Expressions		Core Expressions
Level 1	*Ja,* 'Well,'	*mata* 'again'		*Sayonara.* 'Goodbye.'
Level 2	*Sore ja,* 'Well then,'	*mata* 'again'	*(ato de* 'later')	*Sayōnara.* (Non-business) *Otsukaresama.** 'lit., You should be tired.' *Shitsurei shimasu.* 'Goodbye.'
			(ashita 'tomorrow')	
			(suiyōbi 'Wednesday')	
			(raishū 'next week')	
		osaki ni 'lit., before you'		
Level 3	*Sore dewa,* 'Well then,'	*mata* 'again'	*(nochihodo* 'later')	*Shitsurei itashimasu.* 'Goodbye.'

*Otsukaresama used to be used only for leave taking, that is, people said this to someone who was leaving the office, but recently, it is used throughout the day when people see each other and corresponds to 'Hello' in English.

f. Expressing gratitude   —*Arigatō gozaimasu.*   'Thank you.'

Speech Level	Non-past	Past
Level 1	*Arigatō./Dōmo.* 'Thanks.'	—
Level 2	*Arigatō gozaimasu.* 'Thank you.'	*Arigatō gozaimashita.* 'Thank you for what you've done for me.'
Level 3	*Dōmo arigatō gozaimasu.* 'Thank you very much.'	*Dōmo arigatō gozaimashita.* 'Thank you very much for what you have done.'

◆　　◆　　◆

A Conversation Drills

Drill 1. Complete the following conversations.

1. Introduce yourself to Mr. Akagawa, who is from another company.

    Akagawa: QQ *kagaku no Akagawa desu.*

    You: (a) _____ (Greet properly.)

                  (b) _____ (Say your name and company name.)

                  (c) _____ (Greet properly.)

    Akagawa: *Kochira koso yoroshiku onegaishimasu.*

2. Introduce Ms. Shiroyama, your colleague, to Mr. Takagi, who is from another company (EFG Trading).

    You: (a) _____ (Say that you're going to introduce.)

                  (b) _____ (Give your colleague's name.)

                  (c) _____ (Introduce Mr. Takagi.)

    Shiroyama: *Shiroyama to mōshimasu. Dōzo yoroshiku onegaishimasu.*

    Takagi: EFG *shōji no Takagi desu. Kochira koso yoroshiku onegaishimasu.*

3. Introduce yourself at a party.

    Japanese: [Your name]-*san okuni wa dochira desu ka.*

    You: (a) _____ *desu.*

    Japanese: [Your country] *no dochira desu ka.*

    You: (b) _____ *desu.* (Give the name of the city you are from.)

    Japanese: *Aa sō desu ka. Ii tokoro desu ne.*

4. Your colleague is still working hard at around 8 p.m. on Friday night, and you are going to leave.

    You: (a) _____ (Say you're leaving before your colleague.)

    Colleague: *Otsukaresama deshita.*

    You: (b) _____ (Say you will see each other next week.)

5. You are getting ready to leave after dinner at the Kawashima's residence.

    You: (a) _____ (Say it's almost time to leave.)

                  (b) _____ (Say thank you for the dinner.)

    Ms. Kawashima: *Aa sō desu ka. Mata irasshatte kudasai ne.* 'Please come again.'

    You: (c) _____ (Express your gratitude.)

                  Ojama shimashita. (lit., Sorry to have bothered you.)

Vocabulary

1. *shōji:* trading company   *dochira:* where   *Gochisōsama deshita.:* Thank you
    (o)kuni: country   *sorosoro:* almost time to do   for the dinner.

B Grammar & Vocabulary Building Drills

Drill 2. Make sentences by substituting the underlined parts with the words given.

1. Introduce Mr. Yamamoto, from your company, to a person from another company.

> *Goshōkai shimasu. <u>Kachō</u> no Yamamoto desu.*

(a) *buchō*   (b) *tantō*   (c) *dōryō*   (d) *sutaffu*   (e) *jōshi*

2. Introduce your family to your boss.

> *Buchō, goshōkai shimasu. <u>Tsuma</u> desu.*

(a) *shujin*   (b) *musume*   (c) *musuko*   (d) *chichi*   (e) *haha*

3. Tell someone what your job is.

> *(O)shigoto wa nan desu ka. — <u>Ginkōin</u> desu.*

(a) *kaishain*   (b) *eigo no kyōshi*   (c) *isha*

(d) *bengoshi*   (e) *shufu*

C Listening Tasks

Drill 3. Listen to the CD and choose the appropriate pictures for the statements.

1. (   )   2. (   )   3. (   )   4. (   )   5. (   )

a.	b.	c.	d.	e.
KK *Ginkō*	KK *Ginkō*	JJ *Shōken*	JJ *Shōken*	JJ *Hoken*
Kanada	*Igirisu*	*Ōsutoraria*	*Amerika*	*Doitsu*

Vocabulary

2. *kachō:* section manager
  buchō: department manager
  tantō: person in charge of a task
  dōryō: colleague
  jōshi: boss
  tsuma: wife
  shujin: husband

  musume: daughter
  musuko: son
  chichi: father
  haha: mother
  ginkōin: bank employee
  kaishain: company employee
  eigo no kyōshi: English teacher

  isha: doctor
  bengoshi: lawyer
  shufu: housewife
3. *shōken:* securities company
  hoken: insurance

Drill 4. Listen to the CD and choose the appropriate pictures for the dialogues.

1. (   )   2. (   )   3. (   )   4. (   )   5. (   )

D Review Drills

Drill 5. Read the following instructions and make sentences.

How would you:

1. introduce yourself to your client?

2. respond to #1?

3. introduce Ms. Tsukada from QQ Chemistry to your colleague?

4. introduce your wife/husband to your boss?

5. greet someone when you leave the office earlier than anybody else?

6. respond to #5?

7. express your gratitude to someone for what has been done?

8. greet someone on a nice day?

Drill 6. Match the responses with the questions/remarks.

1. *Okuni wa dochira desu ka.*   ·   · a. *Iie kochira koso.*
2. *Senjitsu wa iroiro arigatō gozaimashita.* ·   · b. *Hontō ni samui desu ne.*
3. *Ohayō gozaimasu. Samui desu ne.*   ·   · c. *Ostukaresama.*
4. *Osaki ni shitsurei shimasu.*   ·   · d. *Kanada desu.*

13

Drill 7. Complete the dialogues by changing the following sentences to the correct order.

1. (a) → (   ) → (   ) → (   )

    a. *Shitsurei shimasu, watakushi kō iu mono desu ga . . .*

    b. Bill *to yonde kudasai.*

    c. OLS *ginkō no Yamamoto-san desu ka. Hajimemashite,* EFG *shōji no* William Brassington *desu. Dōzo yoroshiku.*

    d. Brassington-*san . . . desu ka.*

2. (b) → (   ) → (   ) → (   )

    a. *Tonpuson desu. Dōzo yoroshiku.*

    b. *Tonpuson-san, tsuma desu. Kochira* YY *ginkō no Tonpuson-san.*

    c. *Hajimemashite, Akagawa no kanai de gozaimasu.*

    d. *Shujin ga itsumo osewa ni natte orimasu.* 'Thank you for your support to my husband.'

Vocabulary
7. *kō iu mono:*   like this

(After work, some of the staff of QQ Chemistry are having an informal welcome party at a *yakitori* place.)

Akagawa: *Shōkai suru yo. Tsukada-san, Shiroyama-san, Kuroda-san, Aoshima-san.*
Kochira Jonasan.

Shiroyama: *Jonasan nani?*

Howaito: *Jonasan Howaito desu. Jon to yonde kudasai.*
Yoroshiku onegaishimasu.

Nihonjin: *Tsukada desu./Shiroyama desu./Kuroda desu./Aoshima desu. . . . Yoroshiku!*

Akagawa: *Jā, kanpai!*

******

Aoshima: *Sore de, Jon, itsu kita n desu ka.*

Howaito: *(?!)*

Shiroyama: *Itsu Nihon e kimashita ka.*

Howaito: *(?!)*

Kuroda: *Kuni wa Amerika?*

Howaito: *Iie, chigaimasu. Kanada desu.*

赤川： しょうかいするよ。塚田さん、白山さ
ん、黒田さん、青島さん。
こちら　ジョナサン。

白山： ジョナサン　なに？

ホワイト：ジョナサン・ホワイトです。ジョンと
よんでください。
よろしく　おねがいします。

日本人： 塚田です。／白山です。／黒田です。／
青島です。……よろしく！

赤川： じゃあ、かんぱい！

******

青島： それで、ジョン、いつ　きたんですか。

ホワイト：(?!)

白山： いつ　日本へ　きましたか。

ホワイト：(?!)

黒田： くには　アメリカ？

ホワイト：いいえ、ちがいます。カナダです。

Mr. Akagawa:	(Jonathan,) I'll introduce (your colleagues to you). (They are) Ms. Tsukada, Ms. Shiroyama, Mr. Kuroda and Mr. Aoshima. (To everybody) This is Jonathan.
Ms. Shiroyama:	Jonathan who? (lit., Jonathan what?)
Mr. White:	(My name is) Jonathan White. Call me Jon. Nice to meet everybody.
Japanese Staff:	(I'm) Tsukada/(I'm) Shiroyama/(I'm) Kuroda/(I'm) Aoshima. . . . Nice to meet you, too.
Mr. Akagawa:	Well then, cheers!

******

Mr. Aoshima:	Jon, when did you come (to Japan)?
Mr. White:	(?!)
Ms. Shiroyama:	When did you come to Japan?
Mr. White:	(?!)
Mr. Kuroda:	Are you from the States? (lit., Is your country the U.S.A?)
Mr. White:	No, (lit., that's different) I'm from Canada.

CULTURE NOTE 1

How do Japanese people refer to each other in Japanese?

The way that the Japanese call and address other people changes depending on the group to which one belongs. Note that there exists the conceptual distinction of *uchi* 'inside, in-groups' and *soto* 'outside, non-in-groups' in Japanese society. When you speak with someone from a non-in-group, that person must be respected, and the in-group humbled. Within one's immediate in-group, i.e., in a family traditionally, there is a hierarchy. The father is at the top of the pyramid, followed by the mother, the oldest son, the second son and the older sister and the youngest sister in the order mentioned. Children call their father and mother, respectfully, *otōsan* 'father' and *okāsan* 'mother' in the family, which are polite terms. However, when they talk about their own father and mother in public, they are trained to mention humbly *chichi* for 'father' and *haha* for 'mother.'

One can observe that father and mother call each other *otōsan* and *okāsan* from the children's point of view in the family as well as in public. Thus, oddly enough outside the family *otōsan* and *okāsan* are used when sales clerks are addressing men and women in a shopping arcade. A funny situation is observed: In a foreign country, a sales girl who spoke Japanese reasonably well was trying to sell a leather coat to a Japanese man, saying 'Otōsan, this coat looks good on you,' or 'Otōsan, you should buy this.' Then, her boss who was standing by her, and must have understood Japanese well asked her, "Why do you call him 'Otōsan'? He is not your father."

Also, the second person pronoun *anata* 'you' is rarely used in daily conversation, but some wives use it with their husbands. Here is a famous old story: An old-fashioned husband calls his wife just "Oi (Hey!)." Everyday he says, "Oi, ocha, furo, meshi. (Hey, [give me] tea, [I'll take] a bath and [I'll eat] dinner)" to his wife.

The same distinction between in-group members and non-in-group members is true for other groups such as companies. In your company, the department where you belong is your in-group but a different department becomes non-in-group. At some traditional Japanese companies, titles such as *shachō* 'president,' *senmu* 'senior managing director,' *jōmu* 'managing director,' *buchō* 'department head' and *kachō* 'section manager' are used around the office instead of the persons' names. And -*san*/-*sama* will be added to those titles for people from other departments/companies. Here is a real story: there was a foreign-owned company in Otemachi in Tokyo, where a Japanese person was appointed president for the first time. He made a clear announcement that he would encourage people to use -*san* around the office no matter what titles s/he may have as -*san* is gender free, rank free, and age free as well as marriage-status free.

16

LESSON 2:   NUMBERS
—*Kodomo-san wa nan-nin desu ka.*
'How many children do you have?'

Dialogue 1 Exchanging personal information · · · · · · Formal

(Ryozo Kawashima and David Thompson are at a dinner party after some presentations.)

Kawashima (R): A, Tonpuson-san, senjitsu wa dōmo.

Tonpuson: Kawashima-san deshita ne.

 Kochira koso dōmo arigatō gozaimashita. Takusan hito ga imasu ne. Nan-nin kurai desu ka.

Kawashima: Sō desu ne, nihyaku-nin kurai deshō ka.

******

Kawashima: Tokorode, Tonpuson-san . . .

Tonpuson: Dēbiddo to yonde kudasai.

Kawashima: A, hai. Tokorode Dēbiddo-san no gokazoku wa ogenki desu ka.

Tonpuson: Ee, okagesama de.

Kawashima: Shitsurei desu ga, kodomo-san wa nan-nin desu ka.

Tonpuson: Musuko ga yo-nin desu.

Kawashima: Sō desu ka. Nigiyaka desu ne. Nan-sai desu ka.

Tonpuson: Jūis-sai to has-sai to roku-sai to yon-sai desu.

Kawashima: Sō desu ka.

> Mr. Ryozo Kawashima: Hello, Mr. Thompson. Thank you for (what you've done for me) the other day.
> Mr. Thompson: Well, (as I recall,) you are (lit., were) Mr. Kawashima. Good to see you again. There are so many people here today. I wonder how many.
> Mr. Kawashima: Let me see, I wonder, there might probably be 200 people here.
> ******
> Mr. Kawashima: By the way, Mr. Thompson, . . .
> Mr. Thompson: Call me David.
> Mr. Kawashima Oh, yes. By the way, how is your family, David?
> Mr. Thompson: They are very well, thanks.

Vocabulary

a: oh	*-nin:* [counter for people]	asking)
dōmo: thanks	*kurai/gurai:* about	*shitsurei desu ga:* excuse me (lit., I
takusan: many	*sō desu ne:* let me see	maybe rude, but)
hito: people	*tokorode:* by the way	*sō desu ka:* is that right?
iru (imasu): to be	*ee:* yes	*nigiyaka:* lively
nan-nin: how many people	*okagesama de:* yes, thank you (for	*-sai:* [counter for age]

17

> Mr. Kawashima: (lit., I maybe rude, but) how many children do you have?
> Mr. Thompson: I have four sons.
> Mr. Kawashima: That's terrific! They must be very active. How old are they?
> Mr. Thompson: They are 11, 8, 6 and 4 years old.
> Mr. Kawashima: Is that right?

プレゼン後の ディナーパーティー

川島良三（かわしまりょうぞう）： あ、トンプソンさん、せんじつは　どうも。

トンプソン：川島（かわしま）さんでしたね。こちらこそ　どうも　ありがとうございました。
たくさん　ひとが　いますね。なんにんくらいですか。

川島： そうですね、200 にんくらいでしょうか。
(です)

******

川島： ところで、トンプソンさん……

トンプソン：デービッドと　よんでください。

川島： あ、はい。ところで、デービッドさんの　ごかぞくは　おげんきで
すか。

トンプソン：ええ、おかげさまで。

川島： しつれいですが、こどもさんは　なんにんですか。

トンプソン：むすこが　4にん　です。

川島： そうですか。にぎやかですね。なんさいですか。

トンプソン：11 さいと　8 さいと　6 さいと　4 さいです。

川島： そうですか。

● Comprehension Drill

1. Listen to or read Dialogue 1 and decide if the following statements are true, false or you don't know as not enough information has been given.

1. Mr. Thompson met Mr. Kawashima for the first time.   (T / F / DK)
2. Mr. Kawashima says there might be 200 people at the party. (T / F / DK)
3. Mr. Thompson's family lives in Tokyo.   (T / F / DK)
4. Mr. Thompson has four sons.   (T / F / DK)
5. They are 12, 8, 6 and 3 years old.   (T / F / DK)

2. Put these sentences in the correct order to make a conversation.

(e) → (d) → (b) → (a) → (c)

a. *Jūis-sai to has-sai to roku-sai to yon-sai desu.*
b. *Sō desu ka. Nigiyaka desu ne. Nan-sai desu ka.*
c. *Sō desu ka.*
d. *Musuko ga yo-nin desu.*
e. *Shitsurei desu ga, kodomo-san wa nan-nin desu ka.*

Dialogue 2 · Asking and giving the prices · · · Formal Informal 10

(Jacqueline Richardson, Fuyumi Tsukada and Akiyo Miyasato are checking the prices at a used *kimono* shop.)

Richādoson:	*Sumimasen, kore ikura desu ka.*
Ten'in:	*A, sono obi desu ka. Ichiman-en de gozaimasu.*
Tsukada:	*Jā, kore wa?*
Ten'in:	*Sochira no kimono wa gosen-en de gozaimasu.*
Miyasato:	*Ēh, ii ja nai!*
Ten'in:	*Kochira wa kimono to obi de hassen-en kōnā de gozaimasu.*
Tsukada:	*Sō nē . . .*

(They are looking around in the shop and are leaving.)

San-nin:	*Jā, mata kimasu.*

Ms. Richardson:	Excuse me, how much is this?
Sales clerk:	Oh, you mean that sash. That is 10,000 yen.
Ms. Tsukada:	How about this one?
Sales clerk:	That kimono is 5,000 yen, ma'am.
Ms. Miyasato:	Wow, isn't that a good (price)?
Sales clerk:	This section is the 8,000-yen corner: 8,000 yen for a *kimono* and a sash.
Ms. Tsukada:	That's good, (but) . . .
******	
Customers:	We will be back, thank you.

リチャードソン：	すみません、これ　いくらですか。
店員(てんいん)：	あ、その　おびですか。10,000えんでございます。
塚田(つかだ)：	じゃあ、これは？
店員：	そちらの　きものは　5,000えんでございます。
宮里(みやさと)：	えーっ、いいじゃない！
店員：	こちらは　きものと　おびで　8,000えんコーナーでございます。
塚田：	そうねえ……。
******	
3人(にん)：	じゃあ、また　きます。

Vocabulary

sumimasen: excuse me	*-en:* yen	*ii ja nai!:* isn't it good?
kore: this	*gozaimasu:* is [polite]	*kōnā:* corner; section
ikura: how much	*sochira:* that [polite]	*sō nē:* well, ...
ten'in: sales clerk	*to:* and	*mata kimasu:* will come again
sono: that (thing)	*de:* in total	
obi: sash for *kimono*	*ēh:* wow	

● **Comprehension Drill**

Listen to or read Dialogue 2 and decide if the following statements are true, false or you don't know as not enough information has been given.

1. Ms. Richardson asks the clerk about the price of an *obi*.   (T / F / DK)
2. The clerk cannot answer Ms. Richardson's question.   (T / F / DK)
3. The *obi* is more expensive than the *kimono*.   (T / F / DK)
4. Ms. Miyasato wants to buy a 5,000-yen *kimono*.   (T / F / DK)
5. They bought the *kimono*.   (T / F / DK)

◆   ◆   ◆

Grammar Note 1   How numbers are structured (数の構成)

a. 1 to 99

Memorize the following first.

1	2	3	4	5	6	7	8	9	10
ichi	ni	san	yon/shi	go	roku	nana/shichi	hachi	kyū/ku	jū

Note that in counting the pronunciation "*yon*" for 4, "*nana*" for 7 and "*kyū*" for 9 are commonly used.

			1	2	3	4	5	6	7	8	9
			一	二	三	四	五	六	七	八	九
			ichi	ni	san	yon/shi	go	roku	nana/shichi	hachi	kyū/ku
10	十	jū		12							
20	二十	nijū				24					
30	三十	sanjū						36			
40	四十	yonjū								48	
50	五十	gojū	51								
60	六十	rokujū			63						
70	七十	nanajū					75				
80	八十	hachijū							87		
90	九十	kyūjū									99

Look at the table above. You will see one to nine in a row and ten to ninety in the left column. If you combine numbers in the left column with numbers in the upper row, you can construct the numbers 11 to 99.

b. 100 to 9,000s

	1	2	3	4	5	6	7	8	9
100 百 -hyaku	**100** **hyaku**	200 ni-hyaku	**300** **san-byaku**	400 yon-hyaku	500 go-hyaku	**600** **rop-pyaku**	700 nana-hyaku	**800** **hap-pyaku**	900 kyū-hyaku
1,000 千- -sen	**1,000** **sen**	2,000 ni-sen	**3,000** **san-zen**	4,000 yon-sen	5,000 go-sen	6,000 roku-sen	7,000 nana-sen	**8,000** **has-sen**	9,000 kyū-sen

Look at the table above and observe that the pronunciation changes take place with numbers in bold face. Also note that for 100 and 1,000, *ichi* (1) is not pronounced; so say *hyaku* and *sen*, not *ichi-hyaku* or *ichi-sen*.

c. 1 to 100,000,000,000

			1	ichi	一		ichi	one
			10	jū	十		jū	ten
			100	hyaku	百		hyaku	hundred
			1000	sen	千		sen	1 thousand
		1	0000	man	万 (4 zeros)		ichi-man	10 thousand
		10	0000				jū-man	100 thousand
		100	0000				hyaku-man	1 million
		1000	0000				sen-man	10 million
	1	0000	0000	oku	億 (8 zeros)		ichi-oku	100 million
	10	0000	0000				jū-oku	1 billion
	100	0000	0000				hyaku-oku	10 billion
	1000	0000	0000				sen-oku	100 billion

As you can see from the above, *ichi*, *jū*, *hyaku* and *sen* are repeated with *man*; hence we get *ichi-man* (10,000), *jū-man* (100,000), *hyaku-man* (1,000,000) and *sen-man* (10,000,000), respectively. After *sen-man* we get a new unit, *oku*, which has 8 zeros in it, and *ichi*, *jū*, *hyaku* and *sen* are repeated with *oku* again, before moving on to the next big unit *chō*.

Grammar Note 2 　Using numbers（数字を使う）

The following illustrates how you can use numbers in daily life. The 0 is pronounced "*zero*" or "*rei*" in Japanese when numbers are pronounced separately, as in telephone or room numbers.

a. Telephone numbers

[Someone's telephone number] *(wa) wakarimasu ka.* 'Do you know ~?'

Topic		Verb	SP*
Akagawa-san no keitai bangō	(wa)	wakarimasu	ka.
'Do you know (lit., understand) Mr. Akagawa's mobile phone number?' (Closing Dialogue)			

*SP: Sentence Particle

Used when asking about someone's or a facility's telephone number. The Japanese often use *wakarimasu ka* 'lit., Do you understand?' and *Hai, wakarimasu* 'Yes, I know (lit., understand).'

[Area Code] *no* [*~ no ~*] *desu.*

Area Code		Number	
Tōkyō 03	no	5575 no 3331	desu.
'It's Tokyo 03-5575-3331.'			

(The numbers read "*zero-san no go-go-nana-go no san-san-san-ichi.*")

When you are in a certain area, the area code there is not necessary for a house phone or an office number but it is necessary for a mobile number.

b. Prices

[Item you are pointing to] *wa ikura desu ka.* 'How much ~?'

C.Starter					SP
Sumimasen,	kore	(wa)	ikura	desu	ka.
'Excuse me, but how much is this?' (D-2)					

Price	
10,000-en	de gozaimasu/desu.
'(That) is 10,000 yen.' (D-2)	

c. Room numbers and floors

[Room you want to know] *wa doko/nan-ban desu ka.*

Topic				SP
Kyō no kaigi	wa	doko	desu	ka.
Heya		nan-ban		
'Which room (lit., where) will the meeting be today?' (Closing Dialogue)				
'What is the room number? (lit., As for the room, what is the number?)'				

[Floor] *no* **[Room number]** *desu.*

Floor		Rm No.	
Go-kai	*no*	*503*	*(desu).*
'(It) will be in room 503 on the 5th floor.' (Closing Dialogue)			

Note that "0" in a room number is sometimes pronounced "*maru* (circle)" in Japanese. Therefore, "Room 503" in the example above would be read "*go-maru-san*" in Japanese.

Grammar Note 3   Number of people (人数)

a. Exchanging some information about family

[Children/Siblings] *wa nan-nin desu ka.* 'How many ~ do you have?'

Topic		How many		SP
Gokyōdai	*wa*	*nan-nin*	*desu*	*ka.*
'How many brothers and sisters do you have?'				

[No. of Children/Siblings] *desu.* ' I have ~.'

Comment 1	No. of Siblings	
3-nin desu.	*Otōto ga futari to imōto ga hitori*	*desu.*
'I have three. Two younger brothers and one younger sister.'		

b. Talking about approximate number of people

Nan-nin kurai/gurai desu ka. 'How many people ~, I wonder?'

Comment 1	How many people		SP
Takusan hito ga imasu ne.	*Nan-nin*	*kurai* *desu*	*ka.*
'There are a lot of people here. How many people are here, I wonder?' (D-1)			

Sō desu ne, **[No. of People]** *kurai/gurai deshō ka.*

Starter	No. of People		SP
Sō desu ne,	*200-nin*	*kurai* *deshō*	*ka.*
'Let me see, (I guess) about 200 people are here.' (D-1)			

Two people are talking about the approximate number of people attending a party after a presentation. In that situation, Japanese people often use *kurai/gurai* after the number. And *-deshō ka* is used in this context to avoid definitive remarks.

Grammar Note 4   Particles [*to*] 'and' / [*de*] 'total' (助詞「と」「で」)

a. [Noun 1] *to* [Noun 2] *desu*.

The particle *to* connects two or more words. It means 'and.' Do not use it to connect sentences, adjectives, or verbs.

Noun 1		Noun 2	
Imōto ga hitori	*to*	*otōto ga futari*	*desu.*
kimono	*to*	*obi*	
'(I have) one younger sister and two younger brothers.'			
'*kimono* and sash' (D-2)			

b. [X] *to* [Y] *de ikura desu ka.* 'How much for (the total of) X and Y?'

Noun 1		Noun 2	AM*		SP
Kimono	*to*	*obi*	*de*	*ikura desu*	*ka.*
				8000-en desu	*ϕ.*
'How much for (the total of) the *kimono* and sash?'					
'The *kimono* and sash will be 8,000 yen.'					

*AM: Add-up Marker

The add-up marker *de*, which follows nouns or noun phrases, is the marker for the total number of items. You can use it when you want to know the total price for two or more items.

Grammar Note 5   Counters (助数詞)

In English there are plural forms for nouns with *-s/-es* for countable nouns, and special phrases for uncountable nouns, such as *a sheet of* paper, *a spoonful of* sugar, *two bottles of* wine, *three cups of* coffee, and so on. In that respect, most of the Japanese nouns are uncountable, because a different suffix is used for a different item to express plurality. For example, *-hon* is used for counting bottles and pens, *-mai* for paper, tickets or plates, and so on.

Those suffixes are called "counters." There are quite a few counters, the choice of which will be decided by the shape, material and category of the items, such as cylindrical items, flat items, solid items, people, machinery, liquids, measurements, and so on. The counters given below will be necessary for day to day activities. (For more counters, see Appendix 3 [p.154].)

	Group I		Group II				
	Solid items	People	Japanese currency	Age	Floors	Numbers	Cylindlical items
	-tsu	-ri/-nin	-en	-sai	-kai	-ban	-hon
1	hito-tsu	hito-ri	ichi-en	is*-sai	ik*-kai	ichi-ban	ip*-pon*
2	futa-tsu	futa-ri	ni-en	ni-sai	ni-kai	ni-ban	ni-hon
3	mit-tsu	san-nin	san-en	san-sai	san-kai san-gai*	san-ban	san-bon*
4	yot-tsu	yo*-nin	yo*-en	yon-sai	yon-kai	yon-ban	yon-hon
5	itsu-tsu	go-nin	go-en	go-sai	go-kai	go-ban	go-hon
6	mut-tsu	roku-nin	roku-en	roku-sai	rok*-kai	roku-ban	rop*-pon*
7	nana-tsu	nana-nin shichi-nin	nana-en	nana-sai	nana-kai	nana-ban	nana-hon
8	yat-tsu	hachi-nin	hachi-en	has*-sai	hachi-kai hak*-kai	hachi-ban	hachi-hon hap*-pon*
9	kokono-tsu	kyū-nin	kyū-en	kyū-sai	kyū-kai	kyū-ban	kyū-hon
10	tō	jū-nin	jū-en	jus*-sai jis*-sai	juk*-kai jik*-kai	jū-ban	jup*-pon* jip*-pon*
How many	ikutsu	nan-nin	nan-en/ ikura	nan-sai	nan-kai nan-gai*	nan-ban	nan-bon*

(* indicates pronunciation changes.)

Ⓐ Conversation Drills

Drill 1. Complete the following conversations.

1. Tell someone your phone number.

    Colleague: *Anō . . . denwa bangō wa nan-ban desu ka.*

    You: (a) _____ (Give your phone number.)

    Colleague: *Mō ichido ii desu ka. 03 no . . .*

    You: (b) _____ (Repeat your number.)

    Colleague: *Dōmo arigatō gozaimashita.*

2. Ask the number for a taxi company.

    You: (a) Taxi 会社の tel 番わかりつ790か

        (Ask for the phone number of the taxi company.)

    Colleague: *Ee, chotto matte ne. A, kore kore. 03-3799-9220 desu.*

    You: (b) すみません、もう1度おねがいます

        (Ask your colleague to repeat the number.)

    Colleague: *03-3799-9220.*

    You: (c) ありがとうございい

        (Express your gratitude for what has been done.)

3. Provide information for a delivery.

    You: (a) これはいくらですか _____ (Ask the price.)

    Sales clerk: *Sochira no terebi wa 159,800-en desu.*

    You: (b) これは？ _____ (Point to another one and ask the price.)

    Sales clerk: *Sochira wa 190,000-en desu.*

    You: (c) はいたつおねがいます (Ask politely to deliver the item to your house.)

    Sales clerk: *Gojūsho wa?*

    You: (d) _____ (Give your address.)

    Sales clerk: *Oheya bangō wa?*

    You: (e) _____ (Give your room number.)

    Sales clerk: *Odenwa bangō wa?*

    You: (f) _____ (Give your phone number.)

    Sales clerk: *Hai, kashikomarimasita.*

Vocabulary

1. *anō:* well	*takushī-gaisha:* taxi company	*(go)jūsho:* address
denwa: phone	*wakarimasu ka:* do you know ~?	*(o)heya:* room
bangō: number	*chotto matte:* wait a while [informal]	*Kashikomarimashita.:* Certainly, sir/
nan-ban: what number	*terebi:* TV	ma'am.
mō ichido: once more	*haitatsu:* delivery	

4. Talk about the approximate number of people present.

You: (a) _はじめまして　— です　ヒ一ろしいくあうた・・_

(Introduce yourself and greet another person.)

(b) _あなしね・おとじめめ あうなは？_ (Ask the person's name.)

Mr. Takagi: *Takagi desu. Kochira koso yoroshiku onegaishimasu.*

Takusan hito ga imasu ne. Nan-nin kurai deshō ka.

You: (c) _30人くらいてすが_ (Say that you think there are about

30 people there.)

5. Ask about prices at the CD-ROM corner.

You: (a) _すいません。これはいくらですか_ (Ask the price.)

Sales clerk: *Sochira wa 5-mai de 1000-en de gozaimasu.*

You: (b) _あ。そうですか　これも 5まい_ (Point to another one and ask if

they are the same price.) _1000円ですか_

Sales clerk: *Sochira wa 5-mai de 800-en de gozaimasu.*

You: (c) _どうも_ (Express your appreciation.)

B Grammar & Vocabulary Building Drills

Drill 2. Practice the following dialogue by changing the underlined parts.

> A: *Sumimasen,* (a) *kore* *(wa) ikura desu ka.*
> B: (b) *100-en* *desu.*

1. *kaihi* — ¥7,500

2. *ressun-ryō* — ¥5,000

3. *sumō no chiketto* — ¥11,300

4. *kasa* — ¥3,000

5. *ringo* — ¥150

Vocabulary

1. *-mai:* [counter for flat things]   *sumō:* sumo wrestling   *ringo:* apple
2. *kaihi:* charge for party, etc.   *chiketto:* ticket
  ressun-ryō: tuition   *kasa:* umbrella

27

Drill 3. Practice the following dialogue by changing the underlined parts.

> A: (a) _Kyō no kaigi_ wa doko desu ka.
> B: (b) _5_-kai no (c) _503_ desu.
> A: _Nan-nin gurai desu ka._
> B: (d) _20_-nin gurai deshō ka.
> A: _Tokorode, Yasui-san no keitai bangō wa nanban desu ka._
> B: (e) _090-2664-3137_ desu yo.

1. (a) _uchiawase_   (b) _2_   (c) _201_   (d) _10_   (e) _090-5771-1355_
2. (a) _tenjikai_   (b) _8_   (c) _803_   (d) _30_   (e) _090-8722-3934_
3. (a) _ashita no kaigi_   (b) _7_   (c) _710_   (d) _5_   (e) _090-9131-4877_

Drill 4. Give the total price based on the pictures below.

> _Kimono to obi de 8,000-en desu._

e.g. _kimono & obi / 8,000-en_   1. _kēki & kōhī / 1,200-en_   2. _pasokon & purintā / 220,000-en_

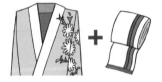  

3. _chiketto 2-mai / 9,000-en_   4. _setto / 550-en_   5. _zenbu / 15,000-en_

Vocabulary

3. _kyō:_ today
  keitai: mobile phone
  uchiawase: meeting

tenjikai: exhibition
4. _kēki:_ cake
  pasokon: personal computer

purintā: printer
setto: set
zenbu: all together

C Listening Tasks

Drill 5. Listen to the CD and choose the appropriate pictures for the dialogues. **11**

1. (d) 2. (a) 3. (c) 4. (b) 5. (e)

a.	b.	c.	d.	e.
 *musuko* × 1 *musume* × 2	 *ane* × 2 *ani* × 1	*ani* × 2	*musume* × 1 *musuko* × 1	*imōto* × 1 *otōto* × 2

Drill 6. Listen to the dialogue and fill in the blanks of the price list below. **12**

1. *shokupan*	2. *kōhī*	3. *gyūnyū*	4. *banana*	5. *yōguruto*
(250)-en	(560)-en	(230)-en	(180)-en	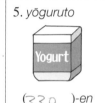 (330)-en

バナナにはぅーと

じゃあこのフーセは
サービスんです それはちがいます

D Review Drills

Drill 7. Read the following instructions and make sentences.

How would you:

1. ask Ms. Tsukada for Mr. Kawashima's phone number?

さんの でんわ ばんごうは わかりますか

2. ask about the room number where the meeting will be held today?

今日の かいきは どこですか

3. ask someone properly his/her daughter's age?

失礼ですか 娘さんは 何さいですか

4. say that your daughter is three years old?✗

娘は 3才です

5. ask how much this is by pointing?

これは いくらですか

6. ask someone how many siblings s/he has?

ごきょうだいは なんにんですか

7. tell someone you have three siblings, one older sister and two younger brothers?

3人です   姉が１人と 弟が 2人です

8. tell someone that you will come again?

じゃ また きます

Drill 8. Match the responses with the questions.

1. *Shitsurei desu ga, otōsan wa nan-sai desu ka.*

2. *Kuroda-san no heya wa nan-kai desu ka.*

3. *Kodomo-san wa nan-nin desu ka.*

4. *Kabuki no chiketto wa ikura desu ka.*

a. *15,000-en desu.*

b. *Musume ga hitori desu.*

c. *68-sai desu.*

d. *6-kai desu.*

Drill 9. Complete the dialogues by changing the following sentences to the correct order.

1. (c) → (a) → (d) → (e) → (b)

a. *Sochira wa 10,000-en desu.*

b. *Ja, kore onegaishimasu.*

c. *Sumimasen, kono būtsu wa ikura desu ka.*

d. *Kono būtsu mo?*

e. *Ee, sō desu. Sochira no wa zenbu 10,000-en desu.*

2. (a) → (e) → (b) → (f) → (d) → (c)

a. *Sumimasen, kore haitatsu onegai dekimasu ka.*

b. *Brassington desu. Denwa wa 03-6278-9912 desu.*

c. *Hai, uketamawarimashita.*   承る   *おきまじほほに その通りにます*

d. *Shibuya-ku Ebisu 1-22-3 desu.*

e. *Hai. Dewa onamae to odenwa bangō o onegaishimasu.*

f. *Gojūsho mo onegaishimasu.*

Vocabulary

7. *(go)kyōdai:* siblings	*kodomo-san:* (your) children	*uketamawarimashita:* Certainly.
8. *otōsan:* father	9. *būtsu:* boots	*(o)namae:* name

Confirming a meeting room number and a mobile phone number

13

(At the office.)

Howaito:	*Sumimasen, kyō no kaigi wa doko desu ka.*
Tsukada:	*Go-kai no go-maru-san.*
Howaito:	*Go-maru-san desu ne. Wakarimashita.*
	Sore to, ano, Akagawa-san no keitai bangō, wakarimasu ka.
Tsukada:	*Un, wakaru yo. Chotto matte.*
	Ēto, zero-kyū-zero no hachi-ichi-san-roku no nana-go-ni-ichi.
Howaito:	*Mō ichi-do, ii desu ka. Zero-kyū-zero no?*
Tsukada:	*Hachi-ichi-san-roku no nana-go-ni-ichi. Kakō ka?*
Howaito:	*Sumimasen, onegaishimasu.*

ホワイト：すみません、きょうの　かいぎは
　　　　　どこですか。
塚田：　　5かいの　503。
ホワイト：503 ですね。わかりました。
　　　　　それと、あの、赤川さんの　けいたい
　　　　　ばんごう、わかりますか。
塚田：　　うん、わかるよ。ちょっと　まって。
　　　　　えーと、090-8136-7521。
ホワイト：もういちど、いいですか。090 の？
塚田：　　8136-7521。かこうか？
ホワイト：すみません、おねがいします。

Mr. White:	Excuse me, but where will the meeting be today?
Ms. Tsukada:	Room 503 on the 5th floor.
Mr. White:	Thank you. It's going to be in room 503, OK.
	And do you know (lit., understand) Mr. Akagawa's mobile phone number?
Ms. Tsukada:	Yeah, one moment. Here we go, it's 090-8136-7521.
Mr. White:	Would you mind repeating that once more, please? 090 and . . .
Ms. Tsukada:	8136-7521. Do you want me to write it down?
Mr. White:	Yes, please. Thank you (lit., Sorry to bother you).

LESSON 3: TIME EXPRESSIONS
—*Jikan wa nan-ji kara nan-ji made desu ka.*
'What are your hours?'

Dialogue 1 Asking about business hours · · · · · · · · · Formal

(Jonathan White calls a library.)

Toshokan'in:	*Hai, kuritsu toshokan desu.*
Howaito:	*Sumimasen, yasumi wa nan-yōbi desu ka.*
Toshokan'in:	*Getsuyōbi desu.*
Howaito:	*Sō desu ka. Jikan wa nan-ji kara nan-ji made desu ka.*
Toshokan'in:	*Asa wa hachi-ji han kara desu. Yoru wa shichi-ji made desu ga,*
	suiyōbi dake go-ji han made desu.
Howaito:	*Sō desu ka. Arigatō gozaimashita.*
Toshokan'in:	*Dō itashimashite.*

Librarian: Good morning, Public (lit., Ward) Library. May I help you?
Mr. White: Yes (lit., Sorry), when do you close during the week?
Librarian: (Our library will be closed) on Mondays.
Mr. White: Thank you. And what are your hours?
Librarian: (We are open) from 8:30 in the morning untill 7 o'clock in the evening.
But, we close at 5:30 in the evening (only) on Wednesdays.
Mr. White: OK. Thank you.
Librarian: You're welcome.

Vocabulary

toshokan'in: librarian	*jikan:* time; hours	*yoru:* night
kuritsu: ward-run (municipal)	*-ji:* o'clock	*ga:* but
toshokan: library	*kara:* from	*dake:* only
yasumi: holiday	*made:* to	*Dō itashimashite.:* You're welcome.
-yōbi: day of the week	*asa:* morning	
getsuyōbi: Monday	*han:* half (an hour)	

32

図書館員：　はい、くりつとしょかんです。

ホワイト：　すみません、やすみは　なんようびですか。

図書館員：　げつようびです。

ホワイト：　そうですか。じかんは　なんじから　なんじまで　ですか。

図書館員：　あさは　8じはんからです。よるは　7じまでですが、すいようび
だけ　5じはんまでです。

ホワイト：　そうですか。ありがとうございました。

図書館員：　どういたしまして。

● **Comprehension Drill**

1. Listen to or read Dialogue 1 and decide if the following statements are true, false or you don't know as not enough information has been given.

1. Mr. White is at the library. (T /F/ DK)
2. Mr. White wants to borrow a business book. (T / F /DK)
3. Mr. White asks what day of the week the library is closed. (T/ F / DK)
4. The library is open from 7:30 in the morning. (T /F/ DK)
5. The library is closed earlier on Wednesdays. (T/ F / DK)

2. Put these sentences in the correct order to make a telephone conversation.

(d) → (b) → (a) → (e) → (c)

a. *Sō desu ka. Jikan wa nan-ji kara nan-ji made desu ka.*
b. *Getsuyōbi desu.*
c. *Sō desu ka. Arigatō gozaimashita.*
d. *Sumimasen, yasumi wa nan-yōbi desu ka.*
e. *Gozen jū-ji kara gogo roku-ji han made desu.*

Dialogue 2 Confirming the time and venue of a meeting

· Formal Informal 15

(Ryozo Kawashima, Jonathan White and Fuyumi Tsukada are talking at the office.)

Kawashima (R):	*Ohayō. Samui ne.*
Howaito:	*Ohayō gozaimasu.*
Tsukada:	*Ohayō gozaimasu. Samui desu ne.*
Kawashima:	*Kotoshi wa toku ni samui yo.*
	Kyonen wa konna ni samukunakatta yo ne.
	Tokoro de, kondo no kaigi wa itsu datta ka na.
Tsukada:	*Asatte, mokuyōbi desu yo.*
Howaito:	*Nan-ji kara desu ka.*
Tsukada:	*Jū-ji kara, kyū-kai no*
	kyū-maru-ichi kaigishitsu yo.

Mr. Ryozo Kawashima: Good morning! It's cold, isn't it?
Mr. White: Good morning.
Ms. Tsukada: Good morning, yes, it is cold.
Mr. Kawashima: It's especially cold this year. It wasn't this cold last year, was it? By the way, I'd like to confirm the date of the next meeting.
Ms. Tsukada: (It is scheduled) on Thursday, which is the day after tomorrow.
Mr. White: What time?
Ms. Tsukada: (The meeting will begin) at 10 a.m. in Room 901, on the 9th floor.

Adj

川島良三（かわしまりょうぞう）：	おはよう。さむいね。
ホワイト：	おはようございます。
塚田（つかだ）：	おはようございます。さむいですね。
川島：	ことしは　とくに　さむいよ。きょねんは　こんなに　さむくなかったよね。ところで　こんどの　かいぎは　いつ　だったかな。
塚田：	あさって、もくようびですよ。
ホワイト：	なんじからですか。
塚田：	10じから、9かいの　901かいぎしつよ。

Vocabulary

samui: cold	*kyonen:* last year	*mokuyōbi:* Thursday
kotoshi: this year	*konna ni:* like this	*kaigishitsu:* meeting room
toku ni: especially	*kondo:* next time	
yo: you know	*asatte:* the day after tomorrow	

● **Comprehension Drill**

Listen to or read Dialogue 2 and decide if the following statements are true, false or you don't know as not enough information has been given.

1. Mr. Kawashima says it is really cold this year.   ((T)/ F / DK)
2. The next meeting will be held the day after tomorrow.   ((T)/ F / DK)
3. Mr. White asks where the meeting will be held.   (T /(F)/ DK)
4. The meeting will start at 9 a.m.   (T /(F)/ DK)
5. Ms. Tsukada will attend the meeting.   (T / F /(DK))

Grammar Note 1   Specific time （特定の時）

a. Specific time and general time

There are two types of time expressions, which we will call "specific time" and "general time" in this textbook. The specific time expressions, such as "11 o'clock," "August 22" and "the year 2007," mark points of time in a stream of time from the past to the future. On the other hand, general time expressions such as "today," "tomorrow" and "yesterday" have a certain time span or duration.

b. Asking about/giving the day of the week that a business is not open

Sunday	Monday	Tuesday	Wednesday	Thursday	Friday	Saturday
日	月	火	水	木	金	土
nichiyōbi	*getsuyōbi*	*kayōbi*	*suiyōbi*	*mokuyōbi*	*kin'yōbi*	*doyōbi*
					1	2
3	4	5	6	7	8	9
10	11	12	13	14	15	16
17	18	19	20	21	22	23
24	25	26	27	28	29	30
31						

In asking when a department store, museum, or a fitness club, etc. is closed, expressions for days of the week and dates of the month are necessary. All of those expressions are specific time expressions. Study the table above:

e.g. 1   A: *Sochira wa yasumi wa itsu desu ka.*   'What day do you close (in a week)?'
      B: ***Getsuyōbi*** *desu.*   'We close on Mondays.' (D-1)

e.g. 2   A: *Sochira wa yasumi wa itsu desu ka.*   'What day do you close (in a month)?'
      B: ***5-ka***, ***15-nichi***, ***25-nichi*** *de gozaimasu.*   'We close on the 5th, 15th and 25th.'

Grammar Note 2 Asking/telling someone about the service hours or office hours (営業時間)

a. Months, days of the month, hours and minutes

	Month	Days of the month	Hours	Minutes
	-gatsu	-ka/nichi	-ji	-fun/-pun
1	ichi-gatsu	tsuitachi	ichi-ji	ip-pun
2	ni-gatsu	futsu-ka	ni-ji	ni-fun
3	san-gatsu	mik-ka	san-ji	san-pun
4	shi-gatsu	yok-ka	yo-ji	yon-pun
5	go-gatsu	itsu-ka	go-ji	go-fun
6	roku-gatsu	mui-ka	roku-ji	rop-pun
7	shichi-gatsu	nano-ka	shichi-ji	nana-fun
8	hachi-gatsu	yō-ka	hachi-ji	hap-pun
9	ku-gatsu	kokono-ka	ku-ji	kyū-fun
10	jū-gatsu	tō-ka	jū-ji	jup/jip-pun
11	jūichi-gatsu	jūichi-nichi	jūichi-ji	jūip-pun
12	jūni-gatsu	jūni-nichi	jūni-ji*	jūni-fun
.				
.				
14		jūyok-ka	jūyo-ji	jūyon-pun
15		jūgo-nichi	jūgo-ji	jūgo-fun
.				
20		hatsu-ka	nijū-ji	nijup-pun/nijip-pun
.				
24		nijūyok-ka	nijūyo-ji*	nijūyon-pun
.				
30		sanjū-nichi		sanjup-pun/ sanjip-pun/ han 'half'
31		sanjūichi-nichi		
nan?	nan-gatsu 'what month?'	nan-nichi 'what day of the month?'	nan-ji 'what time?'	nan-pun 'how many minutes?'

*Rei, which means 'zero,' with the counter -ji is used for '12:00 noon' and '12:00 midnight,' as in gogo rei-ji '12:00 noon' and gozen rei-ji '0 a.m. (= 12:00 midnight).'

b. Starting time and ending time

~ *wa* [Starting Time] *kara* [Ending Time] *made desu*. '(It's) from ~ to ~.'

Topic		Starting Time		Ending Time			SP
Jikan	*wa*	*nan-ji*	*kara*	*nan-ji*	*made*	*desu*	*ka.*
'What are (your) hours?' (D-1)							

Topic		Starting Time			Topic		Ending Time		
Asa	*wa*	*hachi-ji han*	*kara*	*desu.*	*Yoru*	*wa*	*shichi-ji*	*made*	*desu.*
'(We open) at (lit., from) 8:30 in the morning,					(and) until 7 o'clock in the evening.' (D-1)				

Use the pattern *~ kara ~ made* when asking/telling someone about the time span which has a starting time and ending time, such as business hours or office hours.

c. Duration of time

In expressing duration of time, add *kan* to weeks, days and hours. For months, *-kagetsu* is added to the numbers.

	Months	Weeks	Days	Hours
	-kagetsu	*-shūkan*	*-kakan/-nichikan*	*-jikan*
1	*ik-kagetsu*	*is-shūkan*	*ichi-nichi**	*ichi-jikan*
2	*ni-kagetsu*	*ni-shūkan*	*futsu-kakan*	*ni-jikan*
3	*san-kagetsu*	*san-shūkan*	*mik-kakan*	*san-jikan*
4	*yon-kagetsu*	*yon-shūkan*	*yok-kakan*	*yo-jikan*
5	*go-kagetsu*	*go-shūkan*	*itsu-kakan*	*go-jikan*
6	*rok-kagetsu*	*roku-shūkan*	*mui-kakan*	*roku-jikan*
7	*nana-kagetsu*	*nana-shūkan*	*nano-kakan*	*nana-jikan*
8	*hak-kagetsu*	*has-shūkan*	*yō-kakan*	*hachi-jikan*
9	*kyū-kagetsu*	*kyū-shūkan*	*kokono-kakan*	*ku-jikan*
10	*juk/jik-kagetsu*	*jus/jis-shūkan*	*tō-kakan*	*jū-jikan*
11	*jūik-kagetsu*	*jūis-shūkan*	*jūichi-nichikan*	*jūichi-jikan*
12	*jūni-kagetsu*	*jūni-shūkan*	*jūni-nichikan*	*jūni-jikan*
nan?	*nan-kagetsu* 'how many months?'	*nan-shūkan* 'how many weeks?'	*nan-nichikan* 'how many days?'	*nan-jikan* 'how many hours?'
	dono kurai/gurai 'how long?'			

*Kan is not necessary.

Grammar Note 3 Talking about weekly schedules, birthdays and holidays (週の予定・誕生日・休み)

Use the following pattern when you talk about a specific date:

~ wa [Date] *desu.* 'It is [Date].'

Topic		Date	
Tanjōbi	wa	5-gatsu 29-nichi	desu.
'(My) birthday is May 29.'			

~ wa [Starting Date/Time] *kara* [Ending Date/Time] *made desu.*

Topic		Starting Date/Time		Ending Date/Time		
Nyū Yōku no shutchō	wa	10-gatsu 12-nichi	kara	27-nichi	made	desu.
Kaigi		10-ji		11-ji		
'(My) business trip to New York is from October 12 to 27.'						
'The meeting is from 10 to 11.'						

Grammar Note 4 General time (一般的な時)

The following table shows general times, such as years, months, weeks, and so on.

Year	kyonen 'last year'	kotoshi 'this year'	rainen 'next year'
Month	sengetsu 'last month'	kongetsu 'this month'	raigetsu 'next month'
Week	senshū 'last week'	konshū 'this week'	raishū 'next week'
Day	kinō 'yesterday'	kyō 'today'	ashita 'tomorrow'
Morning	kinō no asa 'yesterday morning'	kesa / kyō no asa 'this morning'	ashita no asa 'tomorrow morning'
Noon	kinō no hiru 'yesterday noon'	kyō no hiru 'this noon'	ashita no hiru 'tomorrow noon'
Afternoon	kinō no gogo 'yesterday afternoon'	kyō no gogo 'this afternoon'	ashita no gogo 'tomorrow afternoon'
Evening	kinō no ban / yūbe 'yesterday evening'	kyō no ban / konban 'this evening'	ashita no ban 'tomorrow evening'
When?	itsu		

e.g. *Kaigi wa **asatte**, mokuyōbi desu.* 'The meeting will be on Thursday, the day after tomorrow.' (D-2)

*Pātī wa **ashita no ban** desu.* 'The party will be tomorrow evening.'

◆   ◆   ◆

Ⓐ Conversation Drills

Drill 1. Complete the following conversations.

1. Call a restaurant and ask about business hours.

Restaurant: *Hai, Resutoran OLK de gozaimasu.*

You: *Sumimasen,* (a) ディナーは何時からですか

    (Ask what time dinner time starts.)

Restaurant: *5-ji kara de gozaimasu.*

You: (b) 何時まで ですか (Ask what time the restaurant

    is closed for the day.)

Restaurant: *11-ji made desu.*

You: (c) 休みは何曜日ですか (Ask what day of the week

    the restaurant is closed.)

Restaurant: *Mukyū desu.* 'Open 7 days a week.'

You: *Sō desu ka, arigatō gozaimashita.*

2. In a shop, ask a sales clerk about business hours.

You: (a) ここは何時まで ですか (Ask until what time the shop is open.)

Sales clerk: *8-ji made desu.*

You: (b) 休みは何曜日ですか (Ask what day of the week

    this shop is closed.)

Sales clerk: *Getsuyōbi desu.*

You: *Dōmo.*

3. At the office, ask your subordinate about next presentation.

You: *Ohayō, kyō wa ii tenki desu ne.*

部下 Subordinate: *Sō desu ne.*

You: *Tokorode,* (a) こんどの プレゼンテーションはいつですか

    (Ask when the next presentation is.)

Subordinate: *Asatte, kin'yōbi desu.*

You: (b) 何時からですか (Ask what time it starts.)

Subordinate: *10-ji han kara desu.*

You: (c) どこですか (Ask where it is held.)

Subordinate: *2-kai no 201-kaigishitsu desu.*

You: (d) ああそうですか、ありがとう (Say, "Oh, I see, thank you.")

Vocabulary

1. *resutoran:* restaurant   *mukyū:* 7 days a week (lit., no   *sō desu ne.:* It is.; I agree.
dinā: dinner   holidays)   *purezentēshon:* presentation

4. Ask your colleague about another colleague's birthday.

You: (a) _____ (Ask when Yasui-san's birthday is.)

Colleague: *6-gatsu 10-ka, raishū no kin'yōbi da yo.*

You: (b) _____ (Ask where they are having Yasui-

san's birthday party.)

Colleague: *Shinagawa no Resutoran* OLK.

You: (c) _____ (Say thank you.)

5. Ask your friend about his/her next business trip.

You: (a) _____ (Ask when his/her next business

trip is.)

Friend: *Raigetsu no 10-ka kara.*

You: (b) _____ (Ask until when.)

Friend: *17-nichi made.*

You: (c) _____ (Confirm it will be one week.)

Friend: *Sō da ne.*

Ⓑ Grammar & Vocabulary Building Drills

Drill 2. Look at the pictures and tell someone the time.

e.g.

1.

2.

3.

4.

5.

e.g. _____*7-ji 15-fun*_____ *desu.*

Vocabulary

1. *tanjōbi:* birthday   *pātī:* party

1. _____ desu.   4. _•_____ desu.

2. _____ desu.   5. _____ desu.

3. _____ desu.

Drill 3. Answer the questions based on the clocks below.

e.g.

(a.m.)   (p.m.)

A: *Toshokan wa nan-ji kara nanji made desu ka.*

B: <u>*Gozen 10-ji kara gogo 6-ji made desu.*</u>

1.

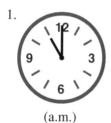

(a.m.)

2.

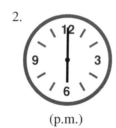

(p.m.)

3.

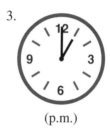

(p.m.)

4.

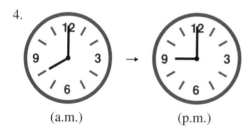

(a.m.)   (p.m.)

5.

(a.m. [midnight])

1. A: *Depāto wa nan-ji kara desu ka.*

    B: _____

2. A: *Shigoto wa nan-ji made desu ka.*

    B: _____

3. A: *Kaigi wa nan-ji kara desu ka.*

    B: _____

Vocabulary

3. *gozen:* a.m.   *yonaka:*   around midnight
   gogo: p.m.; afternoon   *depāto:*   department store

4. A: *Kafe wa nan-ji kara nan-ji made desu ka.*

   B: _____

5. A: *Sūpā wa nan-ji made desu ka.*

   B: _____

Drill 4. Practice the following dialogue by changing the underlined parts.

> A: *Hai, (a) <u>toritsu-bijutsukan</u> desu.*
> B: *Sumimasen, yasumi wa (b) <u>nan'yōbi</u> desu ka.*
> A: *(c) <u>Getsuyōbi</u> desu.*
> B: *Sō desu ka. Jikan wa nan-ji kara nan-ji made desu ka.*
> A: *(d) <u>Gozen 10-ji kara gogo 6-ji made</u> desu ga, (e) <u>kin'yōbi dake gogo 7-ji</u> made desu.*
> B: *Sō desu ka. Arigatō gozaimashita.*
> A: *Dō itashimashite.*

1. (a) *Edo-shiryōkan*　　　　　(b) *itsu*　　　　(c) *nichiyōbi*
   (d) *gozen 8-ji han kara gogo 5-ji han made*　　(e) *doyōbi dake 3-ji*

2. (a) *Ribāsaido* (Riverside) *resutoran*　(b) *nan'yōbi*　(c) *suiyōbi*
   (d) *hiru 11-ji kara yoru 10-ji han made*　　(e) *nichiyōbi dake 9-ji*

3. (a) *Midori depāto*　　　　　(b) *itsu*　　　　(c) *mokuyōbi*
   (d) *gozen 10-ji kara gogo 8-ji made*　(e) *nichiyōbi dake gogo 7-ji*

⒞ Listening Tasks

Drill 5. Listen to the CD and choose the appropriate answers for the questions.

1. a. *Nichiyōbi desu.*　　　b. *5-jikan desu.*　　　c. *Gogo 2-ji desu.*

2. a. *3-ji kara desu.*　　　b. *4-jikan desu.*　　　c. *5-ji made desu.*

3. a. *Hai, sō desu.*　　　b. *Iie, 10-ji kara desu.*　　c. *10-ji kara desu.*

4. a. *Ashita desu.*　　　b. *5-kai no 501 desu.*　　c. *Mokuyōbi kara desu.*

5. a. *6-ji goro desu.*　　　b. *6-ji kara desu.*　　　c. *6-ji made desu.*

Vocabulary

4. *toritsu:*　metropolitan　　　　*bijutsukan:*　museum; art gallary　　　*shiryōkan:*　culture museum

Drill 6. Listen to the CD and choose the appropriate pictures for the dialogues.

1. (   )   2. (   )   3. (   )   4. (   )   5. (   )

 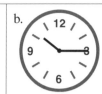  

a.   b.   c.   d.   e.

5:20

Ⓓ Review Drills

Drill 7. Read the following instructions and make sentences.

How would you:

1. ask what day of the week they close?

2. ask what time they open?

3. ask until what time they are open?

4. say your day off is Wednesday?

5. say you start working at 8:30 a.m.?

6. say you finish working at 6:45 p.m.?

7. ask when the next meeting is?

8. say the meeting starts at 11 a.m.?

Drill 8. Match the responses with the questions.

1. *Kondo no kaigi wa itsu desu ka.*   ·   · a. *11-ji kara desu.*
2. *Sumimasen, tesuto wa nan-ji kara desu ka.* ·   · b. *Getsuyōbi.*
3. *Nomikai no basho wa doko desu ka.*   ·   · c. *Ginza no izakaya desu yo.*
4. *Kyō wa nan'yōbi?*   ·   · d. *Ashita, mokuyōbi desu yo.*

Vocabulary

8. *tesuto:*   test; exam   *nomikai:*   drinking party   *izakaya:*   Japanese-style bar

Drill 9. Complete the dialogues by changing the following sentences to the correct order.

1. (a) → (   ) → (   ) → (   )

    a. *Kondo no mītingu wa itsu desu ka.*

    b. *Dō itashimashite.*

    c. *Ā, sō deshita ne. Itsumo arigatō.*

    d. *Raishū no getsuyōbi desu yo.*

2. (b) → (   ) → (   ) → (   ) → (   )

    a. *Ashita wa nan-ji kara desu ka.*

    b. *Tsukada-san, kyō wa nan-ji made shigoto desu ka.*

    c. *Tabun, 10-ji goro made desu.*

    d. *Sō desu ka. Taihen desu ne.*

    e. *Asa 8-ji kara desu.*

Vocabulary

9. *mītingu:* meeting   *tabun:* maybe   *Taihen desu ne.:* It's tough, isn't it?

(At Ms. Miyasato's residence.)

Kumaru: *Sengetsu, Yōroppa ni ikimashita.*

Miyasato: *Itsu kara itsu made?*

Kumaru: *Tōka kara sanjūichi-nichi made desu.*

Unabara: *Tōka kara sanjūichi-nichi made?*
Nagai nē.

Kumaru: *Hai, san-shūkan desu ne.*

Miyasato: *Saisho wa doko?*

Kumaru: *Rondon desu. Tōka no gozen jūichi-ji goro Narita o dete,*
gogo yo-ji han goro Hīsurō ni tsukimashita.

Unabara: *Nan-jikan?*

Kumaru: *Ēto, jūsan-jikan han desu ne.*

Miyasato: *Uwa, jūsan-jikan han? A, kono shashin wa Rondon no . . . ?*

Kumaru: *Pikaderī Sākasu desu. Kono chikaku no kafe de tomodachi to aimashita.*

Unabara: *Nan-ji goro? Mada akarui ne.*

Kumaru: *Roku-ji sukoshi mae gurai desu. Natsu wa ku-ji han kurai made akarui desu yo.*

Miyasato/Unabara: *Hē, sō.*

クマル： せんげつ、ヨーロッパに　いきました。
宮里： いつから　いつまで？
クマル： 10 かから　31 にちまでです。
海原： 10 かから　31 にちまで？　ながいねえ。
クマル： はい、3 しゅうかんですね。
宮里： さいしょは　どこ？
クマル： ロンドンです。10 かの　ごぜん 11 じ　ごろ　成田を　でて、ごご 4 じはんごろ　ヒースローに　つきました。
海原： なんじかん？
クマル： えーと、13 じかんはんですね。
宮里： うわ、13 じかんはん？　あ、この　しゃしんは　ロンドンの……？
クマル： ピカデリーサーカスです。この　ちかくの　カフェで　ともだちと　あいました。
海原： なんじごろ？　まだ　あかるいね。
クマル： 6 じ　すこし　まえ　ぐらい　です。なつは　9 じはんくらいまで　あかるいですよ。
宮里／海原： へえ、そう。

Mr. Kumar: I travelled/went to Europe last month.
Ms. Miyasato: When did you go there? (lit., From when to when did you go there?)
Mr. Kumar: From the 10th to the 31st.
Ms. Unabara: From the 10th to the 31st? That's very long!
Mr. Kumar: Yes, it was three weeks.
Ms. Miyasato: Where did you go first?
Mr. Kumar: First, I went to London. I left Narita Airport at around 11 a.m. on the 10th and arrived at Heathrow Airport at four in the afternoon.
Ms. Unabara: How long did it take to get to London?
Mr. Kumar: Let me see, it took 13 and a half hours.
Ms. Miyasato: Wow, 13 and a half hours! Oh, is this a picture from London?
Mr. Kumar: Yes, that's Piccadilly Circus in London. I met my friend at a café near there.
Ms. Unabara: What time is it then? It still looks bright, like it's daytime.
Mr. Kumar: It was a little before 6 o'clock in the evening. It usually is light until 9:30 at night in the summer time, you know.
Ms. Miyasato/Ms. Unabara: Oh, is that right!

Sumimasen

Some say that Japan is the land of apologies because you will hear "*Sumimasen*" quite frequently on the street, at restaurants, around the office, etc. It seems true that the Japanese apologize far more frequently than Westerners. This probably results from cultural differences. Westerners explain the reason they have to do something under extenuating circumstances. On the other hand, the Japanese simply apologize to expect forgiveness for what s/he has done.

Sumimasen is a humble expression reflecting someone's behavior. Being humble is considered a virtue in Japanese culture as Japanese people respect peace and harmony. In order to avoid blaming others, it is rather easy to apologize and express a humble spirit, which makes everybody happy.

Actually, *sumimasen* basically means "not finished," and implies "to feel bad/in debt." When you draw someone's attention, you feel bad for interrupting them and have him/her pay attention to you; when you express gratitude apologetically, you feel obliged to that person for the favor given to you; and when you express apology, you feel sorry to have caused someone problems. On the other hand, in a similar situation, *arigatō* means a straightforward "thank you."

Thus, *sumimasen* doesn't only mean 'I'm sorry,' but it also means 'Excuse me,' and an apologetic 'Thank you,' depending on the contexts, so it is a versatile word.

There are roughly three functions of *sumimasen*.

1. Drawing someone's attention, or a conversation starter when making a request, like "Excuse me."
2. Expressing apologetic gratitude, like "Thank you."
3. Expressing apology, like "I'm sorry."

Can you recognize the meaning of *sumimasen* in the following examples?

(At a restaurant)
Customer: **Sumimasen.**①
Waitress: *Hai.*
Customer: *Kono gurasu, yogoreteru n desu kedo.* 'This glass is dirty.'
Waitress: **Sumimasen.**②
Sugu ni omochishimasu. 'I'll bring a clean one right away.'
*****
Waitress: **Sumimasen deshita.**③ *Hai, dōzo.*
Customer: **Sumimasen.**④

Answers: ①Excuse me. ②I'm sorry. ③I'm sorry for what has been done. ④(apologetically) Thank you.

LESSON 4: EXPRESSING WHERE YOU WILL GO
—Shūmatsu wa doko e ikimasu ka.
'Where are you going over the weekend?'

Dialogue 1 Talking about travel plans · · · · · · · · · · · · Formal

(Haruko Kawashima is asking David Thompson about his upcoming trip to Kyoto.)

Kawashima (H): Dēbiddo-san, kondo no shūmatsu wa doko e ikimasu ka.

Tonpuson: Kyōto e ikimasu.

Kawashima: Kyōto desu ka.

Tonpuson: Ee. Ryōshin ga Ōsutoraria kara kimasu. Issho ni Kyōto e ikimasu.

Kawashima: Ii desu ne. Goryōshin wa dono kurai Nihon ni imasu ka.

Tonpuson: San-shūkan desu. Raigetsu kaerimasu.

Kawashima: Sō desu ka. Nihon wa hajimete desu ka.

Tonpuson: Iie, ni-kai-me desu. Kyonen mo kimashita.

Kawashima: Kyonen mo Kyōto e ikimashita ka.

Tonpuson: Iie, kyonen wa Hiroshima e ikimashita.

Kawashima: Shinkansen de ikimashita ka.

Tonpuson: Iie, hikōki de ikimashita.

Kawashima: Jā, kondo wa shinkansen desu ka.

Tonpuson: Hai, shinkansen desu.

Ms. Haruko Kawashima: Where are you going over the weekend, David?
Mr. Thompson: (We are) going to Kyoto.
Ms. Kawashima: Oh, Kyoto.
Mr. Thompson: Yes. My parents are coming (to Tokyo) from Australia. We'll go to Kyoto together.
Ms. Kawashima: That's good. How long will they stay in Japan?
Mr. Thompson: For three weeks. They will go back next month.
Ms. Kawashima: I see. Is it the first time for them?
Mr. Thompson: No, it will be the second time. They came last year as well.
Ms. Kawashima: Did you go to Kyoto last year, too?
Mr. Thompson: No, we went to Hiroshima last year.
Ms. Kawashima: Did you go (there) by Shinkansen?
Mr. Thompson: No, we went (there) by plane.
Ms. Kawashima: Well, then, will you go (to Kyoto) by Shinkansen this time?
Mr. Thompson: Yes, (we'll take) Shinkansen.

Vocabulary

shūmatsu: weekend
e: to [direction marker]
iku (ikimasu): to go
ga: [subject marker]
kuru (kimasu): to come

issho ni: together
iru (imasu): to stay
kaeru (kaerimasu): to go home; to be back
hajimete: first time

-kai: [counter for times]
-me: [sequence suffix]
shinkansen: bullet train
de: by [means of transportation]
hikōki: airplane

47

川島春子： デービッドさん、こんどの　しゅうまつは　どこへ　いきますか。

トンプソン： 京都へ　いきます。

川島： 京都ですか。

トンプソン： ええ。りょうしんが　オーストラリアから　きます。いっしょに　京都へ　いきます。

川島： いいですね。ごりょうしんは　どのくらい　日本に　いますか。

トンプソン： ３しゅうかんです。らいげつ　かえります。

川島： そうですか。日本は　はじめてですか。

トンプソン： いいえ、２かいめです。きょねんも　きました。

川島： きょねんも　京都へ　いきましたか。

トンプソン： いいえ、きょねんは　広島へ　いきました。

川島： しんかんせんで　いきましたか。

トンプソン： いいえ、ひこうきで　いきました。

川島： じゃあ、こんどは　しんかんせんですか。

トンプソン： はい、しんかんせんです。

● Comprehension Drill

1. Listen to or read Dialogue 1 and decide if the following statements are true, false or you don't know as not enough information has been given.

    1. David will go to Kyoto this weekend.   (T / F / DK)
    2. David's parents will come to Japan for the first time.   (T / F / DK)
    3. David's parents will stay at David's house.   (T / F / DK)
    4. They also went to Kyoto last year.   (T / F / DK)
    5. They will take Shinkansen to Kyoto this time.   (T / F / DK)

2. Put these sentences in the correct order to make a conversation.

    (   ) → (   ) → (   ) → (   ) → (a)

    a. *Sō desu ka. Goryōshin wa Nihon wa hajimete desu ka.*
    b. *Kyōto e ikimasu.*
    c. *Dēbiddo-san, kondo no shūmatsu wa doko e ikimasu ka.*
    d. *Kyōto desu ka.*
    e. *Ee, ryōshin ga Ōsutoraria kara kimasu.*

Dialogue 2 Asking about lunch plans · · · · · · · · · · · Informal

(Haruko Kawashima, Akiyo Miyasato and Anthony Kumar are talking about going to lunch around noon.)

Kawashima (H):	*Ne, jūni-ji yo. Ohiru, iku?*	
Miyasato:	*Un, iku. Tonī wa?*	
Kumaru:	*Mada, chotto. Osaki ni dōzo.*	
Kawashima/Miyasato:	*Jā, itte kimasu.*	

Ms. Haruko Kawashima: Look! It's 12 o'clock. How about lunch?
Ms. Miyasato: OK, I'm going. How about you, Tony?
Mr. Kumar: Well, not yet (a bit inconvenient). You, go ahead.
Ms. Kawashima/Miyasato: OK, see you. (lit., We're going out now.)

かわしまはる こ
川島春子：　　　ね、12 じよ。おひる、いく？
みやさと
宮里：　　　　　うん、いく。トニーは？
クマル：　　　　まだ、ちょっと。おさきに　どうぞ。
川島／宮里：　　じゃあ、いってきます。

● **Comprehension Drill**

Listen to or read Dialogue 2 and decide if the following statements are true, false or you don't know as not enough information has been given.

1. Ms. Kawashima goes out to lunch with Mr. Kumar.　　(T / F / DK)
2. It's 12 o'clock now.　　(T / F / DK)
3. They have already decided what they will eat.　　(T / F / DK)
4. Three of them will go out together.　　(T / F / DK)
5. Mr. Kumar is not ready for lunch yet.　　(T / F / DK)

Vocabulary

ohiru: lunch　　　　　　　　　　　*Itte kimasu.:*　I'm going out now.

Grammar Note 1 Talking about plans for the weekend （週末の予定）

Ikimasu 'going,' *kimasu* 'coming' and *kaerimasu* 'returning'

Three verbs concerning movement are introduced in this lesson. They are *ikimasu*, *kimasu* and *kaerimasu*. Study their meaning in the table below:

ikimasu	'to go'	movement away from where you originally stood
kimasu	'to come'	movement toward where you stand
kaerimasu	'to return'	movement away from where you are and back to where you originally were

When you talk about the weekend (= the topic), use the three patterns below.

Topic		Place		Verb	SP
Shūmatsu	*wa*	*doko*	*e*	*ikimasu*	*ka.*
'Where are you going over the weekend?' (D-1)					

Subject		Place		Verb
Ryōshin	*ga*	*Ōsutoraria*	*kara*	*kimasu.*
'My parents are coming (to Tokyo) from Australia.' (D-1)				

(Topic)		Time Expression	Verb
(Ryōshin	*wa)*	*raigetsu*	*kaerimasu.*
'(They) will go back home next month.' (D-1)			

The topic in the third pattern is omitted (see also Dialogue 1) because the topic *ryōshin* has been already mentioned in the dialogue. Any information that is understood from the context is likely to be omitted in Japanese.

Grammar Note 2 Verbs （動詞）

a. Non-past and Past

There are two verb forms related to time in Japanese, the Non-past and Past. The Non-past forms cover the present and future, while the Past forms cover the past.

b. Formal and informal verb forms

Also in this lesson, another two verb forms are presented in terms of speech level: the informal verb form (Level 1) and the formal verb form (Level 2). Level 1 is important for you to understand spoken Japanese, but does not have to be used. Level 2 would be appropriate for you to use.

The table below shows the Non-past and Past forms in Level 1 and 2 of the three verbs of movement—*ikimasu*, *kimasu* and *kaerimasu*. Note that in Level 2, verbs end in *-masu* or its variations, whereas in Level 1, the verbs have various endings.

	Non-past		Past	
	Affirmative	Negative	Affirmative	Negative
Level 1 (Informal)	iku kuru kaeru	ikanai konai kaeranai	itta kita kaetta	ikanakatta konakatta kaeranakatta
Level 2 (Formal)	ikimasu kimasu kaerimasu	ikimasen kimasen kaerimasen	ikimashita kimashita kaerimashita	ikimasendeshita kimasendeshita kaerimasendeshita

Grammar Note 3 Particles (助詞)

a. Subject marker [ga]

Subject		Place		Verb
Ryōshin	ga	Ōsutoraria	kara	kimasu.
'My parents are coming (to Tokyo) from Australia.' (D-1)				

A *ga* which follows a noun is a marker that denotes the subject or an agent who does the movement.

b. Direction marker [e]   'to'

Direction (place name)		Verb
Kyōto	e	ikimasu.
'(We are) going to Kyoto.' (D-1)		

The partcle *e* following a place name has the meaning of 'toward/in the direction of' the place.

e.g.   *Issho ni Kyōto e ikimasu.* '(I'm) going to Kyoto together with (my parents).' (D-1)
       Kyonen wa Hiroshima e ikimashita. '(I/we) went to Hiroshima last year.' (D-1)

c. Goal marker [ni]   'to'

Goal (place name)		Verb
Shiga-kōgen	ni	ikimasu.
'(I) will go to Shiga Heights.' (Closing Dialogue)		

Two functions of *ni* will be introduced in this section. One is the goal marker and the other is a particle that indicates purpose of going.

The goal marker *ni* behaves just like the particle *e*. But *e* indicates the direction in more formal situations, while *ni* is used to indicate a specific goal or destination in informal situations.

e.g.   *Doko ni iku no?*   (informal)   'Where are you going?' (Closing Dialogue)
       Doko ni ikimasu ka. (formal)

d. Purpose of going [*ni*]   'will go/come/return to do ~'

Purpose of Going		Verb
Kaimono	*ni*	*ikimasu.*
'(I) will go shopping.'		

Secondly, the particle *ni* following a noun has the connotation of actions and means '(going/coming/going back) to some place to do something.'

e.g. *Raishū wa sukī ni ikimasu.* '(I'll) be going skiing next week.' (Closing Dialogue)

Shinjuku e kaimono ni ikimashita. '(I) went to Shinjuku for shopping.'

e. Inclusion marker [*mo*]   'also'

Inclusion		Place		Verb	SP*
Kyonen	*mo*	*Kyōto*	*e*	*ikimashita*	*ka.*
'Did you go to Kyoto last year, too?' (D-1)					

*SP: Sentence Particle

The particle *mo* means 'also,' 'too' or 'as well.' It denotes that information in the previous sentence will be referred to again.

f. Means of transportation [*de*]   'by means of ~'

Means of Transportation		Verb
Shinkansen	*de*	*ikimashita.*
'(I) went by Shinkansen.'		

The particle *de* is used when talking about going to some place by car/train/plane. Although *de* is used to mark other means, they are not discussed in this lesson.

e.g. *Shinkansen de ikimashita ka.* 'Did you go (there) by Shinkansen?' (D-1)

Iie, hikōki de ikimashita. 'No, I went there by plane.' (D-1)

Grammar Note 4   General time vs. specific time （一般的な時と特定の時）

"General time and specific time" were introduced in Lesson 3. The former is time which has some span, such as *raishū* 'next week,' *kyonen* 'last year' and *shūmatsu* 'weekend,' and the latter is a point in time, such as *12-gatsu* 'December,' *7-ji han* 'seven thirty,' and so on.

Note that specific time expressions need the particle *ni*, but no particle is necessary for general time expressions. Study the following examples.

General Time		Place		Verb
Kyonen	*φ*	*Kyōto*	*e*	*ikimashita.*
'(I) went to Kyoto last year.'				

Specific Time		(Place & Means)				Verb
Asa 7-ji han	*ni*	Shinjuku	kara	basu	de	ikimasu.
'(I will) leave Shinjuku at 7:30 in the morning by bus.'						

e.g.　**(Shūmatsu)** ryōshin ga Ōsutoraria kara kimasu.

'(My) parents are coming from Australia (this weekend).' (D-1)

*3-gatsu 15-nichi **ni** Tōkyō ni kimashita.* '(I) came to Tokyo on March 15th.'

◆　　　◆　　　◆

Ⓐ Conversation Drills

Drill 1. Complete the following conversations.

1. Your colleague asks you about your weekend plans.

Colleague:　*Kondo no shūmatsu wa doko e ikimasu ka.*

You:　　　(a) _____ (Say you will go to Hokkaido.)

Colleague:　*Hokkaidō desu ka. Dare to ikimasu ka.*

You:　　　(b) _____

(Say [you will go there] with your younger brother. He will come from Canada.)

Colleague:　*Sō desu ka. Hikōki de ikimasu ka.*

You:　　　(c) _____ (Say no, you will go by train.)

Colleague:　*E? Densha? Tōi desu yo . . .*

2. Your colleague introduces his/her friend to you.

Colleague:　*Konbanwa.*

You:　　　*Konbanwa.*

Colleague:　*Shōkai shimasu ne. Kochira wa Rī (Lee)-san. Kyō, Kankoku kara kimashita.*

Lee:　　　　*Hajimemashite.*

You:　　　*Hajimemashite.* (a) _____ (Ask if s/he is on a business trip.)

Lee:　　　　*Hai, sō desu.*

You:　　　(b) _____ (Ask when s/he is going back.)

Lee:　　　　*Asatte kaerimasu.*

You:　　　*Mikka-kan desu ka. Isogashii desu ne.*

Vocabulary

1. *densha:* train　　　　　*tōi:* far　　　　　*isogashii:* busy

3. Ask your colleague about the coming weekend.

You: (a) _____

(Ask where your colleague will go this coming weekend.)

Colleague: *Kusatsu e ikimasu. Tomodachi ga Ōsutoraria kara kimasu.*

You: *Ii desu ne.* (b) _____

(Ask if it is the first time for him/her to come to Japan.)

Colleague: *Hai, sō desu.*

You: (c) _____ (Ask if they will go there by car?)

Colleague: *Iie, densha desu.*

4. Your colleague asks you about last weekend. You can answer in the formal speech style.

Colleague: *Shūmatsu wa doko (e) itta no?*

You: (a) _____ (Say you went to Kamakura.)

Colleague: *Dare to itta no?*

You: (b) _____ (Say you went with a friend.)

Colleague: *Sō . . . Kamakura no doko?*

You: (c) _____

(Say you went to Kita-kamakura by train and then visited some temples.)

Colleague: *Nan-ji goro kaetta no?*

You: (d) _____ (Say you came back around 9 at night.)

5. Complete the following conversation about yourself.

Japanese: *Itsu Nihon e kimashita ka.*

You: (a) _____ (Answer when you came to Japan.)

Japanese: *Nihon wa hajimete desu ka.*

You: (b) _____ (Answer Yes or No.)

Japanese: *Ima made ('until now'), doko e ikimashita ka.*

You: (c) _____ (Answer where you have gone,

e.g., Nikko.)

Japanese: *Itsu ikimashita ka.*

You: (d) _____ (Answer when you went there.)

Japanese: *Nan de ikimashita ka.*

You: (e) _____ (Answer how you got there, e.g.,

by train.)

Japanese: *Sō desu ka.*

Vocabulary

1. *tomodachi:* friend   *goro:* around
   (o)tera: temple   *kuruma:* car

54

B Grammar & Vocabulary Building Drills

Drill 2. Write down the verbs for pictures 1-3 below. Also fill in the boxes below with the non-past affirmative/negative and the past affirmative/negative forms of these verbs.

1. (   )   2. (   )   3. (   )

Non-past affirmative	Non-past negative	Past affirmative	Past negative
1.	ikimasen		
2.			kimasendeshita
3.		kaerimashita	

Drill 3. Practice the following dialogue by changing the underlined parts.

> A: (a) <u>Ashita</u> doko e ikimasu ka.
> B: (b) <u>Yoyogi-kōen</u> e ikimasu.

1. (a) *shūmatsu*   (b) *Nikkō*
2. (a) *natsuyasumi*   (b) *Morujibu*
3. (a) *kondo no yasumi*   (b) *Hakone*
4. (a) *ashita*   (b) *Roppongi*
5. (a) *kyō no yoru*   (b) *Ginza*

Vocabulary

3. *natsuyasumi:* summer vacation   *Morujibu:* Maldives

Drill 4. Practice the following dialogue by changing the underlined parts.

> A: *Kondo no shūmatsu wa doko e ikimasu ka.*
>
> B: (a) <u>*Hakone*</u> *e ikimasu.*
>
> A: *Dare to ikimasu ka.*
>
> B: (b) <u>*Dōryō to*</u> *ikimasu.*
>
> A: *Densha desu ka.*
>
> B: *Iie,* (c) <u>*kuruma*</u> *desu.*
>
> A: *Ki o tsukete.* 'Be careful (in driving).'

1. (a) *Izu*   (b) *kazoku to*   (c) *basu*
2. (a) *Shōnan*   (b) *tomodachi to*   (c) *kuruma*
3. (a) *Ginza*   (b) *hitori de*   (c) *jitensha*

Drill 5. Complete the sentences by putting in appropriate particles, or by inserting an ✕ if no particle is necessary.

> e.g. *Watashi* __**wa**__ *ashita* __**✕**__ *Shinjuku* __**e**__ *ikimasu.*

1. *Kawashima-san* _____ *kinō* _____ *Ōsaka* _____ *ikimashita.*
2. *Watashi* _____ *raigetsu* _____ *Amerika* _____ *kaerimasu.*
3. *Tsukada-san* _____ *shūmatsu* _____ *Asakusa* _____ *ikimasendeshita.*
4. *Ryōshin* _____ *raishū* _____ *Nihon* _____ *kimasen.*
5. *Kinō* _____ *uchi* _____ *kaerimasendeshita.*

⒞ Listening Tasks

Drill 6. Listen to the CD and choose the appropriate answers for the questions. `21`

1. a. *Densha desu.*   b. *Un, iku.*   c. *Shibuya e ikimasu.*
2. a. *Iie, 2-kai-me desu.*   b. *Iie, ikimasen.*   c. *Iie, Nihon desu.*
3. a. *Hai, kuruma desu.*   b. *Iie, kuruma desu.*   c. *Iie, shinkansen desu.*
4. a. *Hai, ikimashita.*   b. *Iie, ikimashita.*   c. *Nagoya e ikimashita.*
5. a. *1-shūkan ni 2-kai desu.*   b. *Getsuyōbi to mokuyōbi desu.*   c. *Jimu e ikimasu.*

Vocabulary

4. *dare to:*   with whom   **6.** *1-shūkan ni 2-kai:*   twice a week
    jitensha: bicycle   *jimu:*   training gym

Drill 7. **Listen to the four dialogues and fill in the table with choices from the options given below.** 22

	A. Where the person will go/went	B. With whom s/he will go/went	C. How they will go/ went
Dialogue 1			
Dialogue 2			
Dialogue 3			
Dialogue 4			

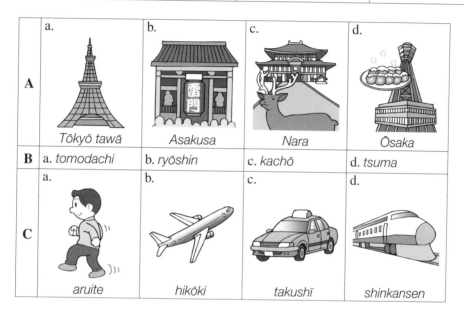

	a.	b.	c.	d.
A	Tōkyō tawā	Asakusa	Nara	Ōsaka
B	a. tomodachi	b. ryōshin	c. kachō	d. tsuma
C	a. aruite	b. hikōki	c. takushī	d. shinkansen

D Review Drills

Drill 8. **Read the following instructions and make sentences.**

How would you:

1. ask where they will go this weekend?

2. say you will go to Kamakura?

3. ask if they will go to the place by train?

4. ask if this will be the first time for someone's parents to come to Japan?

5. say you went to Nagoya last weekend?

6. say you came to Japan last month?

7. say you came to Japan with your family?

8. say you will go shopping in Shinjuku on Sunday?

Drill 9. Match the responses with the questions.

1. *Nihon wa hajimete desu ka.*   ·   · a. *Yamanaka-ko e ikimashita.*
2. *Shinkansen de ikimasu ka.*   ·   · b. *Iie, 3-kai-me desu.*
3. *Shūmatsu wa doko e ikimashita ka.* ·   · c. *4-gatsu desu.*
4. *Goryōshin wa itsu kimasu ka.*   ·   · d. *Iie, hikōki desu.*

Drill 10. Complete the dialogues by changing the following sentences to the correct order.

1.   (b) → (   ) → (   ) → (   )

    a. *Iie, kuruma desu.*

    b. *Ashita doko e ikimasu ka.*

    c. *Densha desu ka.*

    d. *Dizunīrando e ikimasu.*

2.   (e) → (   ) → (   ) → (   ) → (   )

    a. *Sō desu ka. Hikōki de ikimasu ka.*

    b. *Ōshima desu ka.*

    c. *Iie, fune desu.*

    d. *Hai. Ryōshin ga Indo kara kimasu kara.*

    e. *Raishū Ōshima e ikimasu.*

Vocabulary

9. *Yamanaka-ko:* Lake Yamanaka   *Ōshima:* Oshima Island
10. *Dizunīrando:* Disneyland   *fune:* boat; ship

(At a sports club.)

Kumaru: Konnichiwa.

Tsukada: Konnichiwa. Saikin, yoku kimasu ne.

Kumaru: Hai.

Tsukada: Watashi, Tsukada desu. Yoroshiku.

Kumaru: Kumaru desu. Yoroshiku onegaishimasu.

Tsukada: Uchi wa kono chikaku?

Kumaru: Hai, chikaku desu. Demo, koko wa shūmatsu dake kimasu.

Tsukada: A, sō nanda.

Kumaru: Hai. Heijitsu wa shigoto ga isogashii desu kara.

Tsukada: Sō yo ne. Jā, raishū mo kimasu?

Kumaru: Ie, raishū wa sukī ni ikimasu kara, kimasen.

Tsukada: Sukī ka. Doko ni iku no?

Kumaru: Doko? Etto, Shiga-kōgen ni ikimasu.

Tsukada: Ii nā.

クマル ：	こんにちは。
塚田 ：	こんにちは。さいきん、よく　きますね。
クマル ：	はい。
塚田 ：	わたし、塚田です。よろしく。
クマル ：	クマルです。よろしく　おねがいします。
塚田 ：	うちは　この　ちかく？
クマル ：	はい、ちかくです。でも　ここは しゅうまつだけ　きます。
塚田 ：	あ、そうなんだ。
クマル ：	はい。へいじつは　しごとが　いそがし いですから。
塚田 ：	そうよね。じゃあ、らいしゅうも　きま す？
クマル ：	いえ、らいしゅうは　スキーに　いきま すから、きません。
塚田 ：	スキーか。どこに　いくの？
クマル ：	どこ？えっと、志賀高原に　いきます。
塚田 ：	いいなあ。

Mr. Kumar:	Hello.
Ms. Tsukada:	Hello. You come here quite often lately.
Mr. Kumar:	Yes.
Ms. Tsukada:	I'm Tsukada. How are you? (lit., Nice to meet you.)
Mr. Kumar:	I'm Kumar. Nice to meet you, too.
Ms. Tsukada:	Do you live out here?
Mr. Kumar:	Yes, I live near by. But I come here only on weekends.
Ms. Tsukada:	Is that so?
Mr. Kumar:	Because I'm very busy during the week.
Ms. Tsukada:	That's true. I know . . . Are you coming next week, too?
Mr. Kumar:	No, (as a matter of fact) I'm going skiing next weekend.
Ms. Tsukada:	Skiing! Where are you going?
Mr. Kumar:	Where? Let me see . . . I'm going to Shiga Heights.
Ms. Tsukada:	That's very good.

LESSON 5:   REQUESTING

—*Kin'enseki o onegaishimasu.*
'We'd like a table in the non-smoking area.'

Dialogue 1   Ordering food at a restaurant · · · · · · · · · · Formal 24

(David Thompson and Anthony Kumar are going into a restaurant for lunch.)

Weitā:	*Irasshaimase. Ofutari-sama desu ka.*
Kumaru:	*Hai.*
Weitā:	*Otabako wa osui ni narimasu ka.*
Kumaru:	*Iie, kin'enseki o onegaishimasu.*
Weitā:	*Kashikomarimashita. Kochira e dōzo.*

******

Tonpuson:	*Sumimasen, eigo no menyū wa arimasu ka.*
Weitoresu:	*Hai, gozaimasu. Shōshō omachi kudasai.*

******

Weitoresu:	*Gochūmon wa okimari desu ka.*
Tonpuson:	*Hai. B ranchi o hitotsu to, kōhī o onegaishimasu.*
Weitoresu:	*Kōhī wa itsu omochi shimasu ka.*
Tonpuson:	*Ato de onegaishimasu.*
Kumaru:	*Bejitarian no ranchi wa arimasu ka.*
Weitoresu:	*Hai, yasai no karē to tōfu hanbāgu ga gozaimasu.*
Kumaru:	*Jā, tōfu hanbāgu o kudasai.*
Weitoresu:	*Kashikomarimashita.*
Kumaru:	*Sorekara, orenji jūsu mo onegaishimasu.*

******

Vocabulary

weitā: waiter
Irasshaimase.: Hello. (lit., Welcome.)
-sama: [addressing people (polite)]
(o)tabako: cigarette
suu (suimasu): to smoke
kin'enseki: non-smoking seat
menyū: menu
~ wa arimasu ka: do you have ~?

weitoresu: waitress
Shōshō omachi kudasai.: Wait a
   moment, please.
(go)chūmon: order
okimari desu ka: have you decided ~?
ranchi: lunch
hitotsu: one [counting system]

omochi shimasu ka: do we serve/
   bring ~?
ato de: later
bejitarian: vegetarian
yasai: vegetable
karē: curry (and rice)
hanbāgu: burger steak
sorekara: and then

60

(At the cashier.)

Kaikei:	*Goissho desu ka.*
Kumaru:	*Betsubetsu ni onegai dekimasu ka.*
Kaikei:	*Hai.* B *ranchi to kōhī de kyūhyaku-hachijū-en de gozaimasu. Sorekara, tōfu hanbāgu to orenji jūsu de, sen-hachijū-en de gozaimasu.*

Waiter:	Hello, how are you? (lit., Welcome!) Are there two in your party?
Mr. Kumar:	Yes.
Waiter:	Do you smoke?
Mr. Kumar:	No, we'd like a table in the non-smoking area.
Waiter:	Certainly, sir. Come this way, please.
******	
Mr. Thompson:	Excuse me, but do you have an English menu?
Waitress:	Yes, we do. Wait a moment, please.
******	
Waitress:	Are you ready to order?
Mr. Thompson:	Yes, I'd like to have the B-lunch and coffee, please.
Waitress:	When would you like your coffee, sir?
Mr. Thompson:	Later, please.
Mr. Kumar:	Do you have a vegetarian lunch?
Waitress:	Yes, we have vegetable curry and tofu burger steak.
Mr. Kumar:	Good, then, I'd like a tofu burger steak.
Waitress:	Yes, sir.
Mr. Kumar:	Ah, I'd also like an orange juice.
******	
Cashier:	Will this be together?
Mr. Kumar:	Can we pay separately?
Cashier:	Certainly. B-lunch and coffee will be 980 yen. One tofu burger steak and an orange juice will be 1,080 yen.

ウエイター：	いらっしゃいませ。おふたりさまですか。
クマル：	はい。
ウエイター：	おたばこは　おすいになりますか。
クマル：	いいえ、きんえんせきを　おねがいします。
ウエイター：	かしこまりました。こちらへ　どうぞ。
******	
トンプソン：	すみません、えいごの　メニューは　ありますか。
ウエイトレス：	はい、ございます。しょうしょう　おまちください。
******	

Vocabulary

kaikei: cashier	*(go)issho:* together	*betsubetsu ni:* separately

ウエイトレス：ごちゅうもんは　おきまりですか。

トンプソン：　はい。Ｂランチを　ひとつと、コーヒーを　おねがいします。

ウエイトレス：コーヒーは　いつ　おもちしますか。

トンプソン：　あとで　おねがいします。

クマル：　　　ベジタリアンの　ランチは　ありますか。

ウエイトレス：はい、やさいの　カレーと　とうふハンバーグが　ございます。

クマル：　　　じゃあ、とうふハンバーグを　ください。

ウエイトレス：かしこまりました。

クマル：　　　それから、オレンジジュースも　おねがいします。

******

会計：　　　　ごいっしょですか。

クマル：　　　べつべつに　おねがいできますか。

会計：　　　　はい。Ｂランチと　コーヒーで　980 えんでございます。

それから、とうふハンバーグと　オレンジジュースで、1,080 えん

でございます。

●Comprehension Drill

1. Listen to or read Dialogue 1 and decide if the following statements are true, false or you don't know as not enough information has been given.

1. Mr. Thompson asks if an English menu is available. (T / F / DK)
2. They don't have an English menu. (T / F / DK)
3. Mr. Thompson wants to have coffee together with the meal. (T / F / DK)
4. Mr. Kumar wants to have orange juice after the meal. (T / F / DK)
5. They pay the bill separately. (T / F / DK)

2. Put these sentences in the correct order to make a conversation at a restaurant.

(e) → (　) → (　) → (　) → (　)

a. *Kashikomarimashita.*
b. *Bejitarian no ranchi wa arimasu ka.*
c. *Jā, tōfu hanbāgu o kudasai.*
d. *Hai, yasai no karē to tōfu hanbāgu ga gozaimasu.*
e. *Gochūmon wa okimari desu ka.*

Dialogue 2   Confirming and preparing for the meeting

·   Formal   Informal   25

(Ryozo Kawashima, Jonathan White and Fuyumi Tsukada are talking at the office.)

Kawashima (R):	*Jonasan, chotto ii kana.*
Howaito:	*Hai, nan deshō ka.*
Kawashima:	*Kyō gogo no kaigi no shiryō da kedo,*
	jū-nin-bun no kopī no kakunin,
	yoroshiku.
	Sorekara, purezentēshon no junbi wa,
	daijōbu da ne.
Howaito:	*Hai, daijōbu desu.*
	Sukurīn mo konpyūta mo setto shimashita.
Kawashima:	*Sō ka.*
Howaito:	*A, obentō no junbi wa, Tsukada-san, onegai dekimasu ka.*
Tsukada:	*Un, mō yoyaku shita yo. Jūni-ji ni, obentō juk-ko kimasu yo.*
Howaito:	*Ā, sasuga Tsukada-san desu ne. Kore de, zenbu okkē desu.*

Mr. Ryozo Kawashima:	Hi, Jonathan, do you have a minute?
Mr. White:	Sure, what can I do for you?
Mr. Kawashima:	Could you please confirm that the handouts have been completed for 10 people for the meeting this afternoon. Also, is everything ready for the presentation?
Mr. White:	Yes, everything is ready. I have it all set up including a screen and a computer for the presentation.
Mr. Kawashima:	That's good.
Mr. White:	Oh, Ms. Tsukada, could I ask you to prepare lunch boxes?
Ms. Tsukada:	Yes, I've already ordered 10 of them and they will be delivered at 12 noon.
Mr. White:	Excellent! You are an expert, Ms. Tsukada. Then, we are all set.

川島良三 （かわしまりょうぞう）:	ジョナサン、ちょっと　いいかな。
ホワイト：	はい、なんでしょうか。
川島：	きょう　ごごの　かいぎの　しりょうだけど、10にんぶんの コピーの　かくにん、よろしく。それから、プレゼンテーションの じゅんびは、だいじょうぶだね。

Vocabulary

chotto ii kana: do you have a minute? [informal]	*junbi:* preparation	*yoyaku:* reservation
shiryō: materials	*daijōbu:* all right	*-ko:* [counter for things]
-bun: for	*sukurīn:* screen	*sasuga:* indeed; excellent
kopī: copy	*konpyūta:* computer	*okkē:* OK
kakunin: confirmation	*setto suru (shimasu):* to set up	
	(o)bentō: lunch box	

ホワイト：　はい、だいじょうぶです。スクリーンも　コンピューターも　セットしました。

川島：　　　そうか。

ホワイト：　あ、おべんとうの　じゅんびは、塚田さん、おねがいできますか。

塚田：　　　うん、もう　よやくしたよ。12 じに、おべんとう　10 こ　きますよ。

ホワイト：　ああ、さすが　塚田さんですね。これで、ぜんぶ　オッケーです。

● **Comprehension Drill**

Listen to or read Dialogue 2 and decide if the following statements are true, false or you don't know as not enough information has been given.

1. Mr. White's boss asks him to get ready ten handouts for the meeting.　　(T / F / DK)
2. The meeting is planned in the morning.　　(T / F / DK)
3. Ms. Tsukada has already set up for a presentation using a screen and a computer.

　　　(T / F / DK)
4. Ten lunch boxes will be delivered at noon.　　(T / F / DK)
5. Mr. Kawashima will give the presentation.　　(T / F / DK)

◆　　　◆　　　◆

Grammar Note 1　Making requests to service people (注文・依頼)

a. Making an order/request—*Onegaishimasu* vs. *kudasai*

The following two patterns are used when making an order/request.

[Items you want to order/request] *(o) onegaishimasu.* **'(I'd like ~), please.'**

This is used when ordering food or drinks at a restaurant or buying things at a shop. It is also used when asking someone to do something around the office, for example, *Kopī onegaishimasu.* 'Would you copy (this)?' or *Sumisu-san onegaishimasu.* 'Mr. Smith, please.'

[Items you want to order/request] *(o) kudasai.* **'Give me ~, please.'**

This is used when casually ordering food or drinks at a restaurant or a café, or buying things at a shop.

Object		Verb
Kōhī	*(o)*	*onegaishimasu.*
Tōfu hanbāgu		*kudasai.*
'Coffee, please.' (D-1)		
'I'd like a tofu burger steak.' (D-1)		

Inclusion (additional object)		Verb
Orenji jūsu	*mo*	*onegaishimasu.*
		kudasai.
'I'd also like an orange juice.' (D-1)		

The difference in usage between ~ *(o) onegaishimasu* and ~ *(o) kudasai* is that:

(1) ~ *(o) onegaishimasu* is used both when ordering things and requesting intangible things such as services, help or work, but ~ *(o) kudasai* is used only when casually ordering/buying tangible things;

(2) ~ *(o) kudasai* has a nuance of command, so it's English translation is 'Give me ~, please.';

(3) ~ *onegaishimasu* could be used to attract someone's attention but not ~ *kudasai*.

e.g. *Kin'enseki o* **onegaishimasu**. 'We'd like a table in the non-smoking area.' (D-1)
Yoyaku (o) **onegaishimasu**. 'I'd like to make a reservation, please.'
Chīzu bāgā **kudasai**. 'Give me a cheeseburger, please.'
Onegaishimasu! 'Excuse me!'

b. Object marker [o]

The particle *o* following a noun is a marker indicating that the noun is an object of the verb in the sentence. *Onegaishimasu* and *kudasai* need objects with *o*, but this object marker is often omitted in a casual conversation as you can see in the dialogues in this lesson.

Grammar Note 2   How to order/buy things for which you don't know the names (指示詞や番号を使った注文)

a. *Ko-so-a-do* words

When ordering things for which you don't know the names, it is helpful to use the words *kore* 'this one near me,' *sore* 'that one near you' or *are* 'that one over there' by pointing an item on a menu, in a glass case, or on the shelf, etc.

Kore, *sore*, *are* and *dore* 'which one' are words that belong to the set of so-called "*ko-so-a-do* words." More sets of *ko-so-a-do* words (for direction and place, etc.) will be discussed in later lessons.

The *ko-so-a-do* words

	Ko group (near S*)	*So* group (near L**)	*A* group (far from S & L)	*Do* group (question word)
Thing	*kore*	*sore*	*are*	*dore*

*S: Speaker **L: Listener

e.g. **Kore** to **kore** (o) *kudasai*. 'Give me this and this, please.'

b. Giving the number of the items listed on a menu

In looking at the menu and ordering:

e.g. *1-ban to 10-ban* *(o) onegaishimasu.* 'I'd like #1 and #10, please.'

Grammar Note 3 When ordering/buying/requesting more than one thing （複数の注文・購入・依頼）

a. Using numbers with counters

[Items] *o* [Number + Counter] *onegaishimasu/kudasai.* **'Give me no. of ~, please.'**
Kore/Sore/Are o [Number + Counter] *onegaishimasu/kudasai.*
                                            'Give me no. of this/that, please.'

Object		Number + Counter	Verb
Kopī	*o*	*10-mai*	*onegaishimasu.*
Kore		*yottsu*	*kudasai.*
'Ten copies, please.'			
'I'd like four of this, please.'			

If you don't specify how many of the items you want, you will get one. Therefore, if you want to order/buy more than one, specify the number of items by using a number + a counter.

It is important to remember the word order of this pattern. The item you want to order or *kore/sore/are* precede the counters. For example, if you want to have two glasses of draft beer, say the following:

Bīru *(o)* **futatsu** *onegaishimasu/kudasai.* 'I'd like two bottles of beer, please.'
item   number + counter

Caution: Word order
[Items you want or *kore/sore/are*] *(o)* + [How many you want] *onegaishimasu/kudasai.*

b. Connecting sentences [*sorekara*]

If you order two or more items, you can use *to* 'and.' The *to* connects nouns, as was discussed in Lesson 2.

Noun 1		Noun 2		Verb
B *ranchi o hitotsu*	**to**	*kōhī*	*o*	*onegaishimasu.*
				kudasai.
'I'd like to have the B-lunch and coffee, please.' (D-1)				

However, if you want to add another item after you have placed an order, use *sorekara* 'and then; in addition,' which is a conjunction that connects sentences.

Sentence 1	Conjunction	Sentence 2
Tōfu hanbāgu o kudasai.	**Sorekara**	*orenji jūsu mo kudasai.*

e.g.   A: *Tōfu hanbāgu (o) kudasai.*   'I'd like a tofu burger steak.'
         B: *Kashikomarimashita.*   'Yes, sir.'
         A: **Sorekara**, *orenji jūsu mo kudasai.* 'Ah, I'd also like an orange juice.' (D-1)

Grammar Note 4 Asking about the availability of tangible things
（物のある・なし）

a. Asking about availability

[Tangible things] *(wa) arimasu ka.* 'Do you have ~? / Is there a ~ available?'

Topic		Verb of Existence	SP
Eigo no menyū	*wa*	*arimasu*	*ka.*
'Do you have an English menu? (lit., As for an English menu, is there one?)' (D-1)			

~ wa arimasu ka is used to ask if a store has an item you would like to have or to ask if they have some facilities available.

e.g.   A: *Bejitarian no ranchi wa arimasu ka.*   'Do you have a vegetarian lunch? (lit., As for a vegetarian lunch, is there one?) (D-1)

Positive response:
B: *Hai, gozaimasu.* 'Yes, we do.' (D-1)
   Yasai karē to tōfu hanbāgu ga gozaimasu (= *arimasu*).   'Yes, we have vegetable curry and tofu burger steak.' (D-1)

Negative response:
B: *Chotto, nai n desu ga . . .*   'Well, (a bit inconvenient for you, but) we don't have it.' (informal)

If you hear *Chotto . . .* 'Well, a little . . . ,' it means they don't have what you have asked for.

b. Topic marker [*wa*] 'as for'

Topic		Verb	SP
Things	Topic Marker		
Eigo no menyū	**wa**	*arimasu*	*ka.*
		arimasu	ϕ.
		nai n desu	ϕ.
'Do you have an English menu?' (D-1)			
'We have an English menu (, but not a Chinese one).'			
'We don't have an English menu (, but have a Japanese one).'			

In the above examples, the particle *wa* indicates a topic of a sentence with a nuance of contrast, and the verbs following *wa* asks about/explains/denies the topic.

Grammar Note 5   Requesting extra services (特別な依頼)

[Extra Items/Services] *(o) onegai dekimasu ka.* **'Could I ask you to do ~ for me, please?'**

Extra Items/Services	Verb	SP
Betsubetsu ni	*onegai dekimasu*	*ka.*
'Could you please make separate checks for me?' (D-1)		

~ onegai dekimasu ka is used when asking for extra or complicated services, for example, another glass of water, a cup of hot tea, separate checks, etc. This pattern conveys the apologetic nuance of the speaker's request.

e.g.   *Ocha (o) mō ippai onegai dekimasu ka.* 'Could I have another cup of tea, please?'
   Obentō no junbi wa, Tsukada-san, onegai dekimasu ka.
      'Ms. Tsukada, could I ask you to prepare lunch boxes?' (D-2)

◆   ◆   ◆

Ⓐ Conversation Drills

Drill 1. Complete the following conversations.

1. You are at a restaurant with your colleagues for lunch.

   Waitress: *Irasshaimase.*

   You: (a) _____ (Say that there are three in your party.)

   Waitress: *Kochira e dōzo.*

   You: (b) _____ (Ask if an English menu is available.)

   Waitress: *Hai, shōshō omachikudasai. . . . Hai, dōzo.*

   (Place an order for lunch)

   You: (c) _____ (Draw attention.)

   Waitress: *Okimari ni narimashita ka.*

   You: (d) _____ (Order a tempura set menu.)

   Colleague 1: (e) _____ (Order the same one.)

   Colleague 2: (f) _____ (Order the same one.)

   Waitress: *Tempura teishoku mittsu de gozaimasu ne.*

   (At the cashier)

   You: (g) _____

             (Say politely that you'd like to pay separately.)

   Waitress: *Hai, tempura teishoku, 980-en de gozaimasu.*

Vocabulary

1. *tempura teishoku:* tempura set   *onaji:*   same
   (with rice and miso soup)

2. You are at a restaurant, ordering lunch for two.

Waitress:	*Irassahimase. Nan-mei sama desu ka.*	
You:	(a) _____	(Say two people.)
Waitress:	*Otabako wa osui ni narimasu ka.*	
You:	(b) _____	(Ask for a non-smoking seat.)
Waitress:	*Kashikomarimashita. Kochira e dōzo.*	
You:	(c) _____	(Draw attention.)
	(d) _____	
	(Order two lunch sets and two coffees.)	
Waitress:	*Ranchi setto o futatsu to kōhī o futatsu desu ne.*	
	Kōhī wa itsu omochi shimasu ka.	
You:	(e) _____	(Ask her to bring it after the meal.)

(You pay the bill at the table, as you see a sign saying "Please pay at the table.")

You:	(f) _____	(Ask for the check.)
Waitress:	*Hai. Shōshō omachi kudasai.*	

3. Ask about wine and order a bottle for the two of you at a restaurant.

Waiter:	*Wain risuto de gozaimasu.*	
You:	(a) _____	(Ask if they have California wine.)
Waiter:	*Hai, kochira no pēji ga Kariforunia wain de gozaimasu.*	
You:	(b) _____	(Say thank you.)
You:	(c) _____	(Draw attention.)
	(d) _____	(Point out a wine on the list and order it.)
Waiter:	*Kashikomarimashita. Gurasu wa ikutsu omochi shimashō ka.*	
You:	(e) _____	(Ask her to bring two glasses.)

4. Reserve a table for five at a *yakitori-ya* by phone.

Master:	*Hai, arigatō gozaimasu. Torifuji de gozaimasu.*	
You:	*Sumimasen ga,* (a) _____	(Ask to make a reservation.)
Master:	*Hai. Itsu no goyoyaku deshō ka.*	
You:	(b) _____	(Say Saturday this week.)
Master:	*Nan-ji kara deshō ka.*	

Vocabulary

1. *ranchi setto:* lunch set menu	*wain risuto:* wine list	*gurasu:* glass
(o)kaikei: check	*pēji:* page	*ikutsu:* how many

You: (c) _____ (Say from 7:00 p.m.)

Master: *Nan-mei-sama deshō ka.*

You: (d) _____ (Say five people.)

Master: *Shōshō omachi kudasai.*

Konshū no doyōbi, 7-ji kara, go-mei-sama desu ne.

Uketamawarimashita.

Onamae to gorenrakusaki no denwa bangō, onegaishimasu.

You: (e) _____

(Give your name and phone number.)

Master: *Kashikomarimashita. Omachi shite imasu.*

5. Call the *yakitori-ya* and ask to change the reservation.

Master: *Hai, arigatō gozaimasu. Torifuji de gozaimasu.*

You: *Sumimasen ga,* (a) _____

(Ask politely to change the reservation.)

Master: *Hai. Onamae wa?*

You: (b) _____ (Give your name.)

Master: *Itsu no goyoyaku deshō ka.*

You: (c) _____ (Say Saturday this week.)

Master: *Konshū no doyōbi, 7-ji kara, 5-mei-sama no goyoyaku desu ne.*

You: *Hai.* (d) _____

(Ask to change the number of people to six.)

Master: *6-mei-sama desu ne. Kashikomarimashita.*

Ⓑ Grammar & Vocabulary Building Drills

Drill 2. Ask if the following are available.

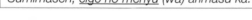

Sumimasen, eigo no menyū (wa) arimasu ka.

1. *shio*   2. *shōyu*   3. *satō*   4. *miruku*   5. *wain risuto*

Vocabulary

1. *(go)renrakusaki:*   contact   **2.** *shio:*   salt   *satō:*   sugar

henkō: change   *shōyu:*   soy sauce   *miruku:*   milk

Drill 3. You are at a restaurant. Ask for the following.

> *Sumimasen, <u>kin'en-seki</u> onegaishimasu.*

1. *mizu*   2. *nama-bīru*   3. *atsukan*   4. *onaji mono*   5. *okaikei*

Drill 4. Ask if the following are available as a special/extra request.

> *Sumimasen, <u>betsubetsu ni</u> onegai dekimasu ka.*

1. *okawari*   2. *ocha mō ippai* 3. *isoide*   4. *kādo de*   5. *ryōshūsho*

Drill 5. Look at the menu on the next page and order something according to the cue.

You:	(a) <u>*Sumimasen.*</u> (Draw attention.)
Waitress:	*Okimari desu ka.*
You:	(b) <u>*Kore hitotsu to kore hitotsu, onegaishimasu.*</u>
	(Order one drink and one set by pointing.)
Waitress:	*Kashikomarimashita.*
You:	*Sorekara,* (c) <u>*3-ban mo onegaishimasu.*</u>
	(Order one dessert in addition by saying the number.)

1. You: (a) Draw attention.
   (b) Order two of #4 and two of #7, by saying the numbers.
   (c) Order one #11, by saying the number.

2. You: (a) Draw attention.
   (b) Order one #1, one #3 and one #8, one #9, by saying the numbers.
   (c) Order one #12, by saying the number.

Vocabulary

3. *mizu:* (cold) water
   nama-bīru: draft beer
   atsukan: hot sake

4. *okawari:* another portion
   ocha: Japanese tea
   mō ippai: another cup of ~

isoide: in a hurry
kādo: card
ryōshūsho: receipt

3. You: (a) Draw attention.
          (b) Order two drinks and two lunch sets by pointing.
          (c) Order two desserts by pointing.

4. You: (a) Draw attention.
          (b) Order two drinks and one dessert by pointing.
          (c) Order one dessert by pointing.

5. You: (a) Draw attention.
          (b) Order one lunch set, one drink and one dessert by pointing.
          (c) Order a glass of water.

Lunch Sets

#1 天ぷら定食　　　#2 とんかつ定食　　　#3 エビフライ定食

#4 コロッケ定食　　　#5 刺身定食

Drinks

#6 コーヒー　　#7 紅茶　　　　#8 ジュース　　#9 ビール　　#10 ワイン

Desserts

#11 アイスクリーム　　　#12 ケーキ　　　　#13 ヨーグルト

Drill 6. Make five dialogues by filling in the blanks with the information given below.

Waiter: *Irasshaimase. Nan-mei-sama desu ka.*

You: (a)_____ *desu.* (b)_____ *onegaishimasu.*

Waiter: *Kashikomarimashita. Kochira e dōzo.*

You: *Sumimasen.* (c)_____ *wa arimasu ka.*

Waiter: *Hai, shōshō omachi kudasai.*

* * * *

Waiter: *Gochūmon wa okimari desu ka.*

You: (d)_____ *to* (e)_____ *onegaishimasu.*

Waiter: *Onomimono wa itsu omochi itashimasu ka.*

You: (f)_____ *onegaishimasu.*

* * * *

Cashier: *Okaikei wa goissho desu ka.*

You: (g)_____ *onegaishimasu.*

	(a)	(b)	(c)	(d)	(e)	(f)	(g)
1			Menu English	A *ranchi* × 2	× 2	after	separately
2			Wine Vin Vino	*aka wain* × 1	× 3		together
3				*chokorēto kēki* × 1	*kōhī zerī* × 1		
4			*koshitsu*	*kitsune udon* × 2	*zarusoba* × 2		
5			*koshitsu*	*nigiri* × 5	× 2	before	

Vocabulary

6. *(o)nomimono:* beverage
  madogawa: window side
  kauntā: counter
  botoru: bottle
  koshitsu: private room

chokorēto kēki: chocolate cake
kitsune udon: udon noodles with
  deep-fried tofu
nigiri: raw fish on rice
kōhī zerī: coffee jelly

zarusoba: buckwheat noodles served
  cold
saki ni: before

ⓒ Listening Tasks

Drill 7. Listen to the CD and choose the appropriate pictures for the dialogues.

1. (　　) 2. (　　) 3. (　　) 4. (　　) 5. (　　)

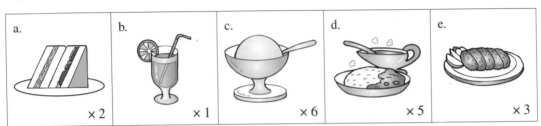

Drill 8. Listen to the CD and choose the appropriate pictures for the dialogues.

1. (　　) 2. (　　) 3. (　　) 4. (　　)

ⓓ Review Drills

Drill 9. Read the following instructions and make sentences.

How would you:

1. ask for an English menu?

2. ask for a glass of water?

3. ask politely to pay separately?

4. ask if vegetarian lunch is available?

5. say that there are three in your party?

Vocabulary

7. *sandoitchi:*　sandwich　　　　*aisu kurīmu:*　ice cream　　　　*tonkatsu:*　pork cutlet

6. ask for a table in the non-smoking area?

7. ask that coffee be brought before the meal?

8. ask if a credit card would be all right?

Drill 10. Match the responses with the questions.

1. *Nan-mei-sama desu ka.*   ·   · a. *Ato de onegaishimasu.*
2. *Gochūmon wa okimari desu ka.*   ·   · b. A *ranchi o hitotsu to kōhī onegaishimasu.*
3. *Otabako wa?*   ·   · c. *Futari desu.*
4. *Kōhī wa itsu omochi shimasu ka.* ·   · d. *Kin'enseki onegaishimasu.*

Drill 11. Complete the dialogues by changing the following sentences to the correct order.

1. (c) → (   ) → (   ) → (   )

    a. *Hai, kashikomarimashita. Shōshō omachi kudasai.*

    b. *Kādo de ii desu ka.*

    c. *Sumimasen, okanjō o onegaishimasu.*

    d. *Hai, Amekkusu ka Biza de onegaishimasu.*

2. (c) → (   ) → (   ) → (   ) → (   ) → (a)

    a. *Dewa, gochūmon o dōzo.*

    b. *Hai. Onamae to gojūsho o onegaishimasu.*

    c. *Piza no deribarī o onegaishimasu.*

    d. *03-1474-9023 desu.*

    e. *Odenwa bangō mo onegaishimasu.*

    f. *Howaito desu. Jūsho wa Ōtemachi 3-1-2 desu.*

Vocabulary

11. *okanjō:* check   *Biza:* Visa   *deribarī:* delivery
     Amekkusu: Amex   *piza:* pizza

CLOSING DIALOGUE
Formal Informal

Eating in or taking out
28

(At a café near the office.)

Ten'in: *Irasshaimase.*

Howaito: *Kyō no kōhī, shōto hitotsu.*

Ten'in: *Omochikaeri desu ka.*

Howaito: *Koko de.*

Ten'in: *Nihyaku-gojū-en de gozaimasu. Sen-en oazukari itashimasu.*

             Nanahyaku-gojū-en no okaeshi de gozaimasu.

             Arigatō gozaimashita.

******

Ten'in: *Tsugi de omachi no okyaku-sama, dōzo.*

Tsukada: *Aisu kafe rate midiamu hitotsu, chīzu·hotto doggu hitotsu, onegaishimasu.*

Ten'in: *Roppyaku-nijū-en de gozaimasu. Kochira de omeshiagari desu ka.*

             Nijūnana-ban de, oseki no hō de omachi kudasai.

<ruby>店員<rt>てんいん</rt></ruby>： いらっしゃいませ。	Staff: Hello. (lit., Welcome to our shop.)
ホワイト： きょうの　コーヒー、ショート　ひとつ。	Mr. White: One small coffee of the day, please.
店員： おもちかえりですか。	Staff: That'll be to go?
ホワイト： ここで。	Mr. White: I'll have it here.
店員： 250 えんでございます。1,000 えん　おあずかりいたします。750 えんの　おかえしでございます。ありがとうございました。	Staff: That'll be 250 yen. You've given me 1,000 yen and here's 750 yen, change. Thank you very much.
******	******
店員： つぎで　おまちの　おきゃくさま、どうぞ。	Staff: Next, please.
<ruby>塚田<rt>つかだ</rt></ruby>： アイスカフェラテ　ミディアム　ひとつ、チーズホットドッグ　ひとつ、おねがいします。	Ms. Tsukada: One medium iced coffee latte, and one cheese dog, please.
店員： 620 えんでございます。こちらで　おめしあがりですか。27 ばんで、おせきの　ほうで　おまちください。	Staff: That'll be 620 yen. Will you be eating here? Please wait at the table with this number, #27.

Noren and Japanese restaurants

*N*oren or "doorway curtains" have been used in Japan for centuries and are unique to this country. They are usually made of traditional Japanese fabrics and are hung between rooms, in entrances, and in windows. In addition to the cloth type, there are rope type *noren*, which are commonly seen at small pubs.

Noren are traditionally used by shops, restaurants, and public bathhouses as a means of protection against the sun, wind, and dust, and also for advertising. *Noren* typically show the name of the establishment or its service, with the words written in *kanji* (Chinese characters) or *hiragana* (Japanese curvy syllabary). They function as signs for the shops and restaurants. A *noren* hung on the outside of an establishment signifies that it is open; when the *noren* withdrawn, the shop is closed for the day.

Noren also have an important meaning in the context of Japanese business customs. Although tangibly they function as signs, conceptually they refer to business ownership. *Noren* date back to the Edo period. When a young employee reached maturity, he was allowed to set up his own store with the same name at his former employer's. This custom was referred to as *noren wake* and is still practiced today. Another traditional practice, in which a former employer provided operating expenses to a new store owner, was called *norendai*. Today *norendai* refers to intangible assets or to goodwill, which results from brand strength, reliance on the original store, etc., and is an important consideration in M&A transactions.

Various types of Japanese restaurants

Izakaya （居酒屋）
The picture shows a rope type *noren* at the doorway. This is an *izakaya* which is a very popular Japanese style drinking and eating place.

Izakaya

Soba-ya （そば屋）
A *soba* shop is a place where you can eat *soba,* which are dark buckwheat noodles. You can see a cloth *noren* with the specialty of the shop written on it in *hiragana*. It reads *osoba* 'dark buckwheat noodles' in a polite way. Also note the display window of dishes shown on the left. Those sample dishes are made of plastic and look quite real.

Soba-ya

Rāmen-ya〔ラーメン屋〕

A *rāmen* shop is a place where you can eat *rāmen*, which are Chinese style noodles. *Rāmen* is believed to have been developed originally in Hokkaido or Kyushu.

   Rāmen-ya are quite different from regular Chinese restaurants. They typically have a counter and only a handful of tables and chairs.

Rāmen-ya

Aka-chōchin

An *aka-chōchin* is a red paper lantern which is hung at the entrance of a Japanese style popular pub. In the picture, the word *yakitori* is written on it in *hiragana*.

Aka-chōchin

Signboards at the entrance

営業中 (*Eigyōchū*): This sign indicates that the restaurant is open.

準備中 (*Junbichū*): This sign indicates that the restaurant is not open yet.

定休日 (*Teikyūbi*): This sign means it is a regular non-business day for the shop. Most restaurants and shops are closed once a week.

LESSON 6: ASKING/GIVING DIRECTIONS
—*Meguro-eki no chikaku made onegaishimasu.*
'To the vicinity of Meguro Station, please.'

Dialogue 1 Taking a taxi · Formal 29

(Anthony Kumar is in a taxi.)

Kumaru: *Sumimasen, Meguro-eki no chikaku made onegaishimasu.*
Untenshu: *Hai.*

(Near Meguro Station.)

Kumaru: *Meguro-dōri o massugu onegaishimasu.*
Untenshu: *Hai.*
Kumaru: *Sorekara, tsugi no tsugi no shingō o migi e onegaishimasu.*
Untenshu: *Futatsu-me no shingō desu ne.*
Kumaru: *Hai, sō desu.*

(After turning right.)

Kumaru: *Tsugi o hidari e magatte,*
sugu ni migi e onegaishimasu.
Untenshu: *Hai.*
Kumaru: *Massugu itte kudasai.*
Untenshu: *Hai.*
Kumaru: *Kono hen de ii desu.*

Mr. Kumar: Excuse me, (take me) to the vicinity of Meguro Station, please.
Driver: Yes, sir.
******

Mr. Kumar: Go straight on Meguro Avenue, please.
Driver: Yes.
Mr. Kumar: Then, turn right at the traffic light after the next one, please.
Driver: OK. (You mean) the second traffic light?
Mr. Kumar: That's right.
******

Vocabulary

eki: station
chikaku: vicinity
untenshu: driver
-dōri: street; avenue
massugu: straight

tsugi: next
shingō: traffic light
migi: right
futatsu-me: second
hidari: left

magaru (magarimasu): to turn
sugu ni: immediately
hen: around (place)

Mr. Kumar:	Turn at the next left and then immediately to the right after that, please.
Driver:	OK.
Mr. Kumar:	Go straight, please.
Driver:	Yes.
Mr. Kumar:	Stop here, please. (lit., Around here will be fine.)

クマル：　すみません、目黒えきの　ちかくまで　おねがいします。

運転手：　はい。

******

クマル：　目黒通りを　まっすぐ　おねがいします。

運転手：　はい。

クマル：　それから、つぎの　つぎの　しんごうを　右へ　おねがいします。

運転手：　ふたつめの　しんごうですね。

クマル：　はい、そうです。

******

クマル：　つぎを　左へ　まがって、すぐに　右へ　おねがいします。

運転手：　はい。

クマル：　まっすぐ　いってください。

運転手：　はい。

クマル：　このへんで　いいです。

● **Comprehension Drill**

1. Listen to or read Dialogue 1 and decide if the following statements are true, false or you don't know as not enough information has been given.

1. Mr. Kumar wants to go to Meguro Station.	(T / F / DK)
2. The driver doesn't know the location of Meguro Station.	(T / F / DK)
3. The taxi takes a right turn at the second traffic light.	(T / F / DK)
4. After turning right, the taxi turns to the left first.	(T / F / DK)
5. Mr. Kumar gets out of the taxi in front of Meguro Station.	(T / F / DK)

2. Put these sentences in the correct order to make a conversation in a taxi.

(　) → (　) → (　) → (　) → (c)

a. *Futatsu-me no shingō desu ne.*

b. *Meguro-dōri o massugu onegaishimasu.*

c. *Hai, sō desu.*

d. *Hai.*

e. *Sorekara, futatsu-me no shingō o migi e onegaishimasu.*

Dialogue 2 Looking for where to get on public transportation · · · · · · · · · · · · ·  Formal Informal 30

(Jacqueline Richardson is talking to a Japanese man on the platform of a train station.)

Richādoson:	*Sumimasen, kono densha, Yūrakuchō ni tomarimasu ka.*
Nihonjin dansei:	*Kore wa tomaranai yo. Yūrakuchō wa mukaigawa no hōmu da yo.*
Richādoson:	*Mukaigawa desu ka.*
Nihonjin dansei:	*Sō sō, atchi.*
Richādoson:	*Arigatō gozaimasu.*

(Ms. Richardson exits the station and is looking for a bus.)

Richādoson:	*Anō, Harumi ni ikitai n desu ga, basutei wa koko desu ka.*
Nihonjin josei:	*Ara, koko ja nai desu yo. Dōro no hantaigawa ni mō hitotsu basutei ga aru deshō? Harumi wa, atchi kara noru no.*
Richādoson:	*Sumimasen. Mō sukoshi yukkuri hanashite kudasai.*
Nihonjin josei:	*Harumi-yuki no basu wa, dōro no hantaigawa desu yo.*
Richādoson:	*Arigatō gozaimasu.*
Nihonjin josei:	*Ki o tsukete ne.*

Ms. Richardson:	Excuse me, does this train stop at Yurakucho Station?
Japanese man:	(Oh, no,) this one doesn't. The train you are looking for will arrive at the opposite platform.
Ms. Richardson:	Oh, on the other side!
Japanese man:	Yes, yes, it's over there.
Ms. Richardson:	Thank you very much for your help.
******	
Ms. Richardson:	Excuse me, I'd like to go to Harumi. Is this the right bus stop?
Japanese woman:	Oh, no, this is the wrong place. Do you see the bus stop across the street from here? That's where you catch the bus to Harumi.
Ms. Richardson:	I'm sorry, but could you speak more slowly, please?
Japanese woman:	A bus bound for Harumi leaves from the other side on the street.
Ms. Richardson:	Thank you very much.
Japanese woman:	Good luck. (lit., Be careful.)

Vocabulary

tomaru (tomarimasu): to stop
dansei: man
mukaigawa: opposite side (face to)
hōmu: platform
atchi: over there
basutei: bus stop
koko: here

josei: woman
ara: oh [female]
dōro: road; street
hantaigawa: opposite side (the other side)
aru (arimasu): to be
noru (norimasu): to get in/on

mō sukoshi: a little bit more
yukkuri: slowly
hanasu (hanashimasu): to speak
-yuki: bound for
Ki o tsukete.: Good luck. (lit., Be careful.)

81

リチャードソン：すみません、この　でんしゃ、有楽町に　とまりますか。

日本人男性：　　これは　とまらないよ。有楽町は　むかいがわの　ホームだよ。

リチャードソン：むかいがわですか。

日本人男性：　　そうそう、あっち。

リチャードソン：ありがとうございます。

******

リチャードソン：あのう、晴海に　いきたいんですが、バスていは　ここですか。

日本人女性：　　あら、ここじゃないですよ。どうろの　はんたいがわに

　　　　　　　　もうひとつ　バスていが　あるでしょう？晴海は、あっちから

　　　　　　　　のるの。

リチャードソン：すみません。もうすこし　ゆっくり　はなしてください。

日本人女性：　　晴海ゆきの　バスは、どうろの　はんたいがわですよ。

リチャードソン：ありがとうございます。

日本人女性：　　きをつけてね。

● Comprehension Drill

Listen to or read Dialogue 2 and decide if the following statements are true, false or you don't know as not enough information has been given.

1. The train that Ms. Richardson is pointing at stops at Yurakucho. (T / F / DK)
2. A man on the platform points Ms. Richardson to the correct track. (T / F / DK)
3. Ms. Richardson wants to go to Harumi by bus. (T / F / DK)
4. There is a conference in Harumi today. (T / F / DK)
5. Ms. Richardson understands the lady's Japanese immediately. (T / F / DK)

◆　　　　◆　　　　◆

Grammar Note 1　Taking a taxi （タクシーに乗る）

Taking a taxi is a convenient way to get somewhere when you are not familiar with the area.

a. Saying your destination

The following two patterns are used to tell a taxi driver where to go.

When you would like to go a specific place, you can use *onegaishimasu*, which you learned in Lesson 5. Say to the taxi driver "[the place where you want to go] + *(made) onegaishimasu*."

[Place you want to go] *(made) onegaishimasu.* **'(Take me) to ~, please.'**

Destination		Verb
Roppongi Hiruzu	*(made)*	onegaishimasu.
'Please take me to Roppongi Hills. (lit., Roppongi Hills, please.)'		

When you would like to go the vicinity of a landmark, you can use ~ *no chikaku* after the landmark.

[Landmark] *no chikaku made onegaishimasu.* **'To the vicinity of ~, please.'**

Destination				Verb	
Landmark					
Meguro-eki	*no*	*chikaku*	*made*	onegaishimasu.	
'(Take me) to the vicinity of Meguro Station, please.' (D-1)					

After that you can give more detailed instructions to the taxi driver. (See Grammar Note 2.)

b. Asking the driver to stop

When you would like to stop, you use ~ *de ii desu* where you want to stop. ~ *de ii desu* literally means '~ is fine.'

[Place] *de ii desu.* **'~ is fine.'**

Place of Action		
Koko		
Kono hen	*de*	*ii desu.*
Soko		
'Stop here. (lit., This will be fine.)'		
'Stop around here. (lit., Around here will be fine.)' (D-1)		
'Stop right there. (lit., That will be fine.)' (Closing Dialogue)		

c. *Koko/soko/asoko* 'here/there/over there'

Koko 'here,' *soko* 'there,' and *asoko* 'over there' are another set of *ko-so-a-do* words which were introduced in Lesson 5.

The *ko-so-a-do* words

	Ko group (near S[*1])	So group (near L[*2])	A group (far from S & L)	Do group (question word)
Thing	kore	sore	are	dore
	kono[*3] + N[*4]	sono + N	ano + N	dono + N
Place	koko	soko	asoko	doko
Area	kono hen	sono hen	ano hen	dono hen

[*1] S: Speaker [*2] L: Listener [*3] kono/sono/ano/dono: Adjective forms of kore/sore/are/dore [*4] N: Noun

Grammar Note 2   Giving directions (道を教える)

a. Giving detailed instructions

When giving more detailed instructions to a taxi driver, use the following patterns.

Place of Motion					Direction		
Tsugi							
Tsugi		*shingō*			*migi*		
Hitotsu-me	*no*	*kōsaten*		*o*		*e*	⇒ **onegaishimasu.**
Futatsu-me		*kado*			*hidari*		
φ		*Hodōkyō*	*no*	*tokoro*			
Yamate-dōri					*massugu*		

e.g.   *Meguro-dōri o massugu onegaishimasu.* 'Go straight on Meguro Avenue, please.' (D-1)

   Tsugi no tsugi no shingō o migi e onegaishimasu. 'Turn right at the traffic light after the next one, please.' (D-1)

   Kōsaten o massugu onegaishimasu. 'Go straight at the intersection, please.'

(Closing Dialogue)

b. Telling the driver where to stop

~ *de ii desu*, introduced in Grammar Note 1-b, can also be used to tell the driver where to stop.

Place of Action						
Tsugi						
Tsugi		*shingō*				
Hitotsu-me	*no*	*kōsaten*		*de*	⇒	**ii desu.**
Futatsu-me		*kado*				
φ		*Hodōkyō*	*no*	*tokoro*		

The following are other verbs that you can use instead of *onegaishimasu* or *ii desu*.

magatte kudasai	'please turn'
itte kudasai	'please go'
tōtte kudasai	'please go through; please take'
tomatte kudasai	'please stop'

e.g.   *Massugu **itte kudasai**.* 'Go straight, please.' (D-1)

   *Soko o hidari e **magatte kudasai**.* 'Turn to the left there, please.' (Closing Dialogue)

Vocabulary

hitotsu-me: first   *kado:* corner   *tokoro:* place
kōsaten: intersection   *hodōkyō:* pedestrian bridge

Grammar Note 3 Taking trains, buses and subways
（電車・バス・地下鉄に乗る）

a. Confirming that a train stops at a certain station

When you want to ask if the train you will take stops at a certain station, you can use the following pattern.

[Transportation] *wa* **[place]** *ni tomarimasu ka.* 'Does (transportation) stop at ~?'

Topic		Place		Verb	SP
Kono densha	(wa)	Yūrakuchō	ni	tomarimasu	ka.
'Does this train stop at Yurakucho Station?' (D-2)					

The responses will be as follows.

Positive response: **Ee, [Verb (affirmative)]** *yo.*

 Ee, tomarimasu yo. (formal) / *Tomaru yo.* (informal) 'Yes, it will stop.'

Negative response: **[Verb (negative)]** *yo.*

 Tomarimasen yo. (formal) / *Tomaranai yo.* (informal) 'This one doesn't.' (D-2)

For variation, when you ask if the public transportation you take will go to a certain place, you can use the verb *ikimasu* instead of *tomarimasu*.

e.g. *Kore wa Shinjuku ni ikimasu ka.* 'Is this going to Shinjuku?'

Grammar Note 4 Particles （助詞）

a. Destination marker [*made*]

Made implies a final destination or goal. This marker is sometimes omitted as in the following because the place name before the marker is obviously a destination.

e.g. *Roppongi Hiruzu (made), onegaishimasu.*

b. Place of motion marker [*o*]

The place of motion marker *o* follows the place where you want to pass and keep moving by in a certain direction, as shown in Grammar Note 2-a.

c. Place of action marker [*de*]

The place of action marker *de* is used to denote a place where actions will take place. The marker *o* is used when you want to keep moving or to pass a point, but *de* is used when you want to stop and do something at the place. Therefore, when a taxi driver hears *o* he keeps driving but as soon as he hears *de*, he will be ready to stop the car.

Grammar Note 5 Conversation strategies: To get to your destination （会話ストラテジー：目的地に行く）

—Asking for information to get to your destination:

Harumi ni ikitai n desu ga, ~. 'I'd like to go to Harumi, but ~.' (D-2)

This implies "Please tell me how to get there," even you don't say it.

—Confirming that the public transportation you will take is the correct one:

Basutei wa koko desu ka. 'Is this the right bus stop?' (D-2)

—When you don't know which is the correct line that you should take:

Shimoda-yuki no densha wa dore desu ka. 'Which is the train bound for Shimoda?'

—Asking for repeating slowly what has just been said:

Mō sukoshi yukkuri hanashite kudasai. 'Could you speak more slowly, please?' (D-2)

◆　　　　◆　　　　◆

Ⓐ Conversation Drills

Drill 1. Complete the following conversations.

1. You are in a taxi to go somewhere near the Kabuki-za theater.

   You: (a) _____

   (Tell the taxi driver to take you near the Kabuki-za theater.)

   Driver: *Hai.*

   You: (b) _____

   (Tell the driver to turn right at the post office.)

   Driver: *Hai.*

   You: (c) _____ (Tell the driver to stop here.)

2. You are in a taxi to go to Ochanomizu Station.

   You: (a) _____

   (Ask the taxi driver to take you to Ochanomizu Station.)

   Driver: *Hai.*

   You: (b) _____

   (Tell the driver to go straight on Sotobori Street.)

   Driver: *Hai.*

   You: (c) _____

   (Tell the driver to turn left at the second intersection.)

Vocabulary

1. *Kabuki-za:* Kabuki-za theater　　*yūbinkyoku:* post office　　*Sotobori-dōri:* Sotobori Street

Driver: *Futatsu-me no kōsaten desu ne.*

3. You are at a station and want to go to Yokohama.

You: (a) _____

(Ask a stranger if this train goes to Yokohama.)

Stranger: *Un, iku yo.*

You: (b) _____ (Express gratitude.)

4. You are at a station and want to go to Kichijoji Station.

You: *Sumimasen,* (a)_____

(Ask if the train stops at Kichijoji Station.)

Stranger: *Kore wa tomaranai yo. Kichijōji wa mukaigawa no hōmu da yo.*

You: (b) _____ (Confirm it's opposite side.)

Stranger: *Sō sō, atchi.*

You: (c) _____ (Say thank you.)

5. You are at a bus terminal and want to go to Ginza.

You: (a) _____

(Ask a stranger if this is the right bus stop to go to Ginza.)

Stranger: *Ara, koko ja nai desu yo. Dōro no hantaigawa desu yo.*

You: (b) _____

(Ask the stranger to speak more slowly.)

Stranger: *Ginza-yuki no basu wa dōro no hantaigawa desu yo.*

You: (c) _____ (Say thank you.)

B Grammar & Vocabulary Building Drills

Drill 2. **Choose the appropriate pictures for the following position words.**

1. ( ) *hidari* 2. ( ) *-dōri* 3. ( ) *kōsaten* 4. ( ) *migi*
5. ( ) *kado* 6. ( ) *hodōkyō* 7. ( ) *shingō* 8. ( ) *tsugi*
9. ( ) *futatsu-me* 10. ( ) *massugu*

Drill 3. Give the destination by changing the underlined part.

> <u>Meguro-eki</u> (made) onegaishimasu.

1. Shibuya

2. Roppongi-kōsaten

3. Hibiya-kōen

4. Shinjuku-eki no minami guchi

5. Akasaka no TBS-biru

Drill 4. Make five dialogues by filling in the blanks with the information given below.

> **You:**   (a)_____ no chikaku made onegaishimasu.
>
> Driver: Hai.
>
> * * * * *
>
> **You:**   (b)_____ onegaishimasu.
>
> Driver: Hai.
>
> **You:**   (c)_____ de ii desu.

	1.	2.	3.	4.	5.
(a)	Tsukiji	KDD-biru	Tōkyō-eki	Ueno-kōen	Roppongi-kōsaten
(b)					
(c)	koko	sono hen	kōban no tokoro	tsugi no shingō	futatsu-me (tsugi no tsugi) no kado

---

Vocabulary

4. kōban: police box   tsukiatari: end of the street

C Listening Tasks

Drill 5. Look at the pictures and listen to the questions. Choose answers from the box below that respond to the questions.

31

a. *Mukaigawa da yo.*	b. *Hai, sō desu.*	c. *Koko ja nai desu yo.*
d. *Ikimasu yo.*	e. *Hai, tomarimasu.*	

1. (　　　)

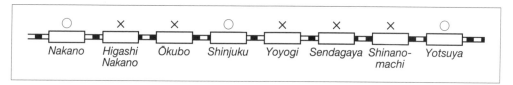

2. (　　　)

3. (　　　)

4. (　　　)

5. (　　　)

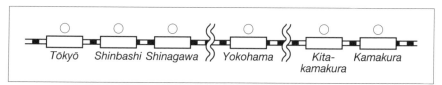

Drill 6. Listen to the three dialogues and fill in the table with choices from the options given below.

32

	A. Destination	B. Street	C. Directions
Dialogue 1			
Dialogue 2			
Dialogue 3			

A. Destination

| Yūrakuchō | Ebisu | Tōkyō-eki | Yoyogi-kōen |

B. Street

C. Directions

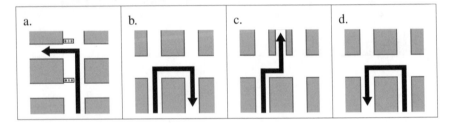

D Review Drills

Drill 7. Read the following instructions and make sentences.

How would you:

1. tell a taxi driver to go near Tokyo Station?

2. tell a taxi driver to turn right at the second (or the one after the next) traffic light?

3. ask a taxi driver to go straight ahead?

4. ask a taxi driver to turn left at the next intersection?

5. ask a taxi driver to stop around here?

6. ask someone if the train stops at Shimbashi Station?

7. tell someone that you want to go to Ginza and ask him/her if this is the right bus stop?

8. ask someone which train is bound for Shimoda?

Drill 8. **Match the responses with the questions/remarks.**

1. *Tsugi no tsugi no shingō desu ne?* ·	· a. *Ara, koko ja nai desu yo.*
2. *Kono densha, Kanda ni tomarimasu ka.* ·	· b. *Kore wa tomaranai desu yo.*
3. *Hiroo ni ikitai n desu ga, basutei wa koko desu ka.* ·	· c. *Massugu desu ne.*
4. *Aoyama-dōri o massugu itte kudasai.* ·	· d. *Hai, futatsu-me desu.*

Drill 9. **Complete the dialogues by changing the following sentences to the correct order.**

1. (a) → ( ) → ( ) → ( ) → ( )

    a. *Sumimasen, Kudan-minami made onegaishimasu.*

    b. *Sono kōsaten o hidari ni magatte kudasai.*

    c. *Hai.*

    d. *Hidari desu ne.*

    e. *Tsugi no shingō no saki de ii desu.*

2. (d) → ( ) → ( ) → ( )

    a. *Hai, ii desu yo.*

    b. *Tōkyō-dōmu wa Sōbu-sen de Suidōbashi made itte kudasai.*

    c. *Sōbu-sen? Sumimasen, rōma-ji de kaite kuremasen ka.*

    d. *Sumimasen, Tōkyō-dōmu e ikitai n desu ga.*

Vocabulary

9. *saki:* beyond   *kaite kuremasen ka:*   would you
                              please write it down?

CLOSING DIALOGUE — Formal

Taking a taxi home and dropping off a colleague on the way

33

(After a business dinner at a restaurant.)

Weitā: Okyaku-sama, takushī ga omachi desu.

Tonpuson: Dewa, sorosoro shitsurei shimasu.

Kawashima (R): Sō desu ka, dewa, mata kondo. Jikai wa karaoke ni ikimashō.

Tonpuson/Kumaru: Kyō wa dōmo gochisōsama deshita. Osaki ni shitsurei shimasu.

(In a taxi.)

Tonpuson: Roppongi kōsaten no chikaku made onegai-
             shimasu. Tochū Shirokane ni yotte kudasai.

(At Shirokane.)

Kumaru: Soko o hidari e magatte kudasai.
            Saisho no hosoi michi o migi desu.
            . . . Tsukiatari no manshon desu.

(Near Roppongi intersection.)

Tonpuson: Ēto, kōsaten o massugu onegaishimasu. Hitotsu-me o hidari e magatte kudasai.
            Tsukiatari o migi e onegaishimasu. Hidarigawa ni kōen ga arimasu. Soko de ii desu.

ウエイター：おきゃくさま、タクシーが おまちです。	Restaurant staff: Excuse me, but your taxi is here.
トンプソン：では、そろそろ しつれいします。	Mr. Thompson: OK. It's time to be leaving.
川島良三：そうですか、では、また こんど。じか いは カラオケに いきましょう。	Mr. Kawashima: We'll get together again soon (lit., next time) We'll go to a karaoke bar, next time, shall we?
トンプソン／クマル：きょうは どうも ごちそうさ までした。おさきに しつれいします。	Mr. Thompson & Mr. Kumar: It was a very good dinner, thank you (for a pleasant evening) today. Goodbye. (lit., Excuse us for leaving before you.)
******	******
トンプソン：六本木こうさてんの ちかくまで おね がいします。とちゅう 白金に よって ください。	Mr. Thompson: Go toward (lit., near) the Roppongi intersection, (and) on the way, drop by at Shirokane, please.
******	******
クマル：そこを 左へ まがってください。さい しょの ほそい みちを 右です。 ……つきあたりの マンションです。	Mr. Kumar: Turn to the left there, please. Turn right at the first small street. . . . Here, that's my apartment building at the end of this street.
******	******
トンプソン：えーと、こうさてんを まっすぐ おね がいします。ひとつめを 左へ まがっ てください。つきあたりを 右へ おね がいします。左がわに こうえんが あ ります。そこで いいです。	Mr. Thompson: OK, go straight at the intersection, please. Turn to the left at the first street and then to the right at the T-junction. You'll see a park on your left. Stop right there (lit., That will be fine).

LESSON 7: ASKING/GIVING THE LOCATION OF PEOPLE OR THINGS
—*Toire wa doko desu ka.*
'Where is the ladies'/men's room, please?'

Dialogue 1 — Looking for some place · · · · · · · · · · · · · Formal

(Jacqueline Richardson is on the first floor of a department store.)

Richādoson:	*Anō, toire wa doko desu ka.*
Ten'in:	*Taihen mōshiwake gozaimasen ga, kono kai ni toire wa gozaimasen.*
Richādoson:	*A, sō desu ka.*
Ten'in:	*Kochira no esukarētā de ni-kai ni ikimasu to, kutsu-uriba ga gozaimasu.*
	Toire wa kutsu-uriba no oku desu.
Richādoson:	*Ni-kai desu ne. Dōmo.*

> Ms. Richardson: Excuse me, where is the ladies' room, please?
> Shop clerk: I'm very sorry, but there's no ladies' room on this floor.
> Ms. Richardson: Is that so?
> Shop clerk: If you go up to the second floor by this escalator, you'll see the shoe department. The ladies' room is way at the back of the shoe department.
> Ms. Richardson: Second floor, right? Thank you very much.

> リチャードソン： あのう、トイレは　どこですか。
> 店員：　　　　　 たいへん　もうしわけございませんが、この　かいに　トイレ
> 　　　　　　　　 は　ございません。
> リチャードソン： あ、そうですか。
> 店員：　　　　　 こちらの　エスカレーターで　２かいに　いきますと、くつう
> 　　　　　　　　 りばが　ございます。トイレは　くつうりばの　おくです。
> リチャードソン： ２かいですね。どうも。

Vocabulary

toire: toilet; rest room	*mōshiwake gozaimasen:* sorry [polite]	*kutsu:* shoes
taihen: very	*esukarētā:* escalator	*uriba:* department; corner
		oku: far end

93

● **Comprehension Drill**

1. Listen to or read Dialogue 1 and decide if the following statements are true, false or you don't know as not enough information has been given.

1. There's no ladies' room on the first floor. (T / F / DK)
2. A shop clerk advises Ms. Richardson to take an elevator to the second floor. (T / F / DK)
3. This is the first time that Ms. Richardson has come to this department store. (T / F / DK)
4. The clerk knows the location of the ladies' room. (T / F / DK)
5. The shoe department is on the first floor. (T / F / DK)

2. Put these sentences in the correct order to make a conversation at a department store.

(   ) → (   ) → (   ) → (   ) → (b)

a. *A, sō desu ka.*
b. *Ni-kai desu ne. Dōmo.*
c. *Ni-kai ni kutsu-uriba ga gozaimasu. Toire wa kutsu-uriba no oku desu.*
d. *Anō, toire wa doko desu ka.*
e. *Taihen mōshiwake arimasen ga, kono kai ni toire wa gozaimasen.*

Dialogue 2 Looking for a thing and person

· Formal Informal **35**

(Anthony Kumar, Akiyo Miyasato and Haruko Kawashima are at the office.)

Kumaru:	*Sumimasen.* A4 (ē-yon) *no kopī no kami wa doko ni arimasu ka.*
Miyasato:	*Sono shiroi tana no migigawa ni aru yo.*
Kumaru:	*Arigatō gozaimasu.*

******

Kumaru:	*Are, Dēbiddo wa?*
Kawashima (H):	*E? Sakki made soko ni ita kedo.*
Miyasato:	*Dēbiddo? Ni-san-pun mae ni kafeteria ni ita yo.*
Kumaru:	*Sō? Kafeteria desu ka.*
	Tokoro de, kafeteria wa nan-kai ni arimasu ka.
Miyasato:	*Nijūsan-kai yo. Ik-kai ni kafe ya resutoran ga aru kedo.*

Vocabulary

kami: paper	*migigawa:* right hand side	*kedo:* though ~
aru (arimasu): to be [things]	*sakki:* a while ago	*mae:* before; ago
shiroi: white	*soko:* there	*kafeteria:* cafeteria
tana: shelf	*iru (imasu):* to be [people, animals]	

Mr. Kumar:	Sorry (to bother you), where do we keep A4 paper for printing?
Ms. Miyasato:	It's on the right side of the white shelf.
Mr. Kumar:	Thanks.
******	
Mr. Kumar:	Oh, where is David? (I thought he was here.)
Ms. Kawashima:	Well, he was there a while ago, but . . .
Ms. Miyasato:	(Are you looking for) David? He was at the cafeteria two or three minutes ago.
Mr. Kumar:	Oh, (he is) at the cafeteria. Well, where is the cafeteria? (lit. What floor?)
Miyasato:	(It's) on the 23rd floor. There are also a café and restaurants on the first floor.

クマル：	すみません。Ａ４の　コピーの　かみは　どこに　ありますか。
宮里：	その　しろい　たなの　右がわに　あるよ。
クマル：	ありがとうございます。
******	
クマル：	あれ、デービッドは？
川島春子：	え？　さっきまで　そこに　いたけど。
宮里：	デービッド？　２〜３ぷんまえに　カフェテリアに　いたよ。
クマル：	そう？　カフェテリアですか。
	ところで、カフェテリアは　なんかいに　ありますか。
宮里：	23かいよ。1かいに　カフェや　レストランが　あるけど。

● **Comprehension Drill**

Listen to or read Dialogue 2 and decide if the following statements are true, false or you don't know as not enough information has been given.

1. The paper for copying is on the right side of the white shelf.　　　　　(T / F / DK)
2. Mr. Kumar was at the cafeteria two minutes ago.　　　　　(T / F / DK)
3. David is at the cafeteria now.　　　　　(T / F / DK)
4. Mr. Kumar doesn't know where the cafeteria is.　　　　　(T / F / DK)
5. The cafeteria is located on the first floor.　　　　　(T / F / DK)

Grammar Note 1 Asking where things/facilities are（物の所在をきく）

a. Asking where things are

When you ask where things or facilities are, you can use two patterns: ~ *wa doko desu/deshō ka* and ~ *wa doko ni arimasu ka.*

The pattern using *desu* or *deshō* is as follows:

[Place/facilities you are looking for] *wa doko desu/deshō ka.* **'Where is ~?'**

C.Starter*	Topic		Location		SP
Anō,	toire	wa	doko	desu	ka.
				deshō	
'Excuse me, where is the ladies' room?' (D-1)					

*C.Starter: Conversation Starters

The response to the above is:

Topic		Location			
Toire	wa	kutsu-uriba	no	oku	desu.
					de gozaimasu.
'It's way at the back of the shoe department.' (D-1)					

The pattern using the verb *arimasu* is as follows:

[Thing you are looking for] *wa doko ni arimasu ka.* **'Where is ~?'**

C.Starter	Topic (inanimate)		Location		Verb	SP
Sumimasen,	A4 no kami	wa	doko	ni	arimasu	ka.
'Where is A4 paper for printing?' (D-2)						

The response to the above is:

> [Place] *ni aru yo.* (informal) / [Place] *ni arimasu yo.* (formal)

e.g.   *Sono shiroi tana no migigawa **ni aru yo**.* 'It's on the right side of the white shelf.' (D-2)

b. Position words

You can use the following position words to describe where things/people are. (See the table in Grammar Note 3-c.)

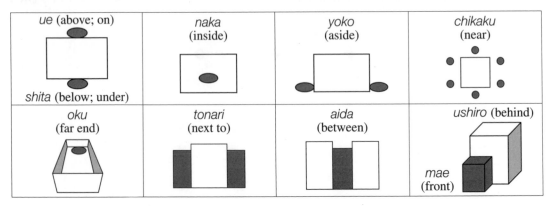

| *ue* (above; on) ... *shita* (below; under) | *naka* (inside) | *yoko* (aside) | *chikaku* (near) |
| *oku* (far end) | *tonari* (next to) | *aida* (between) | *ushiro* (behind) ... *mae* (front) |

c. ~ *deshō ka* vs. ~ *desu ka*

~ *deshō ka* given in **a.** is a more polite way of saying ~ *desu ka*. For instance, when you go to a very formal Japanese restaurant to have a formal Japanese dinner called *kaiseki*, you had better use ~ *deshō ka* in asking its whereabouts, but at a fast food restaurant, it would be polite enough to use ~ *desu ka*.

Grammar Note 2 Asking/telling someone where a person is
(人の所在をきく)

You have learned how to ask and describe where things are by using the verb *arimasu* in Grammar Note 1. In this section you will learn how to locate people with the verb *imasu*. When you are looking for people/animals, use the following pattern.

[The people/animals you are looking for] *wa doko desu ka / ni imasu ka.*

Topic (animate)		Location		Verb	SP
Dēbiddo	*wa*	*doko*	*ni*	*imasu*	*ka.*
				desu	
'Where is David?'					

Doko ni imasu ka or *doko desu ka* could be omitted in informal speech.

   e.g.   *Are, Dēbiddo wa?* 'Oh, where is David?' (D-2)

Grammar Note 3 *Arimasu, imasu* and *desu* (あります・います・です)

a. *Arimasu* vs. *imasu*

Arimasu and *imasu* are the verbs of existence or location. The major difference between them is that *arimasu* is used only with inanimate nouns including trees and flowers, while *imasu* is used with animate nouns such as people, animals, and even moving things like buses and cars.

b. *Desu*

The verb phrase ~ *ni arimasu/imasu* can often be replaced by ~ *desu* as seen below. However, ~ *ni arimasu/imasu* and ~ *desu* are slightly different in nuance; ~ *ni arimasu/imasu* focuses more on the existence of the things/people, while ~ *desu* denotes location with the existence of the things/people assumed.

Topic		Location		Verb	SP
A4 *no kami*	*wa*	*ue*	*ni*	*arimasu*	*yo.*
				aru	
Toire		*doko*		*arimasu*	*ka.*
				desu	

c. Describing location

Now look at the following table and learn how locations are described more in detail.

Location					Verb	SP
Place						
Koko/Soko/Asoko						
Relative Position			Core Position			
Tana Tsukue Kyabinetto Heya Hikidashi Kaidan Erebētā		no	migi/hidari ue/shita naka yoko mae/ushiro chikaku	ni	arimasu aru	yo.

d. *Ko-so-a-do* words for location/directions

The following is a table for *ko-so-a-do* words for location/directions.

		Ko group	So group	A group	Do group
		here/this way (my side)	there/that way (your side)	over there/ that way (the other side)	where/ which way
Informal	Location	koko	soko	asoko	doko
	Direction	kotchi	sotchi	atchi	dotchi
Formal	Location/ Direction	*kochira	*sochira	*achira	*dochira

*These are also used for people.

e. Location marker [*ni*]

When the Location Marker *ni* is used with the verbs *arimasu/imasu*, it indicates the specific place where inanimate or animate things are located or exist. This marker follows the location words as follows:

[Things/people] *wa* **[place]** *ni arimasu/imasu.* 'It/someone is (there) ~.'

Topic		Location				Verb
A4 *no kami*	*wa*	*sono shiroi tana*	*no*	*migigawa*	*ni*	*arimasu.*
Dēbiddo		*jūik-kai*		*kafeteria*		*imashita.*
'It's on the right side of the white shelf.' 'David was at the cafeteria on the 11th floor.'						

Vocabulary

tsukue: desk
kyabinetto: cabinet

hikidashi: drawer
kaidan: stairs

erebētā: elevator

[Place] *ni* **[things/people]** *ga arimasu/imasu.* '**There is/are ~.**'

Location		Subject		Verb	
Ik-kai	*ni*	*kafe ya resutoran*	*ga*	*aru*	*kedo.*

'There are also a café and restaurants on the first floor, though.' (D-2)

The word *kedo* 'though' in the pattern above implies the nuance, 'Is that what you want to know or is there anything else you want to know?'

Grammar Note 4   Formal verb forms vs. informal verb forms
（フォーマル体・インフォーマル体）

When you ask about the location of something using expressions in formal forms, you might receive responses at different speech levels, i.e., very formal or informal. Let's take a look at the following table for some examples.

			Informal	Formal	Very Formal
arimasu	Non-past	aff.	*aru yo*	*arimasu*	*gozaimasu*
		neg.	*nai yo*	*arimasen / nai desu*	*gozaimasen*
	Past	aff.	*atta yo*	*arimashita*	
		neg.	*nakatta yo*	*arimasendeshita*	
imasu	Non-past	aff.	*iru yo*	*imasu*	
		neg.	*inai yo*	*imasen*	
	Past	aff.	*ita yo*	*imashita*	
		neg.	*inakatta yo*	*imasendeshita*	

e.g.   *Shiroi tana no migigawa ni **aru yo**.* (D-2)

*Kutsu-uriba ga **gozaimasu**.* (D-1)

*Kono kai ni wa toire wa **gozaimasen**.* (D-1)

*Kafeteria ni **ita yo**.* (D-2)

Grammar Note 5   Conversation strategy: Starters
（会話ストラテジー：切り出し）

Anō and *sumimasen* 'Excuse me.'

Anō, which is used in the first line in Dialogue 1, is a conversation starter. It functions to draw attention from other people when one wants to ask hesitantly a question that might be embarrassing, offensive or bothersome. *Sumimasen*, which was introduced in Lesson 5, also has the same function, but it is frequently used in more formal situations. You can start questions and requests for help with these two expressions.

◆   ◆   ◆

Ⓐ Conversation Drills

Drill 1. Complete the following conversations.

1. In a department store, ask the sales clerk where the shoe department is located.

    You: (a) _____

                        (Ask properly where the shoe department is.)

    Sales clerk: *Josei-yō deshō ka, dansei-yō deshō ka.*

    You: (b) _____ (Say women's shoes.)

    Sales clerk: *Dewa, 1-kai desu. Koko o massugu itte, migigawa ni arimasu.*

    You: (c) _____ (Express your gratitude.)

2. In a department store, ask the sales clerk where you can find a pen.

    You: (a) _____

                        (Ask properly if they have the same pen as you have now.)

    Sales clerk: *Hai, gozaimasu. 7-kai no bungu-uriba ni gozaimasu.*

    You: (b) _____ (Confirm that it's on the 7th floor.)

3. At the office, ask your colleague where the person you are looking for is.

    You: (a) _____ (Ask if Ms./Mr. Yasui is here.)

    Colleague: *Etto . . . A, imasu yo. Mado no chikaku desu.*

    You: (b) _____ (Say it's true and express gratitude.)

4. Ask several people where the person you are looking for is.

    You: (a) _____ (Ask where Mr. Kawashima is.)

    Colleague 1: *E? Sakki made soko ni ita yo.*

    Colleague 2: *Kawashima-san? 4-5-fun mae ni A-kaigishitsu ni ita kedo.*

    You: (b) _____ (Say it is so.)

5. Ask the sales clerk where the ATM is.

    You: *Anō,* (a) _____ (Ask where ATM is.)

    Sales clerk: *Taihen mōshiwake gozaimasen ga, kono kai ni wa gozaimasen.*

                  ATM wa chika no kauntā no migigawa desu.

    You: (b) _____ (Confirm that it is in the basement.)

                  Dōmo.

Vocabulary

1. *yō:* for   *mado:* window

   bungu: stationery   *chika:* basement

B Grammar & Vocabulary Building Drills

Drill 2. Ask where things/facilities are at a department store by changing the underlined part.

> _Kaidan_ wa doko desu ka.

1. _toire_

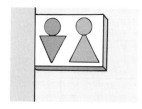

2. _osōzai_

3. _wain-uriba_

4. _kaban-uriba_

5. _erebētā_

Drill 3. Ask where something/someone is around the office by changing the underlined part. Choose the appropriate verb from _arimasu_ or _imasu_ for each sentence.

> _A4 no kami_ wa doko ni **arimasu** ka.
> _Tonī wa_ doko ni **imasu** ka.

1. _hochikisu_

2. _jidō hanbaiki_

3. _shorui_

4. _Takagi buchō_

5. _Yasui-san_

Vocabulary

2. (o)sōzai: deli
erebētā: elevator

3. hochikisu: stapler
jidō hanbaiki: vending machine

shorui: documents

Drill 4. Read the sentences below and choose the number from the picture that corresponds to each sentence.

1. *Posuto wa konbini no mae ni arimasu.*   (   )
2. *Takushī-noriba wa eki no mae ni arimasu.*   (   )
3. *Chūshajō wa kōen no yoko ni arimasu.*   (   )
4. *Toire wa kōen to eki no naka ni arimasu.*   (   )
5. *Kōban wa ano biru no saki ni arimasu.*   (   )

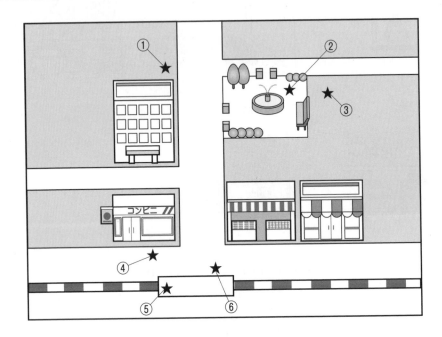

Drill 5. Read the sentences below and choose the number from the picture that corresponds to each sentence.

1. *Hasami wa Akagi-san no tsukue no ue ni arimasu.*   (   )
2. *Fūtō wa tsukue no hikidashi ni arimasu.*   (   )
3. *Yasui-san no keitai wa kaban no naka desu.*   (   )
4. *Aoshima-san wa buchō no heya ni imasu.*   (   )
5. *A4 no kami wa fakkusu no yoko ni arimasu.*   (   )

Vocabulary

4. *posuto:* mailbox
noriba: place to take public transportation

chūshajō: parking lot
5. *hasami:* scissors
fūtō: envelope

kaban: bag
fakkusu: fax

102

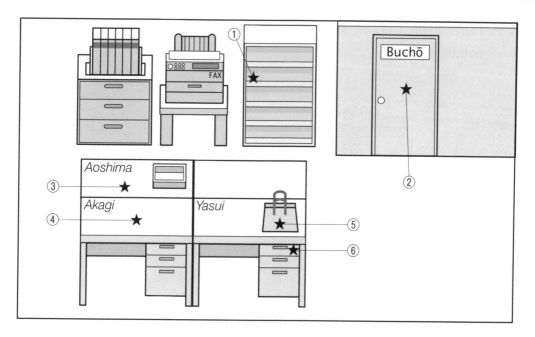

C Listening Tasks

Drill 6. Listen to the five dialogues and choose the number from the picture that corresponds to each dialogue.

36

1. (   )   2. (   )   3. (   )   4. (   )   5. (   )

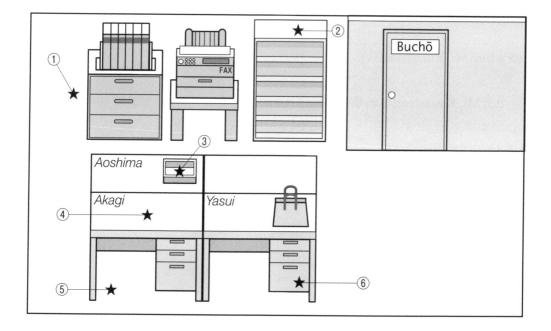

Vocabulary

6. *hako:* box   *gomibako:*   trash can   *chizu:*   map

Drill 7. **Listen to the CD and write the dialogue number in the ( ) , or insert an × if nothing matches.**

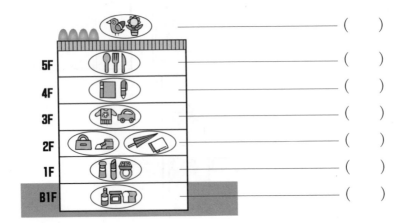

ⓓ Review Drills

Drill 8. **Read the following instructions and make sentences.**

How would you:

1. ask where the pens are?

2. say that the pens are on top of the white cabinet?

3. ask where Ms. Kawashima is?

4. say that Ms. Kawashima is in the meeting room?

5. ask where the toilets are?

6. say that the toilets are next to the elevators?

7. ask where Mr. Akagawa's desk is?

8. say that Mr. White isn't at his desk?

Vocabulary

7. *petto shoppu:* pet shop   *shokuryōhin:* groceries   *omocha:* toys
   okujō: rooftop   *kodomo fuku:* children's clothes

Drill 9. Look at the map below and match the responses with the questions.

1. *Yūbinkyoku wa doko desu ka.* •
2. *Konbini wa doko desu ka.* •
3. *Basutei wa doko desu ka.* •
4. *Hoteru wa doko desu ka.* •

• a. *Eki no mukaigawa ni arimasu.*
• b. *Sūpā no tonari ni arimasu.*
• c. *Byōin no mae ni arimasu.*
• d. *Hana-ya to pan-ya no aida ni arimasu.*

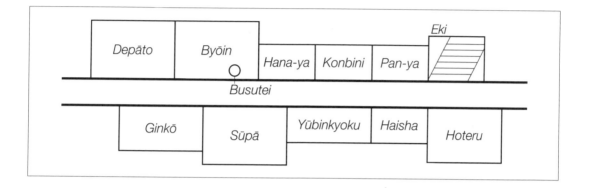

Drill 10. Complete the dialogues by changing the following sentences to the correct order.

1. (   ) → (   ) → (   )

   a. *A, sō desu ka. Dōmo.*

   b. *Hankachi desu ne. Kochira no kutsu-uriba no oku desu.*

   c. *Anō, hankachi-uriba wa doko desu ka.*

2. (d) → (   ) → (   ) → (   ) → (   )

   a. *Sono tonari.*

   b. *Dōmo.*

   c. *Ā, chigau yo. Sotchi.*

   d. *Sumimasen, Kuroda-san no seki wa koko desu ka.*

   e. *Koko desu ka.*

Vocabulary

9. *konbini:* convenience store
hoteru: hotel
hana-ya: florist

pan-ya: bakery
byōin: hospital; clinic
sūpā: supermarket

10. *hankachi:* handkerchief
chigau (chigaimasu): to be
wrong; to be different

CLOSING DIALOGUE   Formal Informal

Looking for something

38

(Mr. Kawashima is in the conference room and calls Ms. Tsukada, but she is not at her desk. So, Mr. White answers.)

Kawashima (R): *Moshimoshi, Kawashima da kedo, Tsukada-san iru?*

Howaito: *Ie, ima imasen ga.*

Kawashima: *Jā, Jonasan, ima kaigichū nan da kedo, chotto shorui o sagashite kureru?*
De, sugu motte kite kurenai? Jūkyū-kai no kaigishitsu.

Howaito: *Hai. Ēto, dono shorui desu ka.*

Kawashima: *YY ginkō no keisansho nan da kedo, tsukue no ue no hako ni nai kanā.*

Howaito: *Ēto, nai desu yo.*

Kawashima: *Jā, mado no soba no tana no ue.*

Howaito: *Tana no ue desu ka.*

Kawashima: *Denakereba, YY ginkō no fairu ni ireta kanā.*

Howaito: *Sono fairu wa kyabinetto no hikidashi no naka desu ne.*
Chotto matte kudasai. A, arimashita.
Sugu motte ikimasu.

Kawashima: *Arigatō. Yoroshiku.*

川島良三：もしもし、川島だけど、塚田さん　いる？

ホワイト：いえ、いま　いませんが。

川島：じゃあ、ジョナサン、いま　かいぎちゅうなんだけど、ちょっと　しょるいを　さがしてくれる？で、すぐ　もってきてくれない？　19かいの　かいぎしつ。

ホワイト：はい。ええと、どの　しょるいですか。

川島：YY銀行の　けいさんしょなんだけど、つくえの　上の　はこに　ないかなあ。

ホワイト：ええと、ないですよ。

川島：じゃあ、まどの　そばの　たなの　上。

ホワイト：たなの　上ですか。

川島：でなければ、YY銀行の　ファイルに　いれたかなあ。

ホワイト：その　ファイルは　キャビネットの　ひきだしの　中ですね。
ちょっと　まってください。あ、ありました。すぐ　もっていきます。

川島：ありがとう。よろしく。

Mr. Kawashima: Hello, this is Kawashima speaking, is Ms. Tsukada there?

Mr. White: No, she's not here at this moment, but . . .

Mr. Kawashima: Is this Jonathan? I'm in the middle of a meeting, but I urgently need a document. Would you find it and bring it to the conference room on the 19th floor?

Mr. White: Yes, sir. But what document?

Mr. Kawashima: It's a statement from YY Bank. I wonder if it is in the in-box on my desk.

Mr. White: No, it's not here.

Mr. Kawashima: Then, look on top the shelf near the window.

Mr. White: On top of the shelf?

Mr. Kawashima: If you can't find it there, I wonder if I put it in the file of YY Bank.

Mr. White: (You mean) the file in the cabinet drawer, right? Wait a minute, here it is. I'll be right over.

Mr. Kawashima: Thanks. Please.

CULTURE NOTE 4

Yoroshiku onegaishimasu

Yoroshiku onegaishimasu is not just 'How do you do? Nice to meet you.' This is one of the most difficult expressions to translate into English. The meaning changes depending on the situation. Let's look at a few examples first.

e.g. 1   YY *Ginkō no Tonpuson desu.* **Yoroshiku onegai shimasu.**
'I'm David Thompson of YY Bank. It is a pleasure to meet you.'

As you can see in example 1, we always say "*Yoroshiku onegaishimasu*" at the end of a self-introduction, implying "Please accept me as one of the members of your group. Please support me and I hope everything will go smoothly in advancing our collaborative activity and our relationship."

e.g. 2   *Kono repōto kin'yōbi made ni dekimasu ka . . .* **Yoroshiku onegaishimasu.**
'Can you finish this report by Friday? . . . Thank you in advance.'

Example 2 illustrates a situation where you ask someone to do something for you, saying 'Please do this for me.' After giving some details, the conversation is closed with *Yoroshiku onegaishimasu*, implying that "I am sorry to trouble you, but I need your help and cooperation. Thank you in advance for your kindness in going out of your way to help me."

e.g. 3   *Sushi (o) 3-nin-mae onegaishimasu.* **Yoroshiku onegaishimasu.**
'Please deliver sushi for three people. Take care of this quickly, please.'

This expression is used when you ask for a service in daily life. For example, when you ask for a delivery of sushi, noodles or pizza, or when you ask for something to be repaired, or when you send some clothes to the dry cleaner, this expression is used after giving some detailed information.

Yoroshiku is an adverb with a number of meanings such as 'willingly,' 'favorably' or 'well.' *Onegaishimasu* is a combination of *onegai* which means 'hope,' 'wish' or 'request,' and *shimasu* which is a verb with the meaning of 'do.'

Thus, *yoroshiku onegaishimasu* would literally be translated into something like the following: 'I'd like to ask a favor of you to support me in a way that is convenient for both of us, in other words I count on your cooperation and consideration.' This implication comes from the group-oriented mentality of Japanese society, where people depend on each other and expect cooperation with each other. In his book *The Anatomy of Dependence*, Dr. Takeo Doi says these expectations evolved from *amae*, which is the feeling of children toward their mother.

LESSON 8: EXPRESSING WHAT YOU WILL DO

—*Kyōto de nani o shimasu ka.*
'What are you going to do in Kyoto?'

Dialogue 1 **Talking about the weekend** · · · · · · · · · · · Formal 39

(Haruko Kawashima, David Thompson and Anthony Kumar are at the office.)

Kawashima (H): Dēbiddo-san, kondo no shūmatsu wa, Kyōto desu ne.
Kyōto de nani o shimasu ka.

Tonpuson: Iroiro shitai desu. Otera o mimasu. Kaimono o shimasu.
Sorekara kaiseki-ryōri o tabemasu.

Kawashima: Ii desu ne. Ja, tanoshinde kudasai.
Kumaru-san wa, shūmatsu wa nani o shimasu ka.

Kumaru: Chikaku no kōen de tenisu o shimasu.
Gogo wa kafe de kōhī o nomimasu.

Kawashima: Dare to tenisu o shimasu ka.

Kumaru: Miyasato-san-tachi to shimasu.
Kawashima-san wa nani o shimasu ka.

Kawashima: Sōji ya sentaku o shimasu.

Ms. Haruko Kawashima: You'll be going to Kyoto this weekend, David. What are you going to do there?

Mr. Thompson: I would like to do many things. I want to (lit., will) see the temples, do some shopping and then, I will be eating a formal Japanese dinner, *kaiseki*.

Ms. Kawashima: That sounds great! Have a good time.
Mr. Kumar, what are you going to do this weekend?

Mr. Kumar: I will be playing tennis at the park near my place and we'll have coffee at a café in the afternoon.

Ms. Kawashima: With whom are you playing tennis?

Mr. Kumar: With Ms. Miyasato and other friends. How about you, Ms. Kawashima?

Ms. Kawashima: I'll be doing house cleaning and laundry.

Vocabulary

suru (shimasu): to do
miru (mimasu): to see
kaiseki-ryōri: formal Japanese dinner
taberu (tabemasu): to eat

tanoshimu (tanoshimimasu): to have fun; to enjoy
nomu (nomimasu): to drink
to: with

sōji: house cleaning
sentaku: laundry

川島春子： 　デービッドさん、こんどの　しゅうまつは、京都ですね。

　　　　　　　京都で　なにを　しますか。

トンプソン： いろいろ　したいです。おてらを　みます。かいものを　します。

　　　　　　　それから　かいせきりょうりを　たべます。

川島： 　　　いいですね。じゃ、たのしんでください。

　　　　　　　クマルさんは、しゅうまつは　なにを　しますか。

クマル： 　　ちかくの　こうえんで　テニスを　します。ごごは　カフェで

　　　　　　　コーヒーを　のみます。

川島： 　　　だれと　テニスを　しますか。

クマル： 　　宮里さんたちと　します。川島さんは　なにを　しますか。

川島： 　　　そうじや　せんたくを　します。

● Comprehension Drill

1. Listen to or read Dialogue 1 and decide if the following statements are true, false or you don't know as not enough information has been given.

    1. David will go to Kyoto this weekend.   (T / F / DK)
    2. David will stay at a *ryokan* in Kyoto.   (T / F / DK)
    3. Mr. Kumar will play tennis this weekend.   (T / F / DK)
    4. Ms. Kawashima will play tennis with Mr. Kumar.   (T / F / DK)
    5. Ms. Kawashima will not do house cleaning and laundry this weekend.   (T / F / DK)

2. Put these sentences in the correct order to make a conversation.

    (c) → (   ) → (   ) → (   ) → (   )

    a. *Otera o mimasu. Kaimono o shimasu. Sorekara kaiseki-ryōri o tabemasu.*
    b. *Ii desu ne. Kumaru-san wa shūmatsu wa nani o shimasu ka.*
    c. *Kondo no shūmatsu wa Kyōto desu ne. Kyōto de nani o shimasu ka.*
    d. *Chikaku no kōen de tenisu o shimasu.*
    e. *Sō desu ka.*

Dialogue 2 Talking about what to buy for lunch · · · Informal

(Akiyo Miyasato, Haruko Kawashima and Anthony Kumar are at their desks.)

Miyasato:	Konbini de obentō katte kuru kedo,
	Kawashima-san, nani ka katte kuru?
Kawashima (H):	Ūn, ja, koko de taberu kana.
	Sandoitchi to jūsu de onegai.
	Warui wa ne.
Miyasato:	Tonī wa?
Kumaru:	Jā, sarada. Sorekara, mizu mo.
Miyasato:	Wakatta. Jā, itte kimasu.

Ms. Miyasato:	(I'll go) and bring back a boxed lunch from the convenience store, but do you want anything, Ms. Kawashima?
Ms. Kawashima:	Oh, OK. I'll eat lunch here at the office. Get me a sandwich and a bottle/can of juice, will you? Thanks.
Ms. Miyasato:	How about you, Tony?
Mr. Kumar:	(May I?) Then, get me a salad. Oh, a bottle of water, too, please.
Ms. Miyazato:	Got it. I'll be back. (lit., I'm going and will be back.)

宮里：	コンビニで　おべんとう　かってくるけど、川島さん、なにか　かってくる？
川島春子：	うーん、じゃ、ここで　たべるかな。サンドイッチと　ジュースでおねがい。わるいわね。
宮里：	トニーは？
クマル：	じゃあ、サラダ。それから、みずも。
宮里：	わかった。じゃあ、いってきます。

● **Comprehension Drill**

Listen to or read Dialogue 2 and decide if the following statements are true, false or you don't know as not enough information has been given.

1. Ms. Miyasato and Ms. Kawashima are going to a convenience store to buy lunch boxes.

(T / F / DK)

2. Ms. Kawashima wants to have sandwiches and juice. (T / F / DK)
3. Mr. Kumar will go out to have lunch. (T / F / DK)
4. Ms. Miyasato will buy sandwiches, too. (T / F / DK)
5. They will eat lunch at the office. (T / F / DK)

Vocabulary

katte kuru (katte kimasu): to buy and bring back	*warui:* bad	*wakatta:* got it
nani ka: something	*warui wa ne:* sorry to have troubled you [informal women's speech]	

◆   ◆   ◆

Grammar Note 1 Asking someone's plans for his/her up-coming days off （休みについてたずねる）

Talking about what you will do over the weekend, during the New Year holidays, Golden Week holidays in May, vacation, etc. seems to be one of the most popular topics to talk about with your colleagues/friends around the office outside of serious business discussions. The following are typical patterns that you can use in asking your colleague about his/her plans for the weekend, etc.

[Up-coming holidays] *wa nani o shimasu ka.* 'What are you going to do ~?'

Topic		Object		Verb	SP
(Kondo no) shūmatsu	*wa*	*nani*	*o*	*shimasu*	*ka.*
'What are you going to do this weekend?' (D-1)					

[Place] *de nani o shimasu ka.* 'What are you going to do (there) ~?'

Place of Action		Object		Verb	SP
Kyōto	*de*	*nani*	*o*	*shimasu*	*ka.*
'What are you going to do in Kyoto?' (D-1)					

Grammar Note 2 Talking about doing things—Action verb （動作動詞）

a. Talking about what you will do

To respond to the questions in Grammar Note 1, you need action verbs such as *mimasu* 'to see,' *tabemasu* 'to eat,' *nomimasu* 'to drink,' and *kaimasu* 'to buy.'

~ o **[Action Verb].**

Object		Action Verb
Otera	*o*	*mimasu.*
'I will see the temples.' (D-1)		

Here are three more examples from Dialogue 1.

e.g. *Kaimono o* **shimasu**. 'I will do some shopping.' (D-1)
  Kaiseki-ryōri o **tabemasu**. 'I will eat a formal Japanese dinner, *kaiseki*.' (D-1)
  Kōhī o **nomimasu**. 'I will drink coffee.' (D-1)

b. Verb conjugations

The following table shows verb conjugations. Note that the formal style verb forms are pretty regular with the *masu* forms, while the informal ones are irregular with different endings.

		Non-past		Past	
		Affirmative	Negative	Affirmative	Negative
Informal	'to do'	*suru*	*shinai*	*shita*	*shinakatta*
	'to eat'	*taberu*	*tabenai*	*tabeta*	*tabenakatta*
	'to drink'	*nomu*	*nomanai*	*nonda*	*nomanakatta*
Formal	'to do'	*shimasu*	*shimasen*	*shimashita*	*shimasendeshita*
	'to eat'	*tabemasu*	*tabemasen*	*tabemashita*	*tabemasendeshita*
	'to drink'	*nomimasu*	*nomimasen*	*nomimashita*	*nomimasendeshita*

In Japanese, the non-past form is used for both present and future time, as discussed in Lesson 4. However, they can be distinguished by using adverbs such as *kyō* 'today' or *ashita* 'tomorrow.'

Grammar Note 3   Additional time expressions (時の表現)

In order to talk about what and when you will do something, you will need action verbs and time expressions. Basic time expressions were introduced in Lesson 3. Here are more time expressions which you can use with the action verbs.

	'every ~'	'end of ~'
Year	*maitoshi*	*nenmatsu*
Month	*maitsuki*	*getsumatsu*
Week	*maishū*	*shūmatsu*
Day	*mainichi*	–
Morning	*maiasa*	–
Evening	*maiban*	–

Grammar Note 4   Particles (助詞)

The following particles will be discussed here.

Place of action marker	*de*	'where you do'
Object marker	*o*	'what you do'
Accompaniment marker	*to*	'with whom you do something'
Conjunction particles	*to*	'and'
	ya	'and so on'

a. Place of action marker [*de*]

This marker comes after place words and denotes where an action occurs. It has the meaning of 'at/in' in English.

Place of Action		Object		Verb
Kōen	*de*	*tenisu*	*o*	*shimasu.*
'I will be playing tennis at the park.' (D-1)				

Here are more examples from the dialogues.

e.g.   *Kyōto de nani o shimasu ka.*   'What are you going to do in Kyoto?' (D-1)
Kafe de kōhī o nomimasu.   'We'll have coffee at a café.' (D-1)
Konbini de obentō katte kuru.   'I'll go and bring back a boxed lunch from the convenience store. (lit., I'm going to buy a boxed lunch at the convenience store and bring it back.)' (D-2)

b. Object marker [*o*]

This comes after nouns designating things and before action verbs.

We already introduced this marker in Lesson 5 as an object marker in/for requesting. Here, we discuss it as a particle that marks the object of action verbs, that is, *what* you do. (See Grammar Note 2-a, for examples.)

c. Accompaniment marker [*to*] '(do ~) with somebody.'

The marker *to* follows the noun designating people, and means 'with somebody.'

Accompaniment		Object		Verb	SP
Dare	*to*	*tenisu*	*o*	*shimasu*	*ka.*
'With whom are you playing tennis?' (D-1)					

e.g.   *Miyasato-san-tachi to shimasu.*   'With Ms. Miyasato and other friends.' (D-1)

d. Particles [*to*] and [*ya*]

To connects two or more words and it means 'and' as we mentioned before. *Ya* also connects two or more words, but it implies that other things are not mentioned and means 'and so on' or 'and the like.' Compare the following examples:

e.g. 1:   *Sandoitchi to jūsu de onegai.*   'Get me a sandwich and a bottle/can of juice, will you?' (D-2)

e.g. 2:   *Sōji ya sentaku o shimasu.*   'I'll be doing house cleaning and laundry (and the like).' (D-1)

Example 1 means that the person wants only a sandwich and a bottle/can of juice. On the other hand, example 2 means that s/he will do laundry and house cleaning, and might do other things that are not mentioned.

Grammar Note 5 Adverbs of frequency and quantity （頻度・量の副詞）

When you want to talk about the frequency or quantity/amount of what you do, you will need adverbs such as "always," "usually," "often," "sometimes," "a lot," " a little" or "not at all." Here is a table of those "adverbs of frequency/quantity."

Adverbs of Frequency		Adverbs of Quantity/Amount	
In an affirmative sentence	In a negative sentence	In an affirmative sentence	In a negative sentence
itsumo 'always'		*takusan* 'a lot'	
taitei 'usually'		*sukoshi* 'a little'	
yoku 'often'			
tokidoki 'sometimes'	*amari* 'not so often'		*amari* 'not so much'
	zenzen 'never'		*zenzen* 'not at all'

Word order in Japanese is not as strict as in English, so you can use these adverbs in the beginning, middle, or even after the main verb.

◆   ◆   ◆

Ⓐ Conversation Drills

Drill 1. Complete the following conversations.

1. Answer your colleague's question about your weekend plans.

    Colleague: *Konshū no nichiyōbi wa nani o shimasu ka.*

    You: (a) _____

        (Say that your in-laws are coming from the USA and that you are going to Kyoto together.)

    Colleague: *Ii desu ne. Kyōto de nani o shimasu ka.*

    You: (b) _____

        (Say that you'd like to do various things. You will see the temples. You will do some shopping.)

    Colleague: *Sō desu ka. Ja, tanoshinde kudasai.*

2. Answer your friend's question about what you usually drink.

    Friend: *Yoru wa nomimasu ka.*

    You: (a) _____ (Say that you drink.)

Vocabulary

1. *giri no ryōshin:* in-laws

Friend: *Nani o nomimasu ka.*

You: (b) _____ (Answer that you drink a little wine.)

Friend: *Okusan/goshujin mo issho ni nomimasu ka.*

You: (c) _____ (Say that your wife/husband doesn't drink.)

3. Answer your colleague's question about what you will do over the weekend.

Colleague: *Ashita wa yasumi desu ne. Nani o shimasu ka.*

You: (a) _____

               (Say that you will go to the park with your family.)

Colleague: *Uchi no chikaku ni kōen ga arimasu ka.*

You: (b) _____

               (Say yes, and tell him/her that you will have lunch there.)

Colleague: *Sō desu ka. Gogo wa nani o shimasu ka.*

You: (c) _____

               (Say that you will listen to music. You will read a book and a magazine, and so on.)

4. Ask your colleague (Yasui-san) what s/he usually has for breakfast.

You: (a) _____

               (Ask Yasui-san what she [usually] eats for breakfast.)

Yasui-san: *Watashi wa taitei orenji jūsu dake desu. Anata wa maiasa nani o tabe-masu ka.*

You: (b) _____

               (Tell her what you usually have for breakfast.)

5. Answer your friend's question about what you did over the weekend.

Friend: *Yasumi wa doko e ikimashita ka.*

You: (a) _____ (Say that you went to Kamakura.)

Friend: *Dare to ikimashita ka.*

You: (b) _____ (Say that you went with your friend.)

Friend: *Kamakura de daibutsu o mimasita ka.*

You: (c) _____ (Say that you didn't.)

Friend: *Sō desu ka. Zannen deshita ne.*

Vocabulary

1. *hiru gohan:* lunch   *hon:* book   *asa gohan:* breakfast
ongaku: music   *zasshi:* magazine   *daibutsu:* Great Buddha
kiku (kikimasu): to listen; to hear   *yomu (yomimasu):* to read   *zannen:* sorry; disapointing

B Grammar & Vocabulary Building Drills

Drill 2. Write down the verbs for pictures 1-5 below. Also fill in the boxes below with the non-past affirmative/negative and the past affirmative/negative forms of these verbs.

e.g. *kaimasu*　　　　1. (　　　　　)　　　2. (　　　　　)

3. (　　　　　)　　　4. (　　　　　)　　　5. (　　　　　)

Non-past affirmative	Non-past negative	Past affirmative	Past negative
e.g. *kaimasu*	*kaimasen*	*kaimashita*	*kaimasendeshita*
1.	*tabemasen*		
2.		*nomimashita*	
3.			*mimasendeshita*
4.	*yomimasen*		
5.		*kikimashita*	

Drill 3. Describe the pictures by using the words shown below and the appropriate verbs from Drill 2.

e.g. *yōguruto*　　　　1. *eiga*　　　　　　2. *shōchū*

Vocabulary

2. *kau (kaimasu):*　to buy　　　**3.** *eiga:*　movie　　　*shōchū:*　Japanese distilled sake

116

3. *ongaku* 4. *shinbun* 5. *sushi*

e.g. *Yōguruto o kaimasu.*

1. *Eiga* _____ 2. *Shōchū* _____

3. *Ongaku* _____ 4. *Shinbun* _____

5. *Sushi* _____

Drill 4. **Complete the five sentences from Drill 3 by adding the time expressions and places shown below.**

	Time expression	Place
e.g.	*nichiyōbi*	*sūpā*
1.	*shūmatsu*	*eigakan*
2.	*konban*	*izakaya*
3.	*mainichi*	*densha no naka*
4.	*maiasa*	*uchi*
5.	*doyōbi*	*resutoran*

e.g. *Nichiyōbi ni sūpā de yōguruto o kaimasu.*

1. _____ *eiga o mimasu.*

2. _____ *shōchū o nomimasu.*

3. _____ *ongaku o kikimasu.*

4. _____ *shinbun o yomimasu.*

5. _____ *sushi o tabemasu.*

Vocabulary

3. *shinbun:* newspaper   *sushi:* raw fish with vinegared rice   **4.** *eigakan:* movie theater

Drill 5. Practice the following dialogue by changing the underlined parts.

> A: *Shūmatsu wa nani o shimasu ka.*
>
> B: *Sō desu nē,* (a) *yoku* (b) *kazoku to* (c) *kaimono o shimasu.*

1. (a) *tokidoki* (b) *tomodachi to* (c) *sukasshu*
2. (a) *taitei* (b) *hitori de* (c) *sōji ya sentaku*
3. (a) *itsumo* (b) *gāru furendo to* (c) *dēto*

Drill 6. Complete the following sentences by adding the appropriate particles, if necessary.

> e.g. *Tokidoki* __x__ *Shinjuku* __de__ *hon* __o__ *kaimasu.*

1. *Nichiyōbi* _____ *yoku* _____ *kazoku* _____ *bōringu* _____ *shimasu.*
2. *Kawashima-san* _____ *itsumo* _____ *kaisha* _____ *shinbun* _____ *yomimasu.*
3. *Watashi* _____ *amari* _____ *uchi* _____ *bangohan* _____ *tabemasen.*
4. *Tsuma to watashi* _____ *doyōbi* _____ *uchi* _____ *sukoshi* _____ *wain* _____ *nomimasu.*
5. *Watashi* _____ *zenzen* _____ *tegami* _____ *kakimasen.*

ⓒ Listening Tasks

Drill 7. Listen to the four dialogues and write the dialogue number in the ( ).

When	( ) tomorrow	( ) next week	( ) this weekend	( ) Saturday
Where	( ) Kamakura	( ) Hokkaido	( ) park in Shinjuku	( ) nearby park
What you'll do	( ) do some shopping	( ) see the blossoms	( ) play soccer	( ) eat crab
With whom	( ) colleagues	( ) girl friend	( ) family	( ) friends

Vocabulary

5. *sukasshu:* squash *gāru furendo:* girl friend **6.** *bōringu:* bowling
hitori de: alone; by oneself *dēto:* dating *tegami:* letter

118

Drill 8. **Listen to the CD and write down the necessary information in the calendar below.**

42

1月						
Sun	**Mon**	**Tue**	**Wed**	**Thu**	**Fri**	**Sat**
				1	2	3
4	5	6	7	8	9	10
11	12	13 **Today**	14	15	16	17
18	19	20	21	22	23 e.g., *Chinese restaurant, with K in Akasaka*	24
25	26	27	28	29	30	31

D Review Drills

Drill 9. **Read the following instructions and make sentences.**

How would you:

1. ask what your colleague will do tomorrow?

2. answer that you will go to the park near your house?

3. ask what your friend will do in the park?

Vocabulary

8. *chūka ryōri:*   Chinese food

4. answer that you will play tennis with your friends?

5. ask your friend what s/he did last Saturday?

6. answer that you went to Asakusa?

7. ask your friend what s/he did at Asakusa?

8. answer that you bought souvenir from Japan?

Drill 10. Match the responses with the questions.

1. *Kyonen no natsuyasumi wa doko e ·*
   ikimashita ka.

2. *Kinō no yoru wa nani o tabemashita ka. ·*

3. *Maiasa jogingu o shimasu ka. ·*

4. *Itsumo doko de kaimono o shimasu ka. ·*

· a. *Rāmen desu.*

· b. *Iie, maiasa ja arimasen.*
     Tokidoki shimasu.

· c. *Eki no mae no sūpā desu.*

· d. *Tai e ikimashita.*

Drill 11. Complete the dialogues by changing the following sentences to the correct order.

1. (d) → (   ) → (   ) → (   )

   a. *Eigakan de mimasu ka.*
   b. *Iie, taitei uchi de DVD o mimasu.*
   c. *Hai, mimasu.*
   d. *Eiga o mimasu ka.*

2. (c) → (   ) → (   ) → (   ) → (   )

   a. *Ueno-kōen desu.*
   b. *Minna de sakura o mimasu. Osake o nomimasu. Oishii mono o tabemasu.*
   c. *Jon-san, konshū no doyōbi ohanami ni ikimasu ka.*
   d. *Ii desu ne. Doko de shimasu ka.*
   e. *Ohanami? Ohanami wa nan desu ka.*

Vocabulary

11. *sakura:* cherry blossoms   *oishii:* tastes good   *(o)hanami:* viewing cherry blossoms

(In the morning.)

Howaito: Ohayō gozaimasu.

Tsukada: Ohayō. Genki nai ne.

Howaito: Iya, futsū desu yo. Tsukada-san ga itsumo genki na n desu yo.

Tsukada: Sō?

Howaito: Tsukada-san wa, dōshite itsumo asa kara genki na n desu ka.

Tsukada: E? Dōshite? Sō nē, chanto asa-gohan o taberu kara kana. Jon wa?

Howaito: Watashi wa taitei kōhī dake desu. Tsukada-san, maiasa nani o tabemasu ka.

Tsukada: Tōsuto to kōhī. Sore ni yōguruto to kudamono. Kyō wa banana.

(Before lunch.)

Howaito: Tsukada-san, hiru-gohan, kyō wa doko de tabemasu ka.

Tsukada: Ano shizenshokuhin no omise wa?

Howaito: Ii desu nē. Ikimashō.

ホワイト：	おはようございます。
塚田：	おはよう。げんき ないね。
ホワイト：	いや、ふつうですよ。塚田さんが いつも げんきなんですよ。
塚田：	そう？
ホワイト：	塚田さんは、どうして いつも あさから げんきなんですか。
塚田：	え？どうして？そうねえ、ちゃんと あさごはんを たべるからかな。ジョンは？
ホワイト：	わたしは たいてい コーヒーだけです。塚田さん、まいあさ なにを たべますか。
塚田：	トーストと コーヒー。それに、ヨーグルトと くだもの。きょうは バナナ。
******	
ホワイト：	塚田さん、ひるごはん、きょうは どこで たべますか。
塚田：	あの しぜんしょくひんの おみせは？

Mr. White:	Good morning.
Ms. Tsukada:	Good morning. You look quiet today.
Mr. White:	I'm fine, just as usual. You are always bouncing, Ms. Tsukada.
Ms. Tsukada:	Oh, am I?
Mr. White:	Why are you always so energetic and cheerful in the morning?
Ms. Tsukada:	Oh, why? I don't know, but maybe it's because I always eat a good breakfast. How about you, Jon?
Mr. White:	I usually just drink coffee for breakfast. What do you eat, Ms. Tsukada?
Ms. Tsukada:	I have a piece of toast, a cup of coffee and then, yoghurt and fruit. I had a banana this morning.
******	
Mr. White:	Where are we going for lunch today, Ms. Tsukada?
Ms. Tsukada:	How about the organic food restaurant?
Mr. White:	Sounds good. Let's go.

LESSON 9: EXPRESSING HOW THINGS ARE/WERE
—*Kyōto wa dō deshita ka.*
'How was (the trip to) Kyoto?'

Dialogue 1 Asking about and commenting on a previous trip
· Formal **44**

(Haruko Kawashima and David Thompson are talking about David's trip to Kyoto.)

Kawashima (H): A, Dēbiddo-san, ohayō gozaimasu. Kyōto wa dō deshita ka.

Tonpuson: Atsukatta desu. Demo, subarashikatta desu.

Kawashima: Sō desu ka. Nani ga yokatta desu ka. Tatoeba?

Tonpuson: Tatoeba, furui otera desu. Shizuka deshita. Yama mo kawa mo
kirei deshita. Kirei na maiko-san mo mimashita yo.

Kawashima: Yokatta desu ne. Goryōshin mo yorokobimashita ka.

Tonpuson: Hai, okagesama de. Kyōto wa tanoshikatta desu.
Demo tsukaremashita. Ryōshin wa kinō kaerimashita.

Kawashima: Otsukaresama deshita.
Sōsō, kaiseki-ryōri wa dō deshita ka.

Tonpuson: Ee, totemo kirei deshita.

Kawashima: Oishikatta desu ka.

Tonpuson: Ee, mā. Demo, takakatta desu.
Kore wa omiyage desu, dōzo.

Kawashima: E! Watashi ni desu ka. Sumimasen.

Tonpuson: Iie, hon no kimochi desu.

<!-- Vocabulary -->
Vocabulary

dō: how
demo: but
subarashii: wonderful; fantastic
tatoeba: for example
furui: old
shizuka: quiet; serene

yama: mountain
kawa: river
kirei: clean; beautiful
yorokobu (yorokobimasu): to be happy
tanoshii: enjoyable
tsukareru (tsukaremasu): to be tired

Ee, mā.: Well, yes.
takai: expensive
(o)miyage: souvenir
hon no kimochi desu: lit., it's a small
token of my gratitude

Ms. Haruko Kawashima: Good morning, David. How was (the trip to) Kyoto?
Mr. Thompson: It was hot, but it was great.
Ms. Kawashima: That's good. What was good, for example?
Mr. Thompson: For example, the old temples. (They) were serene. The mountains were beautiful and so were the rivers. We saw pretty *maiko-san* (young *geisha*), too.
Ms. Kawashima: That's good! Did your parents enjoy the trip, too?
Mr. Thompson: Yes, very much. (lit., Thanks to you.) We had a good time in Kyoto. But I'm tired. My parents went back (to Australia) yesterday.
Ms. Kawashima: You did a lot in a short time. And, how did you like the Japanese formal dinner?
Mr. Thompson: It was very pretty.
Ms. Kawashima: Was it tasty?
Mr. Thompson: Well, yes, but it was expensive. Here is a little something (lit., souvenir) for you.
Ms. Kawashima: Oh my! Is it for me? Thank you.
Mr. Thompson: It's nothing. (lit., It's a small token of my gratitude.)

川島春子（かわしまはるこ）：　あ、デービッドさん、おはようございます。京都（きょうと）は　どうでしたか。
トンプソン：あつかったです。でも、すばらしかったです。
川島：　　　そうですか。なにが　よかったですか。たとえば？
トンプソン：たとえば、ふるい　おてらです。しずかでした。やまも　かわも　きれいでした。きれいな　まいこさんも　みましたよ。
川島：　　　よかったですね。ごりょうしんも　よろこびましたか。
トンプソン：はい、おかげさまで。京都は　たのしかったです。　でも　つかれました。りょうしんは　きのう　かえりました。
川島：　　　おつかれさまでした。　そうそう、かいせきりょうりは　どうでしたか。
トンプソン：ええ、とても　きれいでした。
川島：　　　おいしかったですか。
トンプソン：ええ、まあ。でも、たかかったです。これは　おみやげです、どうぞ。
川島：　　　え！わたしに　ですか。すみません。
トンプソン：いいえ、ほんの　きもちです。

● **Comprehension Drill**

1. Listen to or read Dialogue 1 and decide if the following statements are true, false or you don't know as not enough information has been given.

1. David enjoyed the trip to Kyoto. (T / F / DK)
2. It wasn't very hot there. (T / F / DK)
3. He went there with his friends. (T / F / DK)
4. He thinks *kaiseki* (Japanese formal dinner) was expensive. (T / F / DK)
5. He bought Ms. Kawashima some sweets from Kyoto. (T / F / DK)

2. Put these sentences in the correct order to make a conversation.

(   ) → (   ) → (   ) → (   ) → (c)

a. *Tatoeba, furui otera desu. Shizuka deshita.*
b. *Dēbiddo-san, ohayō gozaimasu. Kyōto wa dō deshita ka.*
c. *Yokatta desu ne.*
d. *Sō desu ka. Nani ga yokatta desu ka. Tatoeba?*
e. *Atsukatta desu. Demo, subarashikatta desu.*

Dialogue 2   Visiting a colleague's house · · · · Formal Informal 45

(Anthony Kumar and Fuyumi Tsukada are invited to Akiyo Miyasato's home. They drop by a florist.)

Kumaru:	*Kirei na hana desu ne!*
Tsukada:	*Tonī wa nani-iro no hana ga suki?*
Kumaru:	*Akai hana desu. Kiiroi hana mo suki desu.*
Tsukada:	*Aoi hanataba mo suteki yo.*
Kumaru:	*Aoi hana desu ka?*
Tsukada:	*Un. Mezurashii kara, ii n ja nai?*
Kumaru:	*Ja, sō shimashō.*

(At the entrance of Ms. Miyasato's house.)

Kumaru:	*Hai, kore.*
Miyasato:	*Uwā, kirei na hana. Suteki na iro ne. Dōmo arigatō.*

(In the living room.)

Miyasato:	*Nēnē, kēki tsukutta n da kedo.*
Tsukada:	*Wā, ureshii! Itadakimasu!*
Miyasato:	*Dō?*
Kumaru:	*Hai, totemo oishii desu. Karui desu ne.*
Miyasato:	*Un, kono kēki wa karui n desu yo. Sore ni, amari amakunai no.*

Mr. Kumar:	They are pretty flowers, aren't they?
Ms. Tsukada:	What color of flowers do you like, Tony?
Mr. Kumar:	I like red flowers, but yellow ones are pretty, too.

Vocabulary

hana: flower	*aoi:* blue	*ureshii:* happy
iro: color	*hanataba:* bouquet	*Itadakimasu.:* lit., I'm going to eat.
suki: to like; favorite	*suteki:* lovely; nice	*karui:* light
akai: red	*mezurashii:* rare; unusual	*sore ni:* in addition; beside
kiiroi: yellow	*tsukuru (tsukurimasu):* to make	*amai:* sweet

Ms. Tsukada:	A blue bouquet is nice, you know.
Mr. Kumar:	Blue flowers? (That's unusual.)
Ms. Tsukada:	Isn't that a good idea, because it's unusual?
Mr. Kumar:	Let's get them.

******

Mr. Kumar:	Here you are (some flowers from us).
Ms. Miyasato:	Wow, they're beautiful and such a nice color, too. Thank you.

******

Ms. Miyasato:	You know, I made this cake, but (I'm not sure if it's good).
Ms. Tsukada:	Oh, that's great! (lit., I'm glad.) Let me have a piece.
Ms. Miyasato:	How is it?
Mr. Kumar:	Very good. It has a light taste.
Ms. Miyasato:	That's right. This cake has a light taste (not so heavy). In addition, it is not so sweet.

クマル：	きれいな　はなですね！
塚田：	トニーは　なにいろの　はなが　すき？
クマル：	あかい　はなです。きいろい　はなも　すきです。
塚田：	あおい　はなたばも　すてきよ。
クマル：	あおい　はなですか？
塚田：	うん。めずらしいから、いいんじゃない？
クマル：	じゃ、そうしましょう。

******

クマル：	はい、これ。
宮里：	うわあ、きれいな　はな。すてきな　いろね。どうも　ありがとう。

******

宮里：	ねえねえ、ケーキ　つくったんだけど。
塚田：	わあ、うれしい！　いただきます！
宮里：	どう？
クマル：	はい、とても　おいしいです。かるいですね。
宮里：	うん、この　ケーキは　かるいんですよ。それに、あまり　あまくないの。

● Comprehension Drill

Listen to or read Dialogue 2 and decide if the following statements are true, false or you don't know as not enough information has been given.

1. Mr. Kumar doesn't like yellow flowers.   (T / F / DK)
2. Mr. Kumar and Ms. Tsukada buy a blue bouquet.   (T / F / DK)
3. Ms. Tsukada has brought a cake to Ms. Miyasato's house.   (T / F / DK)
4. They have tea with their cake.   (T / F / DK)
5. The cake Ms. Miyasato baked is light taste.   (T / F / DK)

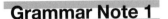

Grammar Note 1 Asking about/commenting on a recent happening
（感想を聞く・述べる）

In Lesson 8, you learned how to discuss what you will be doing over the weekend. After the weekend, you might ask someone what s/he did or say something about what you did during the weekend. When talking about events in the past, you will need the past forms of adjectives or of *desu*.

When asking about a recent happening and getting a general comment:

[Topic] *wa dō deshita ka.* **'How was ~?'**

Topic			SP
Kyōto	*wa*	*dō deshita*	*ka.*
'How was (the trip to) Kyoto?' (D-1)			

e.g.   *Kaiseki-ryōri* **wa dō deshita ka.** 'How did you like the Japanese formal dinner?' (D-1)

When responding to this question:

[*I*-adjective (past)] *desu.* / **[*Na*-adjective]** *deshita.* **'It was ~.'**

(Topic)		Description/Comment 1		Conjunction	Description/Comment 2	
(Kyōto	*wa)*	*atsukatta*	*desu.*	*Demo,*	*subarashikatta*	*desu.*
		totemo kirei	*deshita.*			
'(It) was hot, but (it) was great.' (D-1)						
'(It) was very pretty.'						

The conjunction *demo* means 'but,' and is always used at the beginning of a sentence as shown in the example above.

Grammar Note 2 Asking about/commenting on a recent happening in detail （詳しくたずねる・話す）

a. Asking about and commenting on in detail

In Grammar Note 1, we descussed how to ask general questions about recent events or to comment on them. When you ask about/give comments on events in details, use the following expressions.

Asking in detail:

Nani ga { **[*I*-adjective (past)]** *desu ka.* / **[*Na*-adjective]** *deshita ka.* } *Tatoeba?* **'What was ~, for example?'**

Response		*I*-adj. (past)			Asking for examples
Sō desu ka.	*Nani ga*	*yokatta*	*desu*	*ka.*	*Tatoeba?*
'Is that right? What was good? For example?' (D-1)					

Commenting:

Tatoeba, [Things you are describing] *desu.* $\begin{cases} \text{[}\textit{I}\text{-adjective (past)]} \textbf{\textit{desu.}} \\ \text{[}\textit{Na}\text{-adjective]} \textbf{\textit{deshita.}} \end{cases}$
'For example, something was ~.'

C. Starter	*I*-adj. + N	(non-past)	*Na*-adj.	(past)
Tatoeba,	*furui otera*	*desu.*	*Shizuka*	*deshita.*
'For example, the old temples. (They were) serene.' (D-1)				

[Additional things] *mo* [Additional things] *mo* $\begin{cases} \text{[}\textit{I}\text{-adjective (past)]} \textbf{\textit{desu.}} \\ \text{[}\textit{Na}\text{-adjective]} \textbf{\textit{deshita.}} \end{cases}$
'Something as well as another thing was ~.'

	IM*		IM	*Na*-adj.	(past)
Yama	*mo*	*kawa*	*mo*	*kirei*	*deshita.*
'Mountains as well as rivers were beautiful.' (D-1)					

*IM: Inclusion Marker

Note that instead of *nani* 'what,' as in the first pattern above, you can use other question words like *doko* 'where,' *itsu* 'when' and *dare* 'who' when asking about a specific place, time or person.

b. Asking with yes/no questions

Also, you can ask for specific comments with yes/no questions as in the following:

[*I*-adjective (past)] *desu ka.* / [*Na*-adjective] *deshita ka.* 'Was it ~?'

I-adj. (past)		SP
Oishikatta	*desu*	*ka.*
'Was it tasty?' (D-1)		

c. Giving more than one comment

When you want to make more than one comment, you can connect two sentences using the conjunction *sore ni*, which means 'furthermore' or 'besides,' as in the following:

Comment 1		Conjunction	Comment 2	
Kono kēki wa karui n desu	*yo.*	**Sore ni,**	*amari amakunai*	*no.*
'This cake has a light taste. In addition, it is not so sweet.' (D-2)				

Grammar Note 3   Two types of adjectives in Japanese （2つの形容詞）

There are two types of adjectives in Japanese. One is called the "*i*-adjective" and the other the "*na*-adjective." They behave differently and conjugate differently, but both modify or specify the nouns that come after them.

a. *I*-adjectives vs. *na*-adjectives

Look at the following examples to see the differences between the two types of adjectives.

When both types of adjectives are used as predicates, that is, when they are used with *desu*, they behave the same way:

I-adjective:	*Kyōto wa **atsui/atsukatta** <u>desu</u>.*	'Kyoto is/was hot.'
Na-adjective:	*Yama ga **kirei** <u>desu/deshita</u>.*	'The mountains are/were beautiful.'

However, when they are used as the modifiers, they behave differently; the *i*-adjective keeps the same form before the noun, while the *na*-adjective takes the *-na* ending before the noun, which is the reason for its name. Observe the following examples:

I-adjective:	*Tatoeba, **furui** <u>otera</u> desu.*	'For example, old temples.' (D-1)
Na-adjective:	***Kirei na** <u>maiko-san</u> mo mimashita.*	'We saw pretty young *geisha*, too.' (D-1)

How then can you identify and distinguish between the two types of adjectives? First, all the *i*-adjectives before *desu* end in the consecutive vowels *ai, ii, oi* or *ui*, but not in *ei*.

e.g.	*takai*	'expensive'	*oishii*	'taste good'
	aoi	'blue'	*furui*	'old'
	(*kir<u>ei</u>* 'clean/beautiful' ≠ *i*-adjective)			

Secondly, the *i*-adjective doesn't change its form when it comes before the noun as a modifier, while the *na*-adjective takes a *na*-ending before a noun.

e.g.	***akai** hana*	'red flowers' (D-2)	— *i*-adjective
	***aoi** hanataba*	'a blue bouquet' (D-2)	— *i*-adjective
	***kirei** <u>na</u> hana*	'pretty flowers' (D-2)	— *na*-adjective
	***suteki** <u>na</u> iro*	'nice color' (D-2)	— *na*-adjective

b. Conjugation of *i*-adjectives

A unique feature of Japanese adjectives is that *i*-adjectives conjugate. As mentioned above, *i*-adjectives end in *ai, ii, oi* or *ui*, and the last "*i*" changes as follows:

Conjugation of *I*-adjectives

	Non-past		Past	
	Affirmative	Negative	Affirmative	Negative
Informal	*-i*	*-kunai*	*-katta*	*-kunakatta*
Formal	*-i desu*	*-kunai desu*	*-katta desu*	*-kunakatta desu*

e.g.	'hot' (formal)	*atsui desu – atsukunai desu – atsukatta desu – atsukunakatta desu*
	'hot' (informal)	*atsui – atsukunai – atsukatta – atsukunakatta*
	'good' (informal)	*ii* – yokunai – yokatta – yokunakatta*

As you can see from the above, the formal forms can be made by adding *desu* to the informal forms. The following are examples of formal forms.

e.g.	*Atsukatta **desu**.*	'It was hot.' (D-1)
	*Subarashikatta **desu**.*	'It was great.' (D-1)
	*Yokatta **desu** ka.*	'Was it good?' (D-1)

Oishikatta *desu* ka.   'Was it tasty?' (D-1)
Takakatta *desu*.   'It was expensive.' (D-1)

c. Conjugation of *na*-adjectives

In contrast, *na*-adjectives themselves do not conjugate. The formality and tense of *na*-adjectives are expressed by the conjugation of the *desu* that is attached to them.

Conjugation of *Desu*

	Non-past		Past	
	Affirmative	Negative	Affirmative	Negative
Formal	desu	ja arimasen	deshita	ja arimasendeshita
Informal	da	ja nai	datta	ja nakatta

e.g.   'beautiful' (formal)   *kirei desu – kirei ja arimasen – kirei deshita – kirei ja arimasendeshita*
   'beautiful' (informal)   *kirei da – kirei ja nai – kirei datta – kirei ja nakatta*

Here are two examples from Dialogue 1.

e.g.   *Shizuka deshita.*   'It was serene/quiet.' (D-1)
   Kirei deshita.   'It was beautiful.' (D-1)

Ⓐ Conversation Drills

Drill 1. Complete the following conversations.

1. Ask about the weather yesterday, as you were not in Tokyo.
   You: _____

      (Ask what the weather was like yesterday in Tokyo.)
   Colleague: *Warukatta desu. Ame ga furimashita.*

2. Your colleague asks you about a trip.
   Colleague: *Senshū no ryokō wa dō deshita ka.*
   You: (a) _____

      (Say that it was a good trip and that you had fun.)
   Colleague: *Sore wa yokatta desu ne. Tatoeba, nani ga yokatta desu ka.*
   You: (b) _____

      (Say that the Great Buddha in Nara was fantastic.)

Vocabulary

1. *ame:*   rain   *furu (furimasu):*   to fall (rain/snow)   *ryokō:*   travel

3. As a fairly new resident of Japan, give some comments on how your life is in Japan.

    Japanese: *Nihon no seikatsu wa dō desu ka.*

    You: _____

        (Say that you're busy everyday thanks to you (lit.), and express gratitude.)

    Japanese: *Sō desu ka.*

4. Your friend asks you to show him/her your camera as it looks small and has a nice design.

    Friend: *Kamera chotto misete kudasai.*

    You: (a) _____ (Make sure that your friend is pointing to

        the camera and say go ahead.)

    Friend: *Chiisai desu ne.*

    You: (b) _____ (Agree

        with your friend and say that it's lightweight and you like its design as well.)

    Friend: *Doko no desu ka.*

    You: (c) _____ (Say that it's a Nikon.)

    Friend: *Muzukashii desu ka.*

    You: *Iie, kantan desu yo.*

5. You and your friend are at a gift shop and are deciding on a present for Mr. Kuroda.

    Friend: *Kuroda-san no purezento dore ga ii desu ka.*

    You: (a) _____ (Suggest that we buy a white cup.)

    Friend: *Ā ii desu ne. A, demo kono pinku no mo kawaii desu yo.*

    You: (b) _____

        (Show your hesitation and say it is a little big.)

    Friend: *Sō desu ne. Ja, kuroi no wa dō desu ka.*

    You: (c) _____

        (Say that the black one is a bit heavy.)

        (d) _____

        (You decide on the white one, after all.)

Vocabulary

1. *seikatsu:* life	*kantan:* simple	*kuroi:* black
chiisai: small	*kappu:* cup	*omoi:* heavy
dezain: design	*pinku:* pink	*yappari:* after all
doko no: made in where	*kawaii:* cute	
muzukashii: difficult	*ōkii:* big; large	

B Grammar & Vocabulary Building Drills

Drill 2. Write down the adjectives for pictures 1-10 below. Also fill in the boxes below with the non-past affirmative/negative and the past affirmative/negative forms of these adjectives.

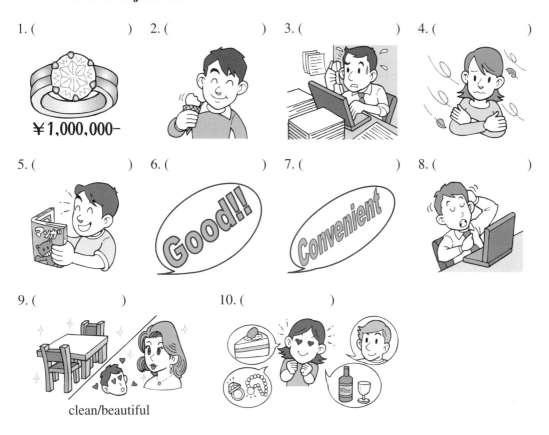

1. ( )
2. ( )
3. ( )
4. ( )
5. ( )
6. ( )
7. ( )
8. ( )
9. ( )

clean/beautiful

10. ( )

Non-past affirmative	Non-past negative	Past affirmative	Past negative
1. *takai desu*			
2.	*oishikunai desu*		
3.		*isogashikatta desu*	
4.			*samukunakatta desu*
5.	*omoshirokunai desu*		
6.		*yokatta desu*	
7. *benri desu*			
8	*hima ja arimasen*		
9.		*kirei deshita*	
10.			*suki ja arimasendeshita*

Vocabulary

2. *omoshiroi:* interesting   *benri:* convenient   *hima:* free; not busy

131

Drill 3. Practice the following dialogue by changing the underlined parts and conjugating the adjectives if necessary.

> A: (a) _Kaiseki-ryōri wa dō deshita ka._
> B: Ē, totemo (b) _kirei deshita._
> A: (c) _Oishikatta desu_ ka.
> B: Ē. (d) _Demo_ (e) _takakatta desu._

1. (a) _wain_   (b) _karui_   (c) _oishii_   (d) _sore ni_   (e) _amakunai_

2. (a) _shutchō_   (b) _ii_   (c) _isogashii_   (d) _demo_   (e) _daijōbu_

3. (a) _atarashii ofisu_   (b) _kirei_   (c) _nigiyaka_   (d) _sore ni_   (e) _benri_

Drill 4. Answer the following questions by using the words given in the parenthesis.

e.g.   _Kinō nani o nomimashita ka._ (_mezurashii / bīru_)
     → **Mezurashii bīru** _o nomimashita._

1. _Kinō nani o tabemashita ka._ (_shinsen / sarada_)

2. _Kyō wa doko e ikimasu ka._ (_shizuka / resutoran_)

3. _Ashita dare ga kimasu ka._ (_furui / tomodachi_)

4. _Dēbiddo-san wa donna hito desu ka._ (_suteki / hito_)

5. _Donna tabemono ga suki desu ka._ (_amai / dezāto_)

Drill 5. Complete the sentences by using the question words given in the box.

> _dō_   _nani_   _donna_

1. Q: _Hokkaidō wa (_   _) deshita ka._
   A: _Totemo subarashikatta desu._

2. Q: _(_   _) ga yokatta desuka?_
   A: _Tabemono ga oishikatta desu._

Vocabulary

3. _atarashii:_   new   **4.** _shinsen:_   fresh

3. Q: (   ) *ryōri o tabemashita ka.*

   A: *Oishii pasuta o tabemashita.*

4. Q: *Kono hon wa* (   ) *deshita ka.*

   A: *Totemo omoshirokatta desu.*

5. Q: *Kinō* (   ) *osake o nomimashita ka.*

   A: *Chūgoku no osake o nomimashita.*

ⓒ Listening Tasks

Drill 6. **Listen to each dialogue and choose the appropriate statement that matches the content.** 🔢46

1. a. *Nikkō wa atsukatta desu.*

   b. *Tōshōgū ga subarashikatta desu.*

   c. *Nikkō wa tsukaremashita.*

2. a. *Sakura wa kirei ja arimasen deshita.*

   b. *Shūmatsu wa hima deshita.*

   c. *Shūmatsu ohanami o shimashita.*

3. a. *Fuyumi-san no neko wa chiisai desu.*

   b. *Jakurīn-san no neko wa kawaii desu.*

   c. *Fuyumi-san wa neko ga suki ja arimasen.*

4. a. *Kabuki wa omoshiroi desu.*

   b. *Kabuki wa muzukashii desu.*

   c. *Kabuki wa nigiyaka desu.*

5. a. *Shōchū wa amai desu.*

   b. *Shōchū wa atsui desu.*

   c. *Shōchū wa oishii desu.*

Vocabulary

6. *neko:* cat

Drill 7. Listen to each dialogue and choose the adjectives you can hear.

1. a. *tanoshikatta*   b. *isogashikatta*   c. *subarashikatta*   d. *yokatta*

2. a. *hima*   b. *nigiyaka*   c. *oishii*   d. *isogashii*

3. a. *isogashii*   b. *suki*   c. *shizuka*   d. *ii*

4. a. *kirei deshita*   b. *atarashikatta*   c. *samukatta*   d. *tanoshikatta*

5. a. *tanoshikatta*   b. *omoshirokatta*   c. *hima deshita*   d. *nigiyaka deshita*

Ⓓ Review Drills

Drill 8. Read the following instructions and make sentences.

How would you:

1. ask someone how his/her summer vacation was?

2. say thank you for asking and answer that it was very enjoyable?

3. ask how the weather was?

4. answer that it was not very pleasant?

5. ask your friend if s/he is busy on Friday?

6. answer that you are not busy on Friday?

7. ask your friend how his/her new house is?

8. answer that it is convenient because it is near the station?

Drill 9. Match the responses with the questions.

1. *Kono osake wa amai desu ka.*   •   • a. *Kibishii desu ga, shinsetsu na hito desu.*

2. *Kono hon wa omoshirokatta desu ka.*   •   • b. *Oishii desu. Demo takai desu.*

3. *Jōshi wa donna hito desu ka.*   •   • c. *Hai, sukoshi amai desu.*

4. *Nihon no tabemono wa dō desu ka.*   •   • d. *Iie, amari omoshirokunakatta desu.*

Vocabulary

9. *kibishii:* severe   *shinsetsu:* nice and kind

Drill 10. Complete the dialogues by changing the following sentences to the correct order.

1. (b) → (   ) → (   ) → (   )

    a. *Kore desu.*

    b. *Sumimasen, ichiban atarashii pasokon wa dore desu ka.*

    c. *Kochira no wa sukoshi yasui desu yo.*

    d. *Demo chotto takai desu ne. Mō sukoshi yasui no wa arimasu ka.*

2. (a) → (   ) → (   ) → (   )

    a. *Kono kutsu kinō kaimashita. Dō desu ka.*

    b. *Sonna ni takakunakatta desu.*

    c. *Ii kaimono o shimashita ne.*

    d. *Suteki desu ne. Takakatta desu ka.*

Vocabulary

10. *yasui:* inexpensive   *sonna ni:* not much

CLOSING DIALOGUE

Formal Informal

48

Talking about last weekend

(At a *yakitori* shop.)

Howaito/Kumaru/Unabara:	*Otsukaresama deshita! Kanpāi!*
Tsukada:	*Jon, Natsue-san, kochira, supōtsu kurabu ga issho no Tonī.*
Kumaru:	*Ansonī Kumaru desu. Yoroshiku. Tonī to yonde kudasai.*
Unabara:	*Unabara desu. Yoroshiku.*
Howaito:	*Jon desu. Yoroshiku.*
Tsukada:	*Taishō! Toriaezu, yakitori, tekitō ni yo-nin-mae.*
Taishō:	*Hai yo.*

(They order something to eat, and start chatting.)

Tsukada:	*Saikin, kawatta koto aru?*
Howaito:	*Ēto, shūmatsu, Kamakura ni ikimashita.*
Tsukada:	*Dō datta?*
Howaito:	*Tanoshikatta desu yo. Nē, Natsue.*
Tsukada:	*Yokatta ne. Tonī wa sengetsu, Shingapōru ni shutchō datta n da yo ne.*
Kumaru:	*Hai, atsukatta desu. Sore ni, totemo isogashikatta desu.*

ホワイト／クマル／海原（うなばら）：	おつかれさまでした！かんぱ〜い！
塚田（つかだ）：	ジョン、夏江（なつえ）さん、こちら、スポーツクラブが いっしょの トニー。
クマル：	アンソニー・クマルです。よろしく。トニーと よんでください。
海原：	海原です。よろしく。
ホワイト：	ジョンです。よろしく。
塚田：	たいしょう！とりあえず、やきとり、てきとうに 4にんまえ。
大将（たいしょう）：	はいよ。
＊＊＊＊＊＊	
塚田：	さいきん、かわったこと ある？
ホワイト：	えーと、しゅうまつ、鎌倉（かまくら）に いきました。
塚田：	どうだった？
ホワイト：	たのしかったですよ。ねえ、夏江。
塚田：	よかったね。トニーは せんげつ、シンガポールに しゅっちょうだったんだよね。
クマル：	はい、あつかったです。それに、とても いそがしかったです。

Mr. White, Kumar & Ms. Unabara:	Here we are! (lit., We've worked hard.) Cheers!
Ms. Tsukada:	Jon and Natsue, this is Tony. I met him at the gym I go to.
Mr. Kumar:	(My name is) Anthony Kumar. Call me Tony.
Ms. Unabara:	I'm Unabara. Nice to meet you.
Mr. White:	I'm Jon. Nice to meet you.
Ms. Tsukada:	Master! First, give me four orders of the *yakitori* of your choice.
Master:	OK.
＊＊＊＊＊＊	
Ms. Tsukada:	Has anything interesting happened recently?
Mr. White:	Yes, (Natsue and I) went to Kamakura last weekend.
Ms. Tsukada:	How was Kamakura?
Mr. White:	It was fun, right, Natsue?
Ms. Tsukada:	That's good. Tony, (as I recall) you were on a business trip to Singapore last month, right?
Mr. Kumar:	Yes, (it was) very hot and (I was very) busy.

LESSON 10: INVITING/RECOMMENDING/ SUGGESTING
—*Sakura wa doko ga ii desu ka.*
'Do you know a good place to see cherry blossoms?'

Dialogue 1 Asking for/giving suggestions and inviting

· Formal 49

(Jonathan White and Fuyumi Tsukada are talking in the break room.)

Howaito:	*Tsukada-san, chotto ii desu ka.*
Tsukada:	*Hai.*
Howaito:	*Shi-gatsu ni kuni kara ryōshin ga kimasu.*
	Sakura wa doko ga ii desu ka.
Tsukada:	*Shi-gatsu no itsu desu ka.*
Howaito:	*Tsuitachi kara tōka made desu.*
Tsukada:	*Sō desu nē. Sono toshi ni yotte chigau kara, muzukashii desu kedo,*
	Aoyama-bochi ya Shinjuku-gyoen ga ii desu yo.
Howaito:	*Sō desu ka. Tsukada-san mo*
	issho ni ikimasen ka.
Tsukada:	*Ii desu ne. Minna de ikimashō.*

Mr. White:	Do you have a minute, Ms. Tsukada?
Ms Tsukada:	Yes, I do.
Mr. White:	My parents are coming to Japan in April. Do you know a good place to see cherry blossoms?
Ms. Tsukada:	When in April are they coming?
Mr. White:	They will be here from the 1st to the 10th.
Ms. Tsukada:	Let me see. It is difficult exactly to say when and where will be good to see cherry blossoms because that depends on the year, but Aoyama Cemetery or Shinjuku-gyoen Park would be good.
Mr. White:	Is that right? Would you like to come with us, Tsukada-san?
Ms. Tsukada:	That's a good idea. Let's all go together!

Vocabulary

chotto ii desu ka: do you have a minute?

toshi: year
~ ni yotte: it depends on ~

minna: everyone

ホワイト：　　塚田さん、ちょっと　いいですか。

塚田：　　　　はい。

ホワイト：　　4がつに　くにから　りょうしんが　きます。さくらは　どこが
　　　　　　　いいですか。

塚田：　　　　4がつの　いつ　ですか。

ホワイト：　　ついたちから　10かまで　です。

塚田：　　　　そうですねえ。その　としによって　ちがうから、むずかしいです
　　　　　　　けど、青山墓地や　新宿御苑が　いいですよ。

ホワイト：　　そうですか。塚田さんも　いっしょに　いきませんか。

塚田：　　　　いいですね。みんなで　いきましょう。

●Comprehension Drill

1. Listen to or read Dialogue 1 and decide if the following statements are true, false or you don't know as not enough information has been given.

    1. Mr. White asks Ms.Tsukada when the cherry blossoms are best for viewing.　(T / F / DK)

    2. Mr. White's parents are coming to Japan in March.　(T / F / DK)

    3. Mr. White's parents are staying in Japan from the 1st to the 10th of April.　(T / F / DK)

    4. Ms. Tsukada has been to Shinjuku-gyoen in the spring before.　(T / F / DK)

    5. Mr. White invites Ms. Tsukada to see the cherry blossoms together.　(T / F / DK)

2. Put these sentences in the correct order to make a conversation.

    (　　　) → (　　　) → (e) → (　　　) → (　　　)

    a. *Shi-gatsu no itsu desu ka.*

    b. *Hai.*

    c. *Tsukada-san, chotto ii desu ka.*

    d. *Tsuitachi kara tōka made desu.*

    e. *Shi-gatsu ni kuni kara ryōshin ga kimasu. Sakura wa doko ga ii desu ka.*

Dialogue 2 Dating · Informal

(Natsue Unabara and Jonathan White are talking about going on a date.)

Unabara:	*Konshū no kin'yōbi, hima?*
Howaito:	*Un, mā ne.*
Unabara:	*Shigoto no ato de, Shibuya no bijutsukan e ikanai?*
	Jon wa Yōroppa no e ga suki deshō?
	Waribikiken ga aru no.
Howaito:	*Shigoto no ato de, bijutsukan? Chotto isogashii yo.*
Unabara:	*Daijōbu. Kin'yōbi to doyōbi wa, yoru ku-ji made da kara.*
Howaito:	*Ā, sō ka. Hoka no hi wa nan-ji made?*
Unabara:	*Shichi-ji da kara, hoka no hi wa, chotto muzukashii ne.*
Howaito:	*Un, sō da ne. Jā, kin'yōbi ni ikō.*
Unabara:	*Shichi-ji ni ni-kai no robī de aō ka. Ato de, bangohan demo dō?*
Howaito:	*A, sō shiyō.*
Unabara:	*Jā, kin'yōbi no shichi-ji ni robī de.*

Ms. Unabara:	Are you free this Friday?
Mr. White:	Yes (at this moment).
Ms. Unabara:	Why don't we go to the museum in Shibuya after work?
	I know you like European paintings and I have discount tickets.
Mr. White:	After work on Friday? It will be a little tight (my schedule).
Ms. Unabara:	No problem, because they are open till 9 p.m. on Fridays and Saturdays.
Mr. White:	Oh, OK. How late are they open on other days of the week?
Ms. Unabara:	(They are open) until 7 p.m., so it will be difficult to go on other days.
Mr. White:	OK, you're right. Let's go this Friday.
Ms. Unabara:	Shall we meet at 7 p.m. in the lobby on the second floor? How about going to dinner or something afterward?
Mr. White:	OK, let's do that.
Ms. Unabara:	Then, (we'll meet) at 7 p.m. on Friday in the lobby.

海原 （うなばら）:	こんしゅうの　きんようび、ひま？
ホワイト：	うん、まあね。
海原：	しごとの　あとで、渋谷（しぶや）の　びじゅつかんへ　いかない？
	ジョンは　ヨーロッパの　えが　すきでしょう？　わりびきけんが　あるの。
ホワイト：	しごとの　あとで、びじゅつかん？　ちょっと　いそがしいよ。

Vocabulary

e:	picture	*hoka:*	other	*au (aimasu):*	to meet
waribikiken:	discount ticket	*robī:*	lobby		

海原：	だいじょうぶ。きんようびと どようびは、よる 9じまでだから。
ホワイト：	ああ、そうか。ほかの ひは なんじまで？
海原：	7じだから、ほかの ひは、ちょっと むずかしいね。
ホワイト：	うん、そうだね。じゃあ、きんようびに いこう。
海原：	7じに 2かいの ロビーで あおうか。あとで、ばんごはんでも どう？
ホワイト：	あ、そうしよう。
海原：	じゃあ、きんようびの 7じに ロビーで。

● **Comprehension Drill**

Listen to or read Dialogue 2 and decide if the following statements are true, false or you don't know as not enough information has been given.

1. Ms. Unabara invites Mr. White to go to see a film.　　　　(T / F / DK)
2. Mr. White likes European art.　　　　(T / F / DK)
3. The art gallery is closed on Sundays.　　　　(T / F / DK)
4. It is difficult to go there on Wednesdays.　　　　(T / F / DK)
5. Ms. Unabara and Mr. White will meet at 7:00 on Saturday.　　　　(T / F / DK)

◆　　　◆　　　◆

Grammar Note 1　Asking for/giving recommendations
（勧めを求める・勧める）

a. Asking for recommendations

Asking in detail:

[What you want to know] *wa doko ga ii desu ka.* '**Where is a good place to/for ~?**'

Topic		Place			SP
Sakura	*wa*	*doko*	*ga*	*ii desu*	*ka.*
'Where is a good place to see cherry blossoms? (lit., As for *sakura*, ~)' (D-1)					

When asking for some recommendations or suggestions regarding a certain place to do something, use the pattern, ~ *wa doko ga ii desu ka.* If you use the word *nani* 'what' instead of *doko* 'where' above, you can ask for recommendations for things to buy, see, eat, and so on. Also, when you want to ask for recommendations for timing, use *itsu* 'when.'

Note that in this pattern, the general topic is marked by *wa*, and *doko*, the question word for the specific information that you want, is marked by *ga*.

b. Giving recommendations

When responding to the question given in the section a., use the following pattern.

[Recommended place/timing/things] *ga ii desu yo.* '~ would be good.'

C.Starter	Places/Things to Recommend			SP
Sō desu nē,	*Aoyama-bochi ya Shinjuku-gyoen*	*ga*	*ii desu*	*yo.*
'Let me see, Aoyama Cemetery or Shinjuku-gyoen Park would be good.' (D-1)				

This pattern is a basic and straightforward response to the question above, and again the specific information you want comes before *ga*.

Grammar Note 2   Inviting someone to join in activities with you (誘う)

a. Inviting someone in a straightforward way

The following pattern is used when inviting someone in a straightforward way. The first example (formal) is used when you invite people such as someone your senior, your boss or a client, while the second (informal) is casually used among colleagues and friends.

[Suggested activity/timing] **[Verb]-*masen ka* / [Verb]-*nai?** 'Won't you ~?'

Time Expression	Place/Events		Verb	SP	
Shigoto no ato de	*Shibuya no bijutsukan*	*e*	*ikimasen*	*ka.*	(formal)
			ikanai	*ɸ ?*	(informal)
'Why don't we go to the museum in Shibuya after work?' (informal) (D-2)					

b. When inviting in a more indirect way or suggesting a plan

[Suggested activity/timing] *dō desu ka* / *dō?* 'How about doing ~?'

Suggestions			SP	
Ato de bangohan	*demo*	*dō desu*	*ka.*	(formal)
		dō	*ɸ ?*	(informal)
'How about going to dinner or something afterward?' (informal) (D-2)				

c. When suggesting something to do

[Suggested activity/timing] **[Verb]-*mashō ka* / [Verb]-*(y)ō ka.** 'Shall we ~?'

Time to Meet		Place to Meet		Verb	SP	
Shichi-ji	*ni*	*2-kai no robī*	*de*	*aimashō*	*ka.*	(formal)
				aō		(informal)
'Shall we meet at 7 p.m. in the lobby on the second floor?' (informal) (D-2)						

The patterns above are used when you make a suggestion or when you want the other person to decide. In other words, you are trying to elicit a decision from the other person, therefore, this is an indirect and polite way of extending an invitation.

d. Taking the initiative on an activity

[Suggested activity/timing] *ni* **[Verb]-*mashō*/[Verb]-*(y)ō*.** **'Let's ~.'**

C.Starter	Suggested Time		Verb	
Jā,	*kin'yōbi*	*ni*	*ikimashō.*	(formal)
			ikō.	(informal)
'Let's go this Friday.' (informal) (D-2)				

Compare the following verb forms for inviting/suggesting.

	Formal Endings	Informal Endings
1. 'Would you like to/Why don't we ~?'	V-*masen ka.*	V-*nai?*
2. 'How about ~ or something?'	N *demo dō desu ka.*	N *demo dō?*
3. 'Shall we ~?'	V-*mashō ka.*	V-*(y)ō ka.*
4. 'Let's ~.'	V-*mashō.*	V-*(y)ō.*

The difference between 3 (V-*mashō ka*/V-*(y)ō ka*) and 4 (V-*mashō*/V-*(y)ō*) is that while the former is used to show some humility to others in decision-making, the latter indicates straightforward initiative by the speaker.

Grammar Note 3 Accepting/declining an invitation (誘いを受ける・断る)

The following are expressions for accepting/declining an invitation.

a. Accepting an invitation

When you accept an invitation, use the same verb as in the invitation. Use the -*mashō* ending when the invitation is in formal speech, and the -*(y)ō* ending when in informal speech.

> e.g. (Informal)
>> A: *Ato de, bangohan demo dō?*   'How about going to dinner or something afterwards?'
>> B: *Sō shiyō.*   'Let's do that.' (D-2)
>
> (Formal)
>> A: *Ato de, bangohan demo dō desu ka.*
>> B: *Sō shimashō.*

b. Declining an invitation

In declining an invitation, you don't have to use a complete sentence, or give a clear reply with "no." Instead use the pattern ~ *wa chotto* to convey a nuance of inconveniences.

> e.g. A: *Doyōbi ni eiga ni ikimasen ka.*
>> B1: *Doyōbi **wa chotto** . . .*   'Saturday will not be good for me.'
>> B2: *Eiga **wa chotto** . . .*   'I'm not in a mood to see movie.'

In summing up, study the following.

Accepting (formal/informal):

Ē, V-*mashō* / V-*y(ō)*.	'Yes, let's ~.'
Ii desu ne. / *Ii ne.*	'That's good.'
Sō shimashō. / *Sō shiyō.*	'Let's do that.'

Declining:

Sō desu ne. Chotto . . .	'Well, it's a bit . . .'
~ *wa chotto.*	'It's a bit inconvenient regarding ~.'
Mata kondo ni shimasu.	'I'll try next time.'

Grammar Note 4 Conversation strategies: Starting and summing up （会話ストラテジー：切り出し・まとめ）

a. Interrupting someone and starting conversation

[Addressing someone], *chotto ii desu ka./ii?* **'Do you have a minute?'**
This pattern is used for starting a conversation smoothly especially when you interrupt someone to ask a favor or a question or to ask for suggestions.

   e.g.   *Tsukada-san, chotto ii desu ka.*
         'Do you have a minute, Ms. Tsukada?' (D-1) (lit., Is it OK if I interrupt you for a minute?)

When your colleague says this to you, you can respond with *Hai.*

b. Asking about someone's availability

[Time expression], *hima desu ka./hima?* **'Are you free ~?'**
This pattern is used to casually ask about someone's availability when you want to invite him/her to join you for something.

   e.g.   *Konshū no kin'yōbi, hima?* 'Are you free this Friday?' (informal) (D-2)
         Konshū no kin'yōbi wa hima desu ka. (formal)

When someone says this to you, you can respond formally and positively, *Hai*, or casually, *Un.*

c. Summing up a date/appointment which has just been set up

Dewa/Jā, [Meeting time] *ni* [Meeting place] *de* (*aimashō*). **'Then, we will meet ~ at ~.'**

C.Starter	Time to Meet		Place to Meet		Verb	
Sore dewa,	*kin'yōbi no shichi-ji*	*ni*	*robī*	*de*	(*aimashō.*)	(formal)
Jā,					(*aō.*)	(informal)
'Then, (we'll meet) at 7 p.m. on Friday in the lobby.' (D-2)						

◆   ◆   ◆

Ⓐ Conversation Drills

Drill 1. Complete the following conversations.

1. Ask your colleague to go to a movie with you.

    You: (a) _____

    (Suggest that your colleague go with you to a movie this Saturday.)

    Colleague: *Ē, ikimashō. Nani o mimasu ka.*

    You: (b) _____

    (Suggest watching a movie that you like.)

    Colleague: *Ii desu ne. Sō shimashō.*

2. Your colleague asks if you have free time for the up-coming weekend.

    Colleague: *Kondo no nichiyōbi wa hima desu ka.*

    You: (a) _____ (Say you are free on Sunday.)

    Colleague: *Tomodachi to shokuji o suru n desu ga, issho ni ikimasen ka.*

    You: (b) _____ (Say yes, by all means, you want to join

    them.)

    Colleague: *Jā, issho ni ikimashō.*

    You: (c) _____ (Ask where you should meet them.)

    Colleague: *Omotesandō de aimashō.*

3. Ask your Japanese friend for his/her suggestions for sightseeing and a souvenir from Tokyo.

    You: (a) _____ (Ask if your friend has time now.)

    Friend: *Hai, nan desu ka.*

    You: (b) _____

    (Ask where the best place is in Tokyo for sightseeing)

    Friend: *Sō desu ne . . . Asakusa wa dō desu ka.*

    You: (c) _____

    (Say that you want to buy a souvenir and ask your friend for some ideas.)

    Friend: *Ningyōyaki wa dō desu ka.*

    You: (d) _____ (Ask what that is.)

    Friend: *Asakusa no yūmei na okashi desu yo.*

Vocabulary

1. *zehi:* by all means   *yūmei:* famous
   kankō: sightseeing   *okashi:* confectionery

4. Your boss is inviting you to a party at his/her house. Accept the invitation.

Boss: *Konshū no doyōbi yotei aru?*

You: (a) _____ (Say you don't have any plans.)

Boss: *Doyōbi ni uchi de pātī o suru n da kedo, konai?*

You: (b) _____ (Say that that sounds like a good idea, and that you be happy to go.)

Boss: *Ja, doyōbi 11-ji ni Shimokitazawa no eki de.*

You: (c) _____ (Say that you consent to the invitation.)

5. Suppose that you are from Australia. Give some suggestions for sightseeing there.

Colleague: *Chotto ii desu ka.*

You: (a) _____ (Say yes, and ask what your colleague wants.)

Colleague: *Kondo no yasumi ni Ōsutoraria e ryokō ni ikimasu.*

You: (b) _____ (Ask where your colleague is going in Australia.)

Colleague: *Shidonī desu. Shidonī no kankō wa doko ga ii desu ka.*

You: (c) _____

(Suggest that your colleague go to the Blue Mountains near Sydney.)

Colleague: *Burū maunten desu ka. Arigatō.*

B Grammar & Vocabulary Building Drills

Drill 2. Practice the following patterns by filling in the blanks.

	Formal		Informal	
	~masen ka	*~mashō*	*~nai?*	*~(y)ō*
1. *ikimasu*	ikimasen ka			
2. *nomimasu*				nomō
3. *aimasu*			awanai?	
4. *tabemasu*		tabemashō		
5. *shimasu*	shimasen ka			
6. *kimasu*		kimashō		

Vocabulary

1. *yotei:* plan; schedule

Drill 3. Complete the following conversations as shown in the example.

e.g. *Shūmatsu tenisu o shimasu.*

→ A: *Shūmatsu tenisu o shimasen ka.*

   B: *Ii desu ne, shimashō.*

1. *Ashita eiga o mimasu.*

→ A: _____

   B: *Hai,* _____

2. *Mō kaerimasu.*

→ A: _____

   B: *Sō desu ne,* _____

3. *Ato de kōhī o nomimasu.*

→ A: _____

   B: *Ii desu yo,* _____

4. *Issho ni bangohan o tabemasu.*

→ A: _____

   B: *Hai,* _____

5. *Raishū, Yokohama e ikimasu.*

→ A: _____

   B: *Hai,* _____

Drill 4. Complete the sentences by using the question words given in the box.

> itsu   doko   dare   nani

1. A: *Yakitori-ya wa (* _____ *) ga ii desu ka.*

   B: *Shinbashi ga ii desu yo.*

2. A: *Sukī wa (* _____ *) ga ii desu ka.*

   B: *12-gatsu kara 2-gatsu ga ii desu.*

3. A: *Kyōkasho wa (* _____ *) ga ii desu ka.*

   B: 'Basic Japanese for Expats' *ga ii desu.*

4. A: *Shikai wa (* _____ *) ga ii desu ka.*

   B: *Akagawa-san ga ii desu ne.*

5. A: *Restutoran wa (* _____ *) ga ii desu ka.*

   B: *Aoyama no mise ga ii desu.*

Drill 5. Practice the following dialogue by changing the underlined parts.

> A: *Roppongi no atarashii* (a) *shoppingu sentā ni ikimashita ka.*
> B: *Iie, mada desu.*
> A: (b)*Kyō, shigoto no ato de ikimasen ka.*
> B: *Ē, ikimashō.*
> A: *Jā,* (c) *6-ji han ni robī de.*

1. (a) *resutoran*   (b) *ashita soko de tabemasu*   (c) *7-ji*
2. (a) *bijutsukan*   (b) *doyōbi issho ni ikimasu*   (c) *11-ji*
3. (a) *kafe*   (b) *ato de kōhī demo nomimasu*   (c) *3-ji han*

C Listening Tasks

Drill 6. Listen to the dialogues and choose the verb form a, b or c, that the first person in each dialogue uses to extend the invitation. `51`

1. a. *minai?*   b. *miyō ka*   c. *miyō*
2. a. *konai?*   b. *koyō ka*   c. *koyō*
3. a. *nomanai?*   b. *nomō ka*   c. *nomō*
4. a. *shinai?*   b. *shiyō ka*   c. *shiyō*
5. a. *ikanai?*   b. *ikō ka*   c. *ikō*

Vocabulary

4. *kyōkasho:* textbook   *shikai:* emcee (MC)

Drill 7. Listen to each question and choose one appropriate answer.

1. a. *Watashi desu.*
   b. *Hai. Nan desu ka.*
   c. *Ima kaigishitsu ni imasu.*

2. a. *4-gatsu ga ii desu yo.*
   b. *Ohanami ga ii desu yo.*
   c. *Inokashira-kōen ga ii desu yo.*

3. a. *Ē. Ikimasu.*
   b. *Iie. Nai desu.*
   c. *Sumimasen. Ima kara kaigi desu.*

4. a. *Ginza ga ii yo.*
   b. *Osaki ni dōzo.*
   c. *Kyō wa chotto . . .*

5. a. *Ē. Sō shimashō.*
   b. *Hai. 200-en desu.*
   c. *Jā, mata kimasu.*

Ⓓ Review Drills

Drill 8. Read the following instructions and make sentences.

How would you:

1. ask someone to suggest when the best time to see the cherry blossoms?

2. suggest that the best time for cherry blossoms is the end of March to April?

3. ask someone if s/he is free this coming weekend?

4. invite someone to go to a restaurant with you? [both formal and informal]

Vocabulary

8. *~ no owari:*   end of ~

5. accept an invitation to go to a restaurant together? [both formal and informal]

6. suggest that you meet him/her at 10 a.m. in the lobby? [both formal and informal]

7. say that it is a bit inconvenient for you at 10 a.m., and suggest that you meet him/her at 11 a.m. instead?

8. confirm that you will meet him/her at 11 a.m. in the lobby?

Drill 9. Match the responses with the questions.

1. *Sukī wa doko ga ii desu ka.*   •   • a. *Un, ikō.*
2. *12-ji ni 1-kai no robī de aō ka.*   •   • b. *Niigata wa dō desu ka.*
3. *Shūmatsu, Ueno no bijutsukan e ikanai?*   •   • c. *Ii desu ne. Tabemashō.*
4. *Ashita, issho ni sushi o tabemasen ka.*   •   • d. *Un, jā 12-ji ni, robī de.*

Drill 10. Complete the dialogues by changing the following sentences to the correct order.

1. (b) → (   ) → (   ) → (   )

    a. *Ii desu ne. Ja, sō shimashō.*

    b. *Kuroda-san ga 10-gatsu ni kekkon shimasu. Nani ka purezento shimasen ka.*

    c. *Sō desu ne. Nani ga ii desu ka.*

    d. *Kōhīmēkā wa dō desu ka.*

2. (c) → (   ) → (   ) → (   )

    a. *Un, sō shiyō.*

    b. *Un. Doko de miru?*

    c. *Doyōbi, issho ni eiga o minai?*

    d. *Roppongi no eigakan wa dō?*

Vocabulary

10. *kekkon suru (shimasu):* to get married   *purezento:* present   *kōhīmēkā:* coffee maker

CLOSING DIALOGUE   Formal Informal

53

Inviting for dinner

(After a meeting.)

Kawashima (R): Ā, nagai kaigi datta! Tsukareta yo.

Kibarashi ni meshi demo dō? Ogoru yo. Konban, yotei aru?

Howaito: Ie, yoru wa aite imasu yo. Tada, korekara Tsukada-san to sukoshi uchiawase ga arimasu ga.

Kawashima: Shiroyama-san wa?

Shiroyama: (Rushing out) Hai, ato de keitai ni renraku shimasu.

(After a while.)

Howaito: A, Shiroyama-san kara mēru desu. "Mata kondo ni shimasu" tte.

Kawashima: Sō ka, zannen da na. Totsuzen datta kara ne.

Ja, Jonasan, uchiawase no ato de, Tsukada-san mo sasotte meshi ni ikō.

Shinagawa no TK biru no 8-kai ni ii sushi-ya ga aru kara.

Howaito: Hai. Zehi.

Kawashima: Watashi wa saki ni itteru yo.

川島良三：ああ、ながい　かいぎだった！　つか
　　　　　れたよ。
　　　　　きばらしに　めしでも　どう？　おご
　　　　　るよ。こんばん、よてい　ある？
ホワイト：いえ、よるは　あいていますよ。ただ、
　　　　　これから　塚田さんと　すこし　うち
　　　　　あわせが　ありますが。
川島：　　白山さんは？
白山：　　はい、あとで　けいたいに　れんらく
　　　　　します。
******
ホワイト：あ、白山さんから　メールです。「ま
　　　　　た　こんどに　します」って。
川島：　　そうか、ざんねんだな。とつぜんだっ
　　　　　たからね。
　　　　　じゃ、ジョナサン、うちあわせの　あ
　　　　　とで、塚田さんも　さそって　めしに
　　　　　いこう。品川の　TK ビルの　8 かい
　　　　　に　いい　すしやが　あるから。
ホワイト：はい。ぜひ。
川島：　　わたしは　さきに　いってるよ。

Mr. Kawashima: Oh boy, that was a long meeting. I'm tired.
To change the mood, how about going out to dinner? It's on me. Do you have other plans tonight?

Mr. White: No, I'm free tonight. But I have a small meeting with Ms. Tsukada after this.

Mr. Kawashima: How about you Ms. Shiroyama?

Ms. Shiroyama: I'll give you a call on your cell phone later.

******

Mr. White: Here's a message from Ms. Shiroyama. She says she will try to make it next time.

Mr. Kawashima: Too bad she can't make it tonight, but it was very short notice.
OK, Jonathan, ask Ms. Tsukada to join us. I know a good sushi restaurant on the 8th floor of the TK Building in Shinagawa.

Mr. White: We'll be there (lit., by all means).

Mr. Kawashima: I'll be going first and will be waiting for you there.

Chotto — A little word with many meanings

The Japanese word *chotto* basically means 'for a moment', 'a bit', 'slightly' and 'just a second', but one hears it dozens of times a day in a variety of situations. Here are some examples of its uses:

Chotto *matte kudasai.*	'Please wait for a moment.'
Chotto *itte kimasu.*	'I'm going out for a moment.'
Chotto *ii desu ka.*	'May I interrupt for a moment?'
Chotto, *sumimasen.*	'Please excuse me.' (used when interrupting someone or when passing in front of someone)
Chotto *takai desu ne.*	'It seems a bit expensive for me.'

Chotto is also used when you want to avoid explaining something clearly because you do not want to embarrass, offend or upset someone, or for some other reason.

e.g. 1   A: *Dō omoimasu ka.* 'What do you think?'
          B: *Sō desu nee,* **chotto** . . . 'Well, let me think, it's a bit . . . (it's inconvenient for me, I don't agree, etc.)'

e.g. 2   A: *Odekake desu ka.* 'Are you going out?'
          B: *Ee,* **chotto** *(soko made).* 'Well, yes, on a short errand nearby.'

e.g. 3   A: *Shūmatsu wa dō shimasu ka.* 'What are your plans for the weekend?'
          B: **Chotto** . . . *(tokuni nani mo nai desu).* 'Well, . . . (I don't really have any plans)'

Chotto can also be used to mean 'No.' It is useful when you are asked to do a favor that you feel would be a little difficult but you don't want to offend the person asking.

e.g. 4   A: *Mō sukoshi yasuku narimasen ka.* 'Can you give me a further discount?'
          B: *Ūn,* **chotto** . . . *(muzukashii desu ne).* 'Well, it's a little difficult right now . . .'

e.g. 5   (When your colleague asks you out for a drink after work but you really must stay in the office and finish your work)
          A: *Kaeri ni ippai dō?* 'Why don't we go for a drink after work?'
          B: *Iyā,* **chotto** . . . *(muri desu ne).* 'Well, it's a little inconvenient for me this evening.'

The above examples are but a few of the many uses of *chotto.* You will probably find yourself becoming more and more accustomed to using this very *benri* or useful Japanese expression, but try to use it sparingly and don't let it become part of your vocabulary, or it will begin to sound like the overused English expressions "Like, you know," "You know," "Like, well, uh yeah."

Appendix 1. Words for jobs and countries <L1>

a. Jobs

	Neutral style	Polite style
company employee	kaishain	—
bank employee	ginkōin	—
doctor	isha	oisha-san / *sensei
housewife	shufu	—
lawyer	bengoshi	bengoshi-san / *sensei
policeman	keikan	omawari-san
shop employee	ten'in	ten'in-san
station employee	ekiin	ekiin-san
teacher	kyōshi	sensei

*Used when addressing.

b. Countries

Japan	Nihon / Nippon	Italy	Itaria
Australia	Ōsutoraria	New Zealand	Nyūjīrando
Brazil	Burajiru	Republic of Korea	Kankoku
Canada	Kanada	Russia	Roshia
China	Chūgoku	Thailand	Tai
France	Furansu	U.K.	Eikoku / Igirisu
Germany	Doitsu	U.S.A.	Amerika
India	Indo	Viet Nam	Betonamu

Appendix 2. Family terms <L1>

	my ~	your ~ / someone else's ~		my ~	your ~ / someone else's ~
family	kazoku	gokazoku	brother (younger)	otōto	otōto-san
husband	otto / shujin	goshujin	sister (older)	ane	onēsan
wife	tsuma / kanai	okusan	sister (younger)	imōto	imōto-san
children	kodomo	kodomo-san / okosan	grandfather	sofu	ojīsan
son	musuko	musuko-san	grandmother	sobo	obāsan
daughter	musume	musume-san / ojōsan	relatives	shinseki	goshinseki
parents	ryōshin	goryōshin	uncle	oji	oji-san
father	chichi	otōsan	aunt	oba	oba-san
mother	haha	okāsan	nephew	oi	oigosan
siblings	kyōdai	gokyōdai	niece	mei	meigosan
brother (older)	ani	onīsan	cousin	itoko	

Appendix 3. Counters <L2>

	Group I		Group II			
	Solid items	People	Japanese currency	Age	Floors	Numbers
	-tsu	*-ri/-nin*	*-en*	*-sai*	*-kai*	*-ban*
1	hito-tsu	hito-ri	ichi-en	is*-sai	ik*-kai	ichi-ban
2	futa-tsu	futa-ri	ni-en	ni-sai	ni-kai	ni-ban
3	mit-tsu	san-nin	san-en	san-sai	san-kai san-gai*	san-ban
4	yot-tsu	yo*-nin	yo*-en	yon-sai	yon-kai	yon-ban
5	itsu-tsu	go-nin	go-en	go-sai	go-kai	go-ban
6	mut-tsu	roku-nin	roku-en	roku-sai	rok*-kai	roku-ban
7	nana-tsu	nana-nin shichi-nin	nana-en	nana-sai	nana-kai	nana-ban
8	yat-tsu	hachi-nin	hachi-en	has*-sai	hachi-kai hak*-kai	hachi-ban
9	kokono-tsu	kyū-nin	kyū-en	kyū-sai	kyū-kai	kyū-ban
10	tō	jū-nin	jū-en	jis*-sai jus*-sai	jik*-kai juk*-kai	jū-ban
How many?	ikutsu (how many things?)	nan-nin nan-mei (how many people?)	nan-en / ikura (how much?)	nan-sai (how old?)	nan-kai nan-gai* (which floor?)	nan-ban (what number?)

	Group II					
	Cylindrical items	Flat items	Machinery	Books	A cup/spoon of	Solid items
	-hon	*-mai*	*-dai*	*-satsu*	*-hai*	*-ko*
1	ip*-pon*	ichi-mai	ichi-dai	is*-satsu	ip*-pai*	ik*-ko
2	ni-hon	ni-mai	ni-dai	ni-satsu	ni-hai	ni-ko
3	san-bon*	san-mai	san-dai	san-satsu	san-bai*	san-ko
4	yon-hon	yon-mai	yon-dai	yon-satsu	yon-hai	yon-ko
5	go-hon	go-mai	go-dai	go-satsu	go-hai	go-ko
6	rop*-pon*	roku-mai	roku-dai	roku-satsu	rop*-pai*	rok*-ko
7	nana-hon	nana-mai	nana-dai	nana-satsu	nana-hai	nana-ko
8	hachi-hon hap*-pon*	hachi-mai	hachi-dai	has*-satsu	hap*-pai*	hak*-ko
9	kyū-hon	kyū-mai	kyū-dai	kyū-satsu	kyū-hai	kyū-ko
10	jip*-pon* jup*-pon*	jū-mai	jū-dai	jis*-satsu jus*-satsu	jip*-pai* jup*-pai*	jik*-ko juk*-ko
How many (items)?	nan-bon*	nan-mai	nan-dai	nan-satsu	nan-bai*	nan-ko

(* indicates pronunciation changes.)

Appendix 4. Interrogatives (Wh-question words)

Basic Wh-question words

who	*dare / donata*	when	*itsu*
what	*nani / nan*	why	*dōshite / naze*
where	*doko*	how	*dō*

More expressions using Wh-question words

<L2>   <L3>

how much	*ikura*	what month	*nan-gatsu*
how old	*nan-sai*	what day of the month	*nan-nichi*
how many times	*nan-kai*	what day of the week	*nan-yōbi*
which floor	*nan-kai / nan-gai*	what time	*nan-ji*
what number	*nan-ban*	how many minutes	*nan-pun*
how many (cylindrical items)	*nan-bon*	how many months	*nan-kagetsu*
		how many weeks	*nan-shūkan*
how many (solid items)	*ikutsu*	how many days	*nan-nichikan*
how many people	*nan-nin/nan-mei*	how many hours	*nan-jikan*

Appendix 5. The *ko-so-a-do* words

		Ko group (near S*)	**So** group (near L**)	**A** group (far from S & L)	**Do** group (question word)
Thing	<L5/L6>	*kore*	*sore*	*are*	*dore*
	<L6>	*kono* + N	*sono* + N	*ano* + N	*dono* + N
Place (informal)	<L6/L7>	*koko*	*soko*	*asoko*	*doko*
Direction (informal)	<L7>	*kotchi*	*sotchi*	*atchi*	*dotchi*
Area	<L6>	*kono hen*	*sono hen*	*ano hen*	*dono hen*
Place/Direction/People (formal)	<L7>	*kochira*	*sochira*	*achira*	*dochira*

*S: Speaker **L: Listener

Appendix 6. Time expressions

a. General time <L3>

	Past ◄		Present		► Future
Year	ototoshi (the year before last)	kyonen (last year)	kotoshi (this year)	rainen (next year)	sarainen (the year after next)
Month	sensengetsu (the month before last)	sengetsu (last month)	kongetsu (this month)	raigetsu (next month)	saraigetsu (the month after next)
Week	sensenshū (the week before last)	senshū (last week)	konshū (this week)	raishū (next week)	saraishū (the week after next)
Day	ototoi (the day before yesterday)	kinō (yesterday)	kyō (today)	ashita (tomorrow)	asatte (the day after tomorrow)
Morning	ototoi no asa (morning of the day before yesterday)	kinō no asa (yesterday morning)	kesa / kyō no asa (this morning)	ashita no asa (tomorrow morning)	asatte no asa (morning of the day after tomorrow)
Noon	ototoi no hiru (noon of the day before yesterday)	kinō no hiru (yesterday noon)	kyō no hiru (this noon)	ashita no hiru (tomorrow noon)	asatte no hiru (noon of the day after tomorrow)
Afternoon	ototoi no gogo (the afternoon of the day before yesterday)	kinō no gogo (yesterday afternoon)	kyō no gogo (this afternoon)	ashita no gogo (tomorrow afternoon)	asatte no gogo (the afternoon of the day after tomorrow)
Evening	ototoi no ban (evening of the day before yesterday)	yūbe / kinō no ban (yesterday evening)	konban/ kyō no ban (this evening)	ashita no ban (tomorrow evening)	asatte no ban (evening of the day after tomorrow)
When?	itsu				

b. Year

The Japanese calendar system uses *gengō* which are eras indicating the reigns of emperors. A new era begins on the day the emperor succeeds to the throne. The current emperor, Akihito, succeeded to the throne on January 8, 1989, as the Showa Era ended on January 7. On the same day, the Cabinet announced the new era name, "Heisei." Since 1868 only one era name has been used by each emperor: the Meiji Era lasted from 1868 to 1912; the Taisho Era from 1912 to 1926; and the Showa Era from 1926 to 1989. However, since the Tokyo Olympic Games in 1964, both the Western and Japanese calendar systems have been commonly used in daily life.

Year	Western Calendar	Japanese Calendar	
1868	*sen-happyaku-rokujū-hachi-nen*	*Meiji gan-nen**	(Meiji 1st year)
.			
1912	*sen-kyūhyaku-jū-ni-nen*	*Taishō gan-nen**	(Taisho 1st year)
.			
1926	*sen-kyūhyaku-nijū-roku-nen*	*Shōwa gan-nen**	(Showa 1st year)
.			
1945	*sen-kyūhyaku-yonjū-go-nen*	*Shōwa nijū nen*	(Showa 20th year)
.			
1989	*sen-kyūhyaku-hachijū-kyū-nen*	*Heisei gan-nen**	(Heisei 1st year)
1992	*sen-kyūhyaku-kyūjū-ni-nen*	*Heisei yo nen*	(Heisei 4th year)
.			
1997	*sen-kyūhyaku-kyūjū-nana-nen*	*Heisei kyū nen*	(Heisei 9th year)
2000	*nisen-nen*	*Heisei jū-ni nen*	(Heisei 12th year)
2005	*nisen-go-nen*	*Heisei jū-nana/ jū-shichi nen*	(Heisei 17th year)
2010	*nisen-jū-nen*	*Heisei nijū-ichi nen*	(Heisei 21st year)
2018	*nisen-jū-hachi-nen*	*Heisei sanjū nen*	(Heisei 30th year)
.			
?	*nan-nen*		

**Gan-nen* is a special way of saying the first year of an emperor's era.

c. National holidays

January 1	*Ganjitsu*	(New Year's Day)
2nd Monday of January	*Seijin no hi*	(Coming of Age Day)
February 11	*Kenkoku kinen no hi*	(National Foundation Day)
March 21*	*Shunbun no hi*	(Vernal Equinox Day)
April 29	*Shōwa no hi*	(Showa Day)
May 3	*Kenpō kinenbi*	(Constitution Day)
May 4	*Midori no hi*	(Greenery Day)
May 5	*Kodomo no hi*	(Children's Day)
3rd Monday of July	*Umi no hi*	(Marine Day)
3rd Monday of September	*Keirō no hi*	(Respect for the Aged Day)
September 23*	*Shūbun no hi*	(Autumnal Equinox Day)
2nd Monday of October	*Taiiku no hi*	(Health and Sports Day)
November 3	*Bunka no hi*	(Culture Day)
November 23	*Kinrō kansha no hi*	(Labor Thanksgiving Day)
December 23	*Tennō tanjōbi*	(The Emperor's Birthday)

*The date differs depending on the year.

Appendix 7. Verb conjugations <L4/L8/L10>

This table shows how verb endings change in non-past/past, affirmative/negative and formal/informal forms.

	Non-past		Past		Inviting (Let's ~)
	Affirmative (do)	Negative (don't)	Affirmative (did)	Negative (didn't)	
Formal [*masu*-form]	-*masu*	-*masen*	-*mashita*	-*masendeshita*	-*mashō*
Informal	-*ru* / -*u* [dictionary form]	-*nai* [*nai*-form]	-*ta* [*ta*-form]	-*nakatta*	-*yō* / -*ō*

The following are examples of conjugations according to verb groups.

a. Group 1

		Non-past		Past		Inviting (Let's ~)
		Affirmative (do)	Negative (don't)	Affirmative (did)	Negative (didn't)	
to meet	F	aimasu	aimasen	aimashita	aimasendeshita	aimashō
	I	au	awanai	atta	awanakatta	aō
to be / to have	F	arimasu	arimasen	arimashita	arimasendeshita	—
	I	aru	nai	atta	nakatta	—
to talk / to speak	F	hanashimasu	hanashimasen	hanashimashita	hanashimasen-deshita	hanashimashō
	I	hanasu	hanasanai	hanashita	hanasanakatta	hanasō
to go	F	ikimasu	ikimasen	ikimashita	ikimasendeshita	ikimashō
	I	iku	ikanai	itta	ikanakatta	ikō
to return	F	kaerimasu	kaerimasen	kaerimashita	kaerimasen-deshita	kaerimashō
	I	kaeru	kaeranai	kaetta	kaeranakatta	kaerō
to buy	F	kaimasu	kaimasen	kaimashita	kaimasendeshita	kaimashō
	I	kau	kawanai	katta	kawanakatta	kaō
to listen	F	kikimasu	kikimasen	kikimashita	kikimasendeshita	kikimashō
	I	kiku	kikanai	kiita	kikanakatta	kikō
to turn	F	magarimasu	magarimasen	magarimashita	magarimasen-deshita	magarimashō
	I	magaru	magaranai	magatta	magaranakatta	magarō
to drink	F	nomimasu	nomimasen	nomimashita	nomimasen-deshita	nomimashō
	I	nomu	nomanai	nonda	nomanakatta	nomō
to get on/in	F	norimasu	norimasen	norimashita	norimasen-deshita	norimashō
	I	noru	noranai	notta	noranakatta	norō
to stop	F	tomarimasu	tomarimasen	tomarimashita	tomarimasen-deshita	tomarimashō
	I	tomaru	tomaranai	tomatta	tomaranakatta	tomarō

to make	F	tsukurimasu	tsukurimasen	tsukurimashita	tsukurimasen-deshita	tsukurimashō
	I	tsukuru	tsukuranai	tsukutta	tsukuranakatta	tsukurō
to read	F	yomimasu	yomimasen	yomimashita	yomimasen-deshita	yomimashō
	I	yomu	yomanai	yonda	yomanakatta	yomō

b. Group 2

		Non-past		Past		Inviting (Let's ~)
		Affirmative (do)	Negative (don't)	Affirmative (did)	Negative (didn't)	
to be / to stay	F	imasu	imasen	imashita	imasendeshita	imashō
	I	iru	inai	ita	inakatta	iyō
to eat	F	tabemasu	tabemasen	tabemashita	tabemasen-deshita	tabemashō
	I	taberu	tabenai	tabeta	tabenakatta	tabeyō
to be tired	F	tsukaremasu	tsukaremasen	tsukaremashita	tsukaremasen-deshita	—
	I	tsukareru	tsukarenai	tsukareta	tsukarenakatta	—
to see	F	mimasu	mimasen	mimashita	mimasen-deshita	mimashō
	I	miru	minai	mita	minakatta	miyō

c. Group 3

		Non-past		Past		Inviting (Let's ~)
		Affirmative (do)	Negative (don't)	Affirmative (did)	Negative (didn't)	
to come	F	kimasu	kimasen	kimashita	kimasendeshita	kimashō
	I	kuru	konai	kita	konakatta	koyō
to do	F	shimasu	shimasen	shimashita	shimasen-deshita	shimashō
	I	suru	shinai	shita	shinakatta	shiyō

Appendix 8. *I*-adjectives and *na*-adjectives <L9>

a. *I*-adjective conjugations (adjectives ending in -ai, -ii, -oi, -ui)

The *i*-adjective ending conjugates as follows.

	Non-past		Past	
	Affirmative	Negative	Affirmative	Negative
Formal	-i desu	-kunai desu	-katta desu	-kunakatta desu
Informal	-i	-kunai	-katta	-kunakatta

Here are examples of *i*-adjective conjugations in informal forms. Formal forms are made by adding *desu* to these forms.

	Non-past		Past	
	Affirmative	Negative	Affirmative	Negative
sweet	amai	amakunai	amakatta	amakunakatta
new	atarashii	atarashikunai	atarashikatta	atarashikunakatta
hot	atsui	atsukunai	atsukatta	atsukunakatta
small	chiisai	chiisakunai	chiisakatta	chiisakunakatta
near	chikai	chikakunai	chikakatta	chikakunakatta
old (things)	furui	furukunai	furukatta	furukunakatta
good	ii /yoi*	yokunai	yokatta	yokunakatta
busy	isogashii	isogashikunai	isogashikatta	isogashikunakatta
light (weight)	karui	karukunai	karukatta	karukunakatta
cute	kawaii	kawaikunai	kawaikatta	kawaikunakatta
rare	mezurashii	mezurashikunai	mezurashikatta	mezurashikunakatta
difficult	muzukashii	musukashikunai	muzukashikatta	muzukashiku-nakatta
taste good	oishii	oishikunai	oishikatta	oishikunakatta
big	ōkii	ōkikunai	ōkikatta	ōkikunakatta
heavy	omoi	omokunai	omokatta	omokunakatta
interesting	omoshiroi	omoshirokunai	omoshirokatta	omoshiroku-nakatta
cold (weather)	samui	samukunai	samukatta	samukunakatta
wonderful	subarashii	subarashikunai	subarashikatta	subarashiku-nakatta
expensive	takai	takakunai	takakatta	takakunakatta
enjoyable	tanoshii	tanoshikunai	tanoshikatta	tanoshikunakatta
happy	ureshii	ureshikunai	ureshikatta	ureshikunakatta
bad	warui	warukunai	warukatta	warukunakatta

* Very formal.

b. *Na*-adjective conjugations (adjectives ending in -*ei* and others)

The *na*-adjective ending conjugates as follows.

	Non-past		Past	
	Affirmative	Negative	Affirmative	Negative
Formal	desu	ja arimasen	deshita	ja arimasendeshita
Informal	da	ja nai	datta	ja nakatta

Here are examples of *na*-adjective conjugations in formal and informal forms.

		Non-past		Past	
		Affirmative	Negative	Affirmative	Negative
convenient	F	benri desu	benri ja arimasen	benri deshita	benri ja arimasendeshita
	I	benri da	benri ja nai	benri datta	benri ja nakatta
free, not busy	F	hima desu	hima ja arimasen	hima deshita	hima ja arimasendeshita
	I	hima da	hima ja nai	hima datta	hima ja nakatta
simple	F	kantan desu	kantan ja arimasen	kantan deshita	kantan ja arimasendeshita
	I	kantan da	kantan ja nai	kantan datta	kantan ja nakatta
clean, beautiful	F	kirei desu	kirei ja arimasen	kirei deshita	kirei ja arimasendeshita
	I	kirei da	kirei ja nai	kirei datta	kirei ja nakatta
lively	F	nigiyaka desu	nigiyaka ja arimasen	nigiyaka deshita	nigiyaka ja arimasendeshita
	I	nigiyaka da	nigiyaka ja nai	nigiyaka datta	nigiyaka ja nakatta
nice and kind	F	shinsetsu desu	shinsetsu ja arimasen	shinsetsu deshita	shinsetsu ja arimasendeshita
	I	shinsetsu da	shinsetsu ja nai	shinsetsu datta	shinsetsu ja nakatta
quiet	F	shizuka desu	shizuka ja arimasen	shizuka deshita	shizuka ja arimasendeshita
	I	shizuka da	shizuka ja nai	shizuka datta	shizuka ja nakatta
like, favorite	F	suki desu	suki ja arimasen	suki deshita	suki ja arimasendeshita
	I	suki da	suki ja nai	suki datta	suki ja nakatta
lovely, nice	F	suteki desu	suteki ja arimasen	suteki deshita	suteki ja arimasendeshita
	I	suteki da	suteki ja nai	suteki datta	suteki ja nakatta
famous	F	yūmei desu	yūmei ja arimasen	yūmei deshita	yūmei ja arimasendeshita
	I	yūmei da	yūmei ja nai	yūmei datta	yūmei ja nakatta

c. Nouns and adjectives for colors

	Noun	Adjective
red	aka	akai
blue	ao	aoi
brown	chairo	chairoi
yellow	kiiro	kiiroi
black	kuro	kuroi
white	shiro	shiroi
green	midori	—
purple	murasaki	—

d. Noun modifying rule

i-adjectives	+	φ	+	noun	→	atarashii hon	(new book)
na-adjective stems		na				kirei na hon	(pretty book)
noun		no				nihongo no hon	(Japanese book)

Appendix 9. Particles

a. Verb-particle relationship

Particle		Meaning	Function	Motion verbs *ikimasu / kimasu / kaerimasu*	Action verbs *tabemasu, nomimasu, kaimasu,* etc.	Existence verbs *arimasu / imasu*
wa	\<L1, L5\>	as for	Topic marker	○	○	○
mo	\<L4\>	also	Inclusion marker	○	○	○
ga	\<L4\>	who/what does	Subject marker	○	○	○
ni	\<L4\>	at/on/in	Specific time marker	○	○	—
kara	\<L3\>	from	Starting point marker	○	—	—
made	\<L3, L6\>	to/until	Ending point marker	○	—	—
e	\<L4\>	to	Direction marker	○	—	—
ni	\<L4\>	to	Goal marker	○	—	—
ni	\<L4\>	for	Purpose of going marker	○	—	—
de	\<L4\>	by	Means of transportation marker	○	—	—
to	\<L8\>	with	Accompaniment marker	○	○	—
o	\<L5, L8\>	what you do	Object marker	—	○	—
de	\<L6, L8\>	at/in	Place of action marker	—	○	—
ni	\<L7\>	at/on	Location marker	—	—	○

b. Noun connecting particles

Particle		Meaning	Function	Examples
no	\<L1\>	of / belonging to	to make a noun modify another noun	YY *ginkō* **no** *Tonpuson*
to	\<L2\>	and	to connect two or more nouns to show all items (exhaustive listing)	*kimono* **to** *obi*
ya	\<L8\>	and so on	to connect two or more nouns to show some of the items (sample listing)	*sōji* **ya** *sentaku*
de	\<L2\>	in total	used with *to* to express total numbers or prices	*kimono to obi* **de** *8000-en*

c. Sentence particles

Particle		Meaning	Function	Examples
ka	\<L1\>	(question marker)	to change a statement to question	*Tonpuson-san desu* **ka**.
ne	\<L1\>	isn't it? / right?	to confirm or obtain a listener's agreement	*Kyō wa ii tenki desu* **ne**.
yo	\<L7\>	You know. / I tell you.	to convey emphatically/friendly one's own ideas to someone	*Harumi-iki no basu wa atchi desu* **yo**.

Appendix 10. Position words <L7>

ue	above, on	*chikaku*	nearby
shita	below, under	*narabi*	on the same side of the street
naka	inside	*mukaigawa*	across the street
soto	outside	*hantaigawa*	opposite side
mae	front	*aida*	between
ushiro	back, behind	*oku*	far end
migi(gawa)	right (side)	*temae*	in front of, before
hidari(gawa)	left (side)	*saki*	after
tonari	next to	*mannaka*	center, in the middle
yoko	aside		

Appendix 11. Adverbs

a. Adverbs of frequency <L8>

high ↑ ↓ low	*itsumo*	(always)	affirmative sentence
	taitei	(usually)	
	yoku	(often)	
	tokidoki	(sometimes)	
	amari	(not so often)	negative sentence
	zenzen	(never)	

b. Adverbs of quantity/amount <L8>

large ↑ ↓ small	*takusan*	(lot)	affirmative sentence
	sukoshi	(little)	
	amari	(not so much)	negative sentence
	zenzen	(not at all)	

c. Adverbs of degree

high ↑ ↓ low	*yoku*	(well/much)	affirmative sentence
	daitai	(mostly)	
	sukoshi	(a little / a few)	
	amari	(not so (much))	negative sentence
	zenzen	(never)	

Appendix 12. Words for eating and drinking

a. Beverages

mizu	水	water
ocha	お茶	Japanese tea
kōhī	コーヒー	coffee
hotto	ホット	hot coffee
aisu kōhī	アイスコーヒー	iced coffee
kōcha	紅茶	tea
jūsu	ジュース	juice
ūron cha	ウーロン茶	oolong tea
bīru	ビール	beer
nama-bīru	生ビール	draft beer
dai-nama	大生	draft beer in large mug
chū-nama	中生	draft beer in medium mug
Nihon-shu	日本酒	Japanese brewed sake
atsukan	熱燗	hot sake
shōchū	焼酎	Japanese distilled sake
chūhai	酎ハイ	*shōchū*-based cocktail
uisukī	ウイスキー	whisky
rokku	ロック	on the rocks
mizuwari	水割り	with water
oyuwari	お湯割り	with hot water
wain	ワイン	wine
aka-wain	赤ワイン	red wine
shiro-wain	白ワイン	white wine

b. Foods (dishes)

yakitori	焼き鳥	grilled chicken on sticks
edamame	枝豆	boiled soybeans
karaage	唐揚げ	deep fried chicken
sashimi	刺身	sliced raw fish
moriawase	盛り合わせ	assorted dish
teishoku	定食	set menu with rice and miso-soup
tenpura	天ぷら	deep fried fish and vegetables
tonkatsu	とんかつ	pork cutlet
ebi furai	エビフライ	deep fried prawn
yakizakana	焼き魚	grilled fish
karē raisu	カレーライス	curry and rice
sushi	寿司	sliced raw fish with vinegared rice
sabinuki	さび抜き	without *wasabi*
nigiri	にぎり	sliced raw fish on bite-sized portions of vinegard rice
chirashi	ちらし	sliced raw fish arrayed on vinegard rice
sukiyaki	すき焼き	beef with vegetables cooked in sweetened soy sauce in a pan

shabushabu	しゃぶしゃぶ	beef cooked on the table in clear broth
yakiniku	焼き肉	Korean barbecue
oden	おでん	fish cake, vegetables and eggs stewed in broth
gyūdon	牛丼	beef and onion on rice in bowl
tendon	天丼	tempura on rice in bowl
tekkadon	鉄火丼	sliced uncooked tuna on rice in bowl
unadon	うな丼	grilled eel on rice in bowl
oyakodon	親子丼	chicken and egg on rice in bowl
katsudon	カツ丼	pork cutlet on rice in bowl
rāmen	ラーメン	Chinese noodles prepared Japanese style
gyōza	餃子	fried ground pork and vegetable dumpling
shūmai	シュウマイ	steamed meatball dumpling
yakisoba	焼きそば	fried Chinese noodles
kitsune udon	きつねうどん	udon noodles with fried bean curd
zarusoba	ざるそば	buckwheat noodles served cold

c. Ingredients

shōyu	醤油	soy sauce
shio	塩	salt
satō	砂糖	sugar
koshō	胡椒	pepper
su	酢	vinegar
miso	味噌	salty soybean paste
kechappu	ケチャップ	ketchup
masutādo	マスタード	mustard
mayonēzu	マヨネーズ	mayonnaise
wasabi	わさび	grated Japanese green horseradish
goma	ごま	sesame
tamago	たまご	egg
tōfu	豆腐	tofu
niku	肉	meat
gyūniku	牛肉	beef
butaniku	豚肉	pork
toriniku	鶏肉	chicken
hikiniku	ひき肉	ground meat
sakana	魚	fish
sake	鮭	salmon
maguro	まぐろ	tuna
anago	あなご	sea eel
ebi	えび	shrimp, prawn
kani	かに	crab
ika	いか	squid
tako	たこ	octopus
yasai	野菜	vegetables

kyabetsu	キャベツ	cabbage
kyūri	きゅうり	cucumber
pīman	ピーマン	green pepper
jagaimo	じゃがいも	potato
satsumaimo	さつまいも	sweet potato
ninjin	にんじん	carrots
nasu	なす	eggplant
naganegi	長ねぎ	long onion
tamanegi	玉ねぎ	onion
ninniku	にんにく	garlic
kudamono	くだもの	fruit(s)
budō	ぶどう	grapes
momo	もも	peach
ringo	りんご	apple
ichigo	いちご	strawberry
mikan	みかん	tangerine orange
suika	すいか	watermelon
nashi	なし	pear

Appendix 13. Formal expressions used by service staff

Irasshaimase.	Welcome to our store.
Nan-mei-sama desu ka.	How many people in your party?
Gochūmon wa, okimari desu ka.	Are you ready to order? (lit., Have you decided what to order?)
Itsu omochi shimasu ka.	When shall I bring ~?
Hai, gozaimasu.	Yes, we have.
Goissho desu ka.	Will this be together?
Kashikomarimashita.	Certainly, sir/ma'am.
Kochira e dōzo.	Come this way, please.
Shōshō omachi kudasai.	Please wait for a moment.
Omochikaeri desu ka.	Will that be to go?
Kochira de omeshiagari desu ka.	Is this to eat in?
Tsugi de omachi no okyaku-sama, dōzo.	Next customer (waiting), please.
1,000-en oazukari itashimasu.	You've given me 1,000 yen.
Okaeshi de gozaimasu.	Here is your change.
Omatase itashimashita.	Sorry to have kept you waiting.
Goyōi dekimasu.	Yes, we can handle that.
Onamae to odenwa bangō o onegai itashimasu.	Could I have your name, and your phone number, please?
Omachi itashite orimasu.	We will be expecting you, madam/sir.
Itsu no goyoyaku deshō ka.	When is this reservation for?
Uketamawarimashita.	Your reservation/order is confirmed.
Taihen mōshiwake gozaimasen.	I'm terribly sorry.
Omachidōsama deshita.	Thank you for waiting.
Otabako wa osui ni narimasu ka.	Do you smoke?

Appendix 14. Samples of short speeches

a. As a newcomer （新しい職場で）

Hajimemashiate, kondo kochira ni osewani narimasu <u>Jonasan Howaito</u> desu. <u>Kanada</u> kara kimashita. Nanimo wakarimasen ga, isshōkenmei ganbarimasu node, yoroshiku onegai shimasu.

はじめまして、今度こちらにお世話になりますジョナサン・ホワイトです。カナダから来ました。何もわかりませんが、一生懸命頑張りますので、よろしくお願いします。

(Hello, my name is Jonathan White. I'm from Canada. I will be working with you here. I am new here, so I may need some assistance from you. I'll do my best.)

b. At a new office where you are transferred （転勤してきた職場で）

<u>Ōsaka</u> kara tenkin-shite kimashita <u>Ansonī Kumaru</u> desu. Kuni wa <u>Igirisu</u> desu ga, <u>Ōsaka</u> ni wa 2-nen imashita. Mada iroiro wakaranai koto ga arimasu node, yoroshiku goshidō o onegaishimasu.

大阪から転勤してきましたアンソニー・クマルです。国はイギリスですが、大阪には2年いました。まだいろいろわからないことがありますので、よろしくご指導をお願いします。

(My name is Anthony Kumaru, originally from England and I have been transferred from Osaka. I worked in Osaka for two years but I'm afraid I'll sometimes have to bother you, so I would appreciate it if you would give me some suggestions and advice. Thank you.)

c. As a manager （上司として）

Kochira wa <u>Jonasan Howaito</u>-san desu. Mada <u>Nihon</u> ni narete inai node, minna tasukete agete kudasai.

こちらは、ジョナサン・ホワイトさんです。まだ日本になれていないので、みんな助けてあげてください。

(This is Jonathan White. Everything is very new to him, so please give him your assistance or advice, would you?)

d. When being transferred to another office （転勤していくとき）

Kondo <u>Ōsaka</u> ni tenkin suru koto ni narimashita. Minasan to owakare suru nowa totemo zannen desu. 2-nen-kan no mijikai aida deshita ga, taihen osewa ni narima-shita. (Talk about some good memories and cultural shocks in English.) <u>Ōsaka</u> ni kitara zehi gorenraku kudasai. Issho ni nomi ni ikimashō. Dōmo iroiro arigatō gozaimashita.

今度大阪に転勤することになりました。皆さんとお別れするのはとても残念です。

2年間の短い間でしたが、大変お世話になりました。(英語で思い出などを話す)
大阪に来たらぜひご連絡ください。一緒に飲みに行きましょう。どうもいろいろ
ありがとうございました。

(It's been decided that I'll be transferred to Osaka. It is very hard to say good bye to you. During the past two years, all of you have been so helpful. (*Some talk in English*.) When you come to Osaka, be sure to contact me and let's go for a drink. Thank you for everything.)

e. When leaving Japan for good （帰国するとき）

Jitsu wa, jōdan de Nihongo de sayonara supīchi o suru to itte shimaimashita node, yakusoku wa mamorimasu.

2-nen mae Nihon ni kite kara minasan ni wa taihen osewa ni narimashita ga, 7-gatsu ni kyū ni kikoku suru koto ni nari, totemo zannen desu. Kawashima-san niwa toku ni purojekuto no koto de, Miyasato-san niwa kazoku no koto de mo iroiro osewa ni narimashita. (More words in English.) Shidonī ni kitara zehi renraku shite kudasai. Dōmo iroiro arigatō gozaimashita.

実は、冗談で日本語でさよならスピーチをすると言ってしまいましたので、約束
はまもります。　2年前日本に来てから皆さんには大変お世話になりましたが、7月に急に帰国
することになり、とても残念です。川島さんには特にプロジェクトのことで、宮里
さんには家族のことでもいろいろお世話になりました。(英語で少し話す)シドニー
に来たらぜひ連絡してください。どうもいろいろありがとうございました。

(Actually, I was joking and said by mistake that I would make a farewell speech in Japanese. So, here I will keep my word.

It's been just two years since I came to Japan and everybody has been so nice and helpful to me. It is too bad that I'll have to return home so urgently in July. I owe you a lot, especially Kawashima-san for her hard work together with the projects and Miyasato-san for her valuable assistance to my family as well. (*More words in English*.) When you come to Sydney, be sure to contact me. Thank you for everything and I'll miss you all.)

f. At a year-end party （忘年会で）

Minasan konbanwa. Kyō wa nen ni ichido no bōnenkai desu. Kotoshi mo okage-samade kaisha ni totte ii toshi deshita. Kon'ya wa shigoto no koto wa wasurete, ōini tanoshimimashō. Soshite, rainen wa motto ii toshi de arimasu yōni. Arigatō gozaimashita.

皆さん、こんばんは。今日は年に一度の忘年会です。今年もおかげさまで会社にとっ
ていい年でした。今夜は仕事のことは忘れて、大いに楽しみましょう。そして、
来年はもっといい年でありますように。ありがとうございました。

(Good evening. Here we are at our annual year-end party. We had a good year due to your hard work this year, too. Let's enjoy ourselves and not worry about work. And may the next year be another good or better year. Thank you.)

g. At a New Year's party（新年会で）

Minasan, akemashite omedetō gozaimasu. Nentō ni atari, hitokoto goaisatsu o mōshiagemasu. (*Some talk in English.*) Saigo ni, kotoshi mo wagasha no issō no hatten to minasan no gokenkō o oinori itashimasu. Arigatō gozaimashita.

皆さん、明けましておめでとうございます。年頭にあたり、一言ご挨拶を申し上げます。（英語で少し話す）最後に、今年もわが社の一層の発展と皆さんのご健康をお祈りいたします。ありがとうございました。

(Happy New Year! I'd like to take this opportunity to say a few words in Japanese. (*Some words in English.*) Lastly, I wish the company's greater success in the New Year and I wish you all the best of health. Thank you.)

h. Kanpai speech at a wedding reception（結婚披露宴での乾杯の音頭）

Soredewa, goshimei ni azukarimashita node, kanpai no ondo o torasete itadakimasu.
　Akagawa Hiroshi-san, Shiroyama Ayano-san, gokekkon omedetō gozaimasu. Ofutari no oshiawase to gokenkō o inotte, kanpai! (Kanpāi! Kanpāi!) Dōmo arigatō gozaimashita.

それでは、ご指名に預かりましたので、乾杯の音頭を取らせていただきます。赤川博史さん、白山綾乃さん、ご結婚おめでとうございます。お二人のお幸せとご健康を祈って、乾杯！（かんぱーい！ かんぱーい！）どうもありがとうございました。

(As I have been chosen for this privelege, let me propose a toast for the happiness and health of newlyweds. Cheers! Thank you.)

Listening Tasks

Lesson 1 (pp. 12-13; Tracks 6-7)

Drill 3. Listen to the CD and choose the appropriate pictures for the statements.

1. はじめまして。JJ 証券のジョン・アンダーソンです。国はアメリカです。
2. はじめまして。JJ 保険のジョン・アンダーソンです。国はドイツです。
3. はじめまして。KK 銀行のジョン・アンダーソンです。国はイギリスです。
4. はじめまして。KK 銀行のジョン・アンダーソンです。国はカナダです。
5. はじめまして。JJ 証券のジョン・アンダーソンです。国はオーストラリアです。

Drill 4. Listen to the CD and choose the appropriate pictures for the dialogues.

1. A：こんにちは。
   B：こんにちは。お仕事ですか。
   A：はい。
   B：いってらっしゃい。
   A：いってきます。
2. A：こんばんは。
   B：こんばんは。ご紹介します。妻のルイスです。
   A：高木です。よろしく。
3. A：こんにちは。今日も寒いですね。
   B：ええ、本当に。
   A：じゃ、また。
4. A：おはようございます。
   B：おはようございます。暑いですね。
   A：ジョギングですか。
   B：ええ。
5. A：すみません、お先に失礼します。
   B：お疲れ様。じゃ、また明日、よろしく。
   A：はい。じゃ、明日。

Lesson 2 (p. 29; Tracks 11-12)

Drill 5. Listen to the CD and choose the appropriate pictures for the dialogues.

1. A：子供さんは何人ですか。
   B：二人です。娘が一人と息子が一人です。
2. A：子供さんは何人ですか。
   B：三人です。息子が一人と娘が二人です。
3. A：ご兄弟は何人ですか。
   B：兄が二人です。
4. A：ご兄弟は何人ですか。
   B：三人です。姉が二人と兄が一人です。
5. A：ご兄弟は何人ですか。
   B：三人です。妹が一人と弟が二人です。

Drill 6. Listen to the dialogue and fill in the blanks of the price list below.

客　：すみません。食パンはいくらですか。
店員：250 円です。
客　：じゃあ、このコーヒーは？
店員：それはサービス品です。560 円ですよ。
客　：本当？ この牛乳もサービス？
店員：ああ、すみません。それは違います。230 円です。
客　：そう……。あっ、フルーツも……りんごはいくら？
店員：それは、5つで 600 円です。
客　：バナナは？
店員：バナナは 180 円です。
客　：バナナにしよう～っと。それから、ヨーグルトね。ヨーグルトはいくら？
店員：330 円です。
客　：どうも。
店員：ありがとうございました。

Lesson 3 (pp. 42-43; Tracks 16-17)

Drill 5. Listen to the CD and choose the appropriate answers for the questions.

1. 休みはいつですか。
   a. 日曜日です。　b. 5時間です。　c. 午後2時です。

2. 今日は何時までですか。
   a. 3時からです。　b. 4時間です。　c. 5時までです。

3. プレゼンテーションは何時からですか。
   a. はい、そうです。　b. いいえ、10時からです。　c. 10時からです。

4. 会議の場所はどこですか。
   a. 明日です。　b. 5階の501です。　c. 木曜日からです。

5. ロンドンは今何時ですか。
   a. 6時ごろです。　b. 6時からです。　c. 6時までです。

Drill 6. Listen to the CD and choose the appropriate pictures for the dialogues.

1. A：すみません、ここは何時までですか。
   B：7時です。
   A：そうですか。どうも。

2. A：会議は何時からですか。
   B：3時です。
   A：わかりました。

3. A：仕事は何時までですか。
   B：5時20分です。
   A：そうですか。

4. A：日本語のレッスンは何時からですか。
   B：10時15分です。
   A：そうですか。がんばってください。

5. A：今、何時ですか。
   B：12時半ですよ。
   A：じゃ、ランチにしましょう。

Lesson 4 (pp. 56-57; Tracks 21-22)

Drill 6. Listen to the CD and choose the appropriate answers for the questions.

1. 明日どこへ行きますか。
   a. 電車です。　b. うん、行く。　c. 渋谷へ行きます。

2. ご家族は日本は初めてですか。
   a. いいえ、2回目です。　b. いいえ、行きません。　c. いいえ、日本です。

3. 名古屋へは新幹線で行きましたか。
   a. はい、車です。　b. いいえ、車です。　c. いいえ、新幹線です。

4. 去年も名古屋へ行きましたか。
   a. はい、行きました。　b. いいえ、行きました。　c. 名古屋へ行きました。

5. いつジムに行きますか。
   a. 1週間に2回です。　b. 月曜日と木曜日です。　c. ジムへ行きます。

Drill 7. Listen to the four dialogues and fill in the table with choices from the options given below.

1. A：明日、どこへ行きますか。
   B：浅草へ行きます。
   A：そうですか。誰と行きますか。
   B：妻と行きます。
   A：地下鉄ですか。
   B：いいえ、歩いて行きます。

2. A：来月、奈良へ行くの。
   B：奈良ですか。誰と行きますか。
   A：両親と行くの。国から両親が来るから。
   B：そうですか。新幹線で行きますか。
   A：うん、そう。

3. A：週末は東京タワーに行ったんだ。
   B：そうですか。いいですね。誰と行きましたか。
   A：友達と。
   B：地下鉄で行きましたか。
   A：ううん、タクシーで。

4. A：来週、出張です。
　　B：そうですか。どこへ行きますか。
　　A：大阪へ行きます。
　　B：一人ですか。
　　A：いいえ、課長と行きます。
　　B：新幹線ですね。
　　A：いいえ、飛行機です。

Lesson 5 (p. 74; Tracks 26-27)

Drill 7. Listen to the CD and choose the appropriate pictures for the dialogues.

1. 店員：いらっしゃいませ。
　　客：　アイスクリームを6つ下さい。
　　店員：かしこまりました。

2. 店員：いらっしゃいませ。
　　客：　ジュースを1つ下さい。
　　店員：かしこまりました。

3. 店員：いらっしゃいませ。
　　客：　カレー5つ下さい。
　　店員：かしこまりました。

4. 店員：いらっしゃいませ。
　　客：　とんかつ3つ下さい。
　　店員：かしこまりました。

5. 店員：いらっしゃいませ。
　　客：　サンドイッチ2つ下さい。
　　店員：かしこまりました。

Drill 8. Listen to the CD and choose the appropriate pictures for the dialogues.

1. 店員：いらっしゃいませ。ご注文は？
　　A：　天ぷら定食お願いします。
　　B：　私は、天ぷらそばお願いします。
　　店員：天ぷら定食と天ぷらそばですね。
　　　　　少々お待ちください。

2. A：あ、もう12時ですよ。
　　B：お昼に行きましょう。

3. A：今日はどこへ行きますか。
　　B：そうですね。今日は和食がいいですね。
　　A：じゃあ、「うめや」へ行きましょう。

4. 店員：1,680円でございます。
　　A：　すみませんが、別々にお願いできますか。
　　店員：はい、天ぷら定食は980円、天ぷらそばは700円でございます。ありがとうございました。

Lesson 6 (pp. 89-90; Tracks 31-32)

Drill 5. Look at the pictures and listen to the questions. Choose answers from the box below that respond to the questions.

1. この電車は新宿に止まりますか。
2. 東京に行きたいんですが、バス停はここですか。
3. 次の次の信号ですね。
4. 日比谷行きはこのホームですか。
5. この電車は鎌倉に行きますか。

Drill 6. Listen to the three dialogues and fill in the table with choices from the options given below.

1. A：すみません、恵比寿駅の近くまで、お願いします。
　　B：はい。
　　A：明治通りをまっすぐお願いします。
　　B：はい。
　　A：次を右へ曲がって、すぐ左へお願いします。
　　B：はい。

2. A：有楽町まで、お願いします。
　　B：はい。
　　A：晴海通りをまっすぐお願いします。
　　B：はい。
　　A：二つ目の信号を左へお願いします。
　　B：はい。

3. A：代々木公園まで、お願いします。
　　B：はい。
　　A：甲州街道をまっすぐお願いします。
　　B：はい。
　　A：次の交差点を右へ曲がって、すぐにまた右へお願いします。
　　B：はい。

Lesson 7 (pp. 103-104; Tracks 36-37)

Drill 6. Listen to the five dialogues and choose the number from the picture that corresponds to each dialogue.

1. A：すみません、ホチキスはどこにありますか。
   B：その箱の中にあるよ。

2. A：すみません、ゴミ箱はどこにありますか。
   B：机の下にあるよ。

3. A：すみません、コピー機はどこにありますか。
   B：あのキャビネットのとなりにあるよ。

4. A：すみません、東京の地図はどこにありますか。
   B：あの棚の上にあるよ。

5. A：すみません、CDはどこにありますか。
   B：あの引き出しの奥にあるよ。

Drill 7. Listen to the CD and write the dialogue number in the (　), or insert an × if nothing matches.

1. A：すみません、ペットショップはどこにありますか。
   B：ペットショップですね。屋上にございます。

2. A：すみません、靴売り場はどこにありますか。
   B：2階にございます。

3. A：あのう、レストランはどこですか。
   B：レストランですね。エレベーターで5階に行きますと、右側にございます。

4. A：すみません、ワイン売り場はどこにありますか。
   B：地下1階の食料品売り場にございます。

5. A：あのう、子供服はどこにありますか。
   B：3階のおもちゃ売り場の奥でございます。

Lesson 8 (pp. 118-119; Tracks 41-42)

Drill 7. Listen to the four dialogues and write the dialogue number in the (　).

1. A：明日、何をしますか。
   B：友達とサッカーをします。
   A：どこでしますか。
   B：うちの近くの公園です。
   A：へえ、そうですか。

2. A：今度の週末は鎌倉ですね。鎌倉で何をしますか。
   B：大仏を見ます。それから、買い物をします。
   A：誰と行きますか。
   B：ガールフレンドと行きます。
   A：いいですね。楽しんでください。

3. A：土曜日、何をするの？
   B：新宿御苑へ行きます。散歩をします。花を見ます。それからカフェでお茶を飲みます。
   A：誰と行くの？
   B：家族と行きます。
   A：そう。いいね。

4. A：来週、北海道へ行きます。
   B：そうですか。北海道で何をしますか。
   A：刺身やかにを食べます。それから、日本のお酒を飲みます。
   B：誰と行きますか。
   A：同僚と行きます。
   B：そうですか。楽しんでください。

Drill 8. Listen to the CD and write down the necessary information in the calendar below.

Example: 来週の金曜日に、川島さんと赤坂で中華料理を食べます。

1. 明日、午後7時から日本語のレッスンがあります。
2. 来週の月曜日と水曜日にテニスをします。
3. 先週の火曜日に、塚田さんと銀座で映画を見ました。
4. 昨日、ビックカメラでテレビを買いました。
5. 今週の土曜日に、課長と新宿でお酒を飲みます。

Lesson 9 (pp. 133-134; Tracks 46-47)

Drill 6. Listen to each dialogue and choose the appropriate statement that matches the content.

1. A：日光はどうでしたか。
   B：寒かったです。でもとてもよかったです。
   A：何がよかったですか。たとえば？
   B：たとえば、東照宮です。素晴らしかったです。

2. A：週末は何をしましたか。
   B：お花見をしました。
   A：そうですか。どうでしたか。
   B：桜がとてもきれいでした。でも疲れました。

3. A：ジャクリーンさん、この写真見てください。
   B：え、何？ わあ、かわいい！ 冬美さんのうちの猫？
   A：ええ。小さいでしょう。

4. A：歌舞伎はおもしろいですか。
   B：おもしろいですよ。衣装もきれいです。
   A：言葉は大丈夫ですか。
   B：歌舞伎座は、いつも英語のイヤホンガイドがありますよ。
   A：そうですか。

5. A：ねえねえ、焼酎あるんだけど。
   B：わあ、うれしい！ いただきます！
   A：どう？
   B：うん、とてもおいしいです。これは甘くないんですね。

Drill 7. Listen to each dialogue and choose the adjectives you can hear.

1. A：夏休みはどうでしたか。
   B：楽しかったです。とてもよかったです。

2. A：大阪は静かなところですか。
   B：いいえ、静かじゃないです。にぎやかなところですよ。あ、それに、食べ物がおいしいです。たとえば、たこ焼きや、お好み焼きです。

3. A：新しい仕事はどうですか。
   B：毎日、とても忙しいです。大変ですよー。でも、今の仕事はすごくいいですから、大丈夫です！

4. A：北海道はどうでしたか。
   B：すごく寒かったです。でも、景色がきれいでした。それに、素晴らしいところでした。

5. A：週末はどうでしたか。
   B：ああ、暇でした。
   A：どこへも行かなかったんですか。
   B：ええ、うちでDVDを見ました。おもしろかったです。

Lesson 10 (pp. 147-148; Tracks 51-52)

Drill 6. Listen to the dialogues and choose the verb form a, b or c, that the first person in each dialogue uses to extend the invitation.

1. A：日曜日、一緒に映画を見ようか。
   B：いいよ。見よう。

2. A：来週、またここへ来ない？
   B：そうだね。来よう。

3. A：疲れたから、コーヒーを飲もう。
   B：うん、飲もう。

4. A：週末、テニスをしない？
   B：いいね、しよう。

5. A：明日の晩、レストランへ行こうか。
   B：うん、行こう。

Drill 7. Listen to each question and choose one appropriate answer.

1. すみません。ちょっといいですか。
2. お花見はどこがいいですか。
3. 来週の土曜日、予定ある？
4. 今日の夜、映画行かない？
5. コーヒーでも飲みましょうか。

Answers

Lesson 1

Comprehension Drill
● **Dialogue 1** (p. 3)
1. 1. T   2. DK   3. F   4. F   5. T
2. (a) → d → c → b → e
● **Dialogue 2** (p. 5)
1. T   2. DK   3. F   4. T   5. F

Drill 1 （解答例） (p. 11)
1. (a) *Hajimemashite.*
   (b) YY *ginkō no Tonpuson desu.*
   (c) *Dōzo yoroshiku onegaishimasu.*
2. (a) *Goshōkai shimasu.*
   (b) *Uchi no Shiroyama desu.*
   (c) *Kochira wa* EFG *shōji no Takagi-san desu.*
3. (a) *Amerika desu.*
   (b) *Sanfuranshisuko desu.*
4. (a) *Osaki ni shitsurei shimasu.*
   (b) *Ja, mata raishū.*
5. (a) *Sorosoro shitsurei shimasu.*
   (b) *Gochisōsama deshita.*
   (c) *Hai. Arigatō gozaimasu.*

Drill 2 （略）
Drill 3 (p. 12)
1. d   2. e   3. b   4. a   5. c
Drill 4 (p. 13)
1. c   2. a   3. e   4. b   5. d
Drill 5 （解答例） (p. 13)
1. *Hajimemashite.* YY *ginkō no Kawashima desu.*
   Dōzo yoroshiku onegaishimasu.
2. *Kochira koso yoroshiku onegaishimasu.*
3. *Kochira wa* QQ *kagaku no Tsukada-san desu.*
4. *Buchō, tsuma/shujin desu.*
5. *Osaki ni shitsurei shimasu.*
6. *Otsukaresama deshita.*
7. *Iroiro arigatō gozaimashita.*
8. *Ii tenki desu ne.*

Drill 6 (p. 13)
1. d   2. a   3. b   4. c

Drill 7 (p. 14)
1. (a) → c → d → b
2. (b) → c → a → d

Lesson 2

Comprehension Drill
● **Dialogue 1** (p. 18)
1. 1. F   2. T   3. DK   4. T   5. F
2. (e) → d → b → a → c
● **Dialogue 2** (p. 20)
1. T   2. F   3. T   4. DK   5. F

Drill 1 （解答例） (p. 26)
1. (a) *03-1234-5678 desu.*
   (b) *1234-5678 desu.*
2. (a) *Takushī gaisha no denwa bangō*
       wakarimasu ka.
   (b) *Sumimasen, mō ichido onegaishimasu.*
   (c) *Arigatō gozaimashita.*
3. (a) *Sumimasen, kore wa ikura desu ka.*
   (b) *Kore wa?*
   (c) *Haitatsu onegaishimasu.*
   (d) *Shibuya-ku Yoyogi 6-25 Uehara Manshon*
       desu.
   (e) *601 desu.*
   (f) *03-9876-5432 desu.*
4. (a) *Hajimemashite. Sumisu to mōshimasu.*
       Dōzo yoroshiku onegaishimasu.
   (b) *Shitsurei desu ga, (onamae wa?)*
   (c) *30-nin gurai deshō ka.*
5. (a) *Sumimasen. Kore ikura desu ka.*
   (b) *Ā sō desu ka. Kore mo 5-mai de 1000-en*
       desu ka.
   (c) *Dōmo.*

Drill 2 （略）
Drill 3 （略）
Drill 4 (p. 28)
1. *Kēki to kōhī* de *1,200-en desu.*

2. _Pasokon to purintā_ de _220,000-en_ desu.

3. _Chiketto 2-mai_ de _9,000-en_ desu.

4. _Setto_ de _550-en_ desu.

5. _Zenbu_ de _15,000-en_ desu.

Drill 5 (p. 29)

1. d   2. a   3. c   4. b   5. e

Drill 6 (p. 29)

1. _250_   2. _560_   3. _230_   4. _180_   5. _330_

Drill 7 （解答例）(p. 29)

1. _Tsukada-san, Kawashima-san no denwa bangō wakarimasu ka._

2. _Kyō no kaigi wa doko desu ka._

3. _Shitsurei desu ga, musume-san wa nan-sai desu ka._

4. _Musume wa 3-sai desu._

5. _Kore wa ikura desu ka._

6. _Gokyōdai wa nan-nin desu ka._

7. _3-nin desu. Ane ga hitori to otōto ga futari desu._

8. _Jā, mata kimasu._

Drill 8 (p. 30)

1. c   2. d   3. b   4. a

Drill 9 (p. 30)

1. (c) → a → d → e → b

2. (a) → e → b → f → d → (c)

Lesson 3

Comprehension Drill

● **Dialogue 1** (p. 33)

1. 1. F   2. DK   3. T   4. F   5. T

2. d → b → a → e → (c)

● **Dialogue 2** (p. 35)

1. T   2. T   3. F   4. F   5. DK

Drill 1 （解答例）(p. 39)

1. (a) _dinā wa nan-ji kara desu ka._

 (b) _Nan-ji made desu ka._

 (c) _Yasumi wa nan-yōbi desu ka._

2. (a) _Koko wa nan-ji made desu ka._

 (b) _Yasumi wa nan-yōbi desu ka._

3. (a) _kondo no purezentēshon wa itsu desu ka._

(b) _Nan-ji kara desu ka._

(c) _Doko desu ka._

(d) _Ā, sō desu ka. Arigatō._

4. (a) _Yasui-san no tanjōbi wa itsu desu ka._

 (b) _Tanjōbi no pātī wa doko desu ka._

 (c) _Ā, arigatō._

5. (a) _Kondo no shutchō wa itsu desu ka._

 (b) _Itsu made desu ka._

 (c) _1-shūkan desu ne._

Drill 2 (p. 40)

1. _8-ji 55-fun desu._   2. _6-ji 10-pun desu._   3. _12-ji 20-pun desu._   4. _1-ji 45-fun desu._   5. _4-ji han desu._

Drill 3 (p. 41)

1. _Gozen 11-ji kara desu._

2. _Gogo 6-ji made desu._

3. _Gogo 1-ji kara desu._

4. _Asa (gozen) 8-ji kara yoru (gogo) 9-ji made desu._

5. _Yonaka no 12-ji made desu._

Drill 4 （略）

Drill 5 (p. 42)

1. a   2. c   3. c   4. b   5. a.

Drill 6 (p. 43)

1. d   2. a   3. e   4. b   5. c

Drill 7 （解答例）(p. 43)

1. _Yasumi wa nan-yōbi desu ka._

2. _Nan-ji kara desu ka._

3. _Nan-ji made desu ka._

4. _Yasumi wa suiyōbi desu._

5. _Shigoto wa gozen 8-ji han kara desu._

6. _Shigoto wa gogo 6-ji 45-fun made desu._

7. _Kondo no mītingu wa itsu desu ka._

8. _Mītingu wa gozen 11-ji kara desu._

Drill 8 (p. 43)

1. d   2. a   3. c   4. b

Drill 9 (p. 44)

1. (a) → d → c → b

2. (b) → c → a → e → d

Lesson 4

Comprehension Drill
● **Dialogue 1** (p. 48)
1. 1. T   2. F   3. DK   4. F   5. T
2. c → b → d → e → (a)
● **Dialogue 2** (p. 49)
1. F   2. T   3. DK   4. F   5. T

Drill 1 （解答例） (p. 53)
1. (a) *Hokkaidō e/ni ikimasu.*
    (b) *Otōto to ikimasu. Kanada kara kimasu.*
    (c) *Iie, densha desu.*
2. (a) *Shutchō desu ka.*
    (b) *Itsu kaerimasu ka.*
3. (a) *Kondo no shūmatsu wa doko e/ni ikimasu ka.*
    (b) *Tomodachi wa Nihon wa hajimete desu ka.*
    (c) *Kuruma de ikimasu ka.*
4. (a) *Kamakura e/ni ikimashita.*
    (b) *Tomodachi to ikimashita.*
    (c) *Kita-Kamakura made densha de ikimashita. Sorekara otera ni ikimashita.*
    (d) *Yoru 9-ji goro kaerimashita.*
5. (a) *1-nen mae ni kimashita.*
    (b) *Hai, sō desu. / Iie, hajimete ja arimasen.*
    (c) *Nikkō e/ni ikimashita.*
    (d) *Sensenshū ikimashita.*
    (e) *Densha de ikimashita.*

Drill 2 (p. 55)
1. *ikimasu* — (*ikimasen*) — *ikimashita* — *ikimasendeshita*
2. *kimasu* — *kimasen* — *kimashita* — (*kimasendeshita*)
3. *kaerimasu* — *kaerimasen* — (*kaerimashita*) — *kaerimasendeshita*

Drill 3 （略）
Drill 4 （略）
Drill 5 (p. 56)
1. *Kawashima-san* <u>wa</u> *kinō* × *Ōsaka* <u>e</u> *ikimashita.*
2. *Watashi* <u>wa</u> *raigetsu* × *Amerika* <u>e</u> *kaerimasu.*
3. *Tsukada-san* <u>wa</u> *shūmatsu* <u>×/wa</u> *Asakusa* <u>e</u> *ikimasendeshita.*
4. *Ryōshin* <u>wa</u> *raishū* <u>×/wa</u> *Nihon* <u>e</u> *kimasen.*
5. *Kinō* <u>wa</u> *uchi* <u>e</u> *kaerimasendeshita.*

Drill 6 (p. 56)
1. c   2. a   3. b   4. a   5. b

Drill 7 (p. 57)

	A	B	C
Dialogue 1	b	d	a
Dialogue 2	c	b	d
Dialogue 3	a	a	c
Dialogue 4	d	c	b

Drill 8 （解答例） (p. 57)
1. *Kondo no shūmatsu wa doko e/ni ikimasu ka.*
2. *Kamakura e/ni ikimasu.*
3. *Densha de ikimasu ka.*
4. *Goryōshin wa Nihon wa hajimete desu ka.*
5. *Shūmatsu Nagoya e/ni ikimashita.*
6. *Sengetsu Nihon e/ni kimashita.*
7. *Kazoku to Nihon e/ni kimashita.*
8. *Nichiyōbi ni Shinjuku e/ni kaimono ni ikimasu.*

Drill 9 (p. 58)
1. b   2. d   3. a   4. c

Drill 10 (p. 58)
1. (b) → d → c → a
2. (e) → b → d → a → c

Lesson 5

Comprehension Drill
● **Dialogue 1** (p. 62)
1. 1. T   2. F   3. F   4. DK   5. T
2. (e) → b → d → c → a
● **Dialogue 2** (p. 64)
1. T   2. F   3. F   4. T   5. DK

Drill 1 （解答例） (p. 68)
1. (a) *3-nin desu.*
    (b) *Eigo no menyū wa arimasu ka.*
    (c) *Sumimasen.*
    (d) *Tenpura-teishoku, onegaishimasu.*
    (e) *Watashi mo.*

(f) *Onaji.*

(g) *Betsubetsu ni, onegai dekimasu ka.*

2. (a) *Futari desu.*

(b) *Kin'enseki, onegaishimasu.*

(c) *Sumimasen.*

(d) *Ranchi setto futatsu to kōhī futatsu, onegaishimasu.*

(e) *Ato de onegaishimasu.*

(f) *Okaikei, onegaishimasu.*

3. (a) *Kariforunia wain, arimasu ka.*

(b) *Arigatō gozaimasu.*

(c) *Sumimasen.*

(d) *Kore, onegaishimasu.*

(e) *Futatsu, onegaishimasu.*

4. (a) *yoyaku, onegaishimasu.*

(b) *Konshū no doyōbi desu.*

(c) *7-ji kara desu.*

(d) *5-nin desu.*

(e) *Howaito desu. Denwa bangō wa 1234-5678 desu.*

5. (a) *yoyaku no henkō, onegai dekimasu ka.*

(b) *Howaito desu.*

(c) *Konshū no doyōbi desu.*

(d) *6-nin ni henkō dekimasu ka.*

Drill 2 (略)

Drill 3 (略)

Drill 4 (略)

Drill 5 (p. 71)

1. (a) *Sumimasen.*

(b) *4-ban futatsu to 7-ban futatsu onegaishimasu.*

(c) *Sorekara, 11-ban mo (hitotsu) onegaishimasu.*

2. (a) *Sumimasen.*

(b) *1-ban (hitotsu) to 3-ban (hitotsu) to 8-ban (hitotsu) to 9-ban (hitotsu) onegaishimasu.*

(c) *Sorekara, 12-ban mo (hitotsu) onegaishimasu.*

3. (a) *Sumimasen.*

(b) *Kore futatsu to kore futatsu onegaishimasu.*

(c) *Sorekara, kore mo futatsu onegaishimasu.*

4. (a) *Sumimasen.*

(b) *Kore futatsu to kore (hitotsu) onegaishimasu.*

(c) *Sorekara, kore mo (hitotsu) onegaishimasu.*

5. (a) *Sumimasen.*

(b) *Kore (hitotsu) to kore (hitotsu) to kore (hitotsu) onegaishimasu.*

(c) *Sorekara, mizu mo (hitotsu) onegaishimasu.*

Drill 6 (p. 73)

1. (a) *Futari* desu.

(b) *Kin'enseki* onegaishimasu.

(c) *Eigo no menyū* wa arimasu ka.

(d) *A-ranchi futatsu* to

(e) *kōhī futatsu* onegaishimasu.

(f) *Ato de* onegaishimasu.

(g) *Betsubetsu ni* onegaishimasu.

2. (a) *3-nin* desu.

(b) *Madogawa no tēburu* onegaishimasu.

(c) *Wain risuto* wa arimasu ka.

(d) *Aka-wain ippon* to

(e) *gurasu mittsu* onegaishimasu.

(f) —

(g) *Issho ni* onegaishimasu.

3. (a) *Futari* desu.

(b) *Kauntā* onegaishimasu.

(c) —

(d) *Chokorēto kēki hitotsu* to

(e) *kōhī zerī hitotsu* onegaishimasu.

(f) —

(g) —

4. (a) *4-nin* desu.

(b) —

(c) *Koshitsu* wa arimasu ka.

(d) *Kitsune udon futatsu* to

(e) *zarusoba futatsu* onegaishimasu.

(f) —

(g) *Betsubetsu ni* onegaishimasu.

5. (a) *5-nin* desu.

(b) —

(c) *Koshitsu* wa arimasu ka.

(d) *Nigiri itsutsu* to

(e) _bīru 2-hon_ onegaishimasu.

(f) _Saki ni_ onegaishimasu.

(g) _Issho ni_ onegaishimasu.

Drill 7 (p. 74)

1. c   2. b   3. d   4. e   5. a

Drill 8 (p. 74)

1. c   2. a   3. b   4. d

Drill 9 （解答例） (p. 74)

1. Eigo no menyū wa arimasu ka.

2. Mizu, onegaishimasu.

3. Betsubetsu ni onegai dekimasu ka.

4. Bejitarian no ranchi wa arimasu ka.

5. 3-nin desu.

6. Kin'enseki, onegaishimasu.

7. Kōhī wa saki ni onegaishimasu.

8. Kādo de onegai dekimasu ka.

Drill 10 (p. 75)

1. c   2. b   3. d   4. a

Drill 11 (p. 75)

1. (c) → a → b → d

2. (c) → b → f → e → d → (a)

Lesson 6

Comprehension Drill

● **Dialogue 1** (p. 80)

1. 1. F   2. DK   3. T   4. T   5. F

2. b → d → e → a → (c)

● **Dialogue 2** (p. 82)

1. F   2. T   3. T   4. DK   5. F

Drill 1 （解答例） (p. 86)

1. (a) Sumimasen, Kabuki-za no chikaku made onegaishimasu.

   (b) Yūbinkyoku no tokoro o migi e onegaishimasu.

   (c) Koko de ii desu.

2. (a) Sumimasen, Ochanomizu-eki made onegaishimasu.

   (b) Sotobori-dōri o massugu itte kudasai.

   (c) Tsugi no tsugi no kōsaten o hidari e onegaishimasu.

3. (a) Sumimasen, kono densha, Yokohama ni ikimasu ka.

   (b) Arigatō gozaimasu.

4. (a) kono densha wa Kichijōji ni tomarimasu ka.

   (b) Mukaigawa desu ka.

   (c) Arigatō gozaimasu.

5. (a) Ginza e ikitai n desu ga, basutei wa koko desu ka.

   (b) Sumimasen, mō sukoshi yukkuri hanashite kudasai.

   (c) Arigatō gozaimasu.

Drill 2 (p. 87)

1. d   2. h   3. i   4. j   5. e   6. g   7. b   8. f

9. c   10. a

Drill 3 （略）

Drill 4 （解答例） (p. 88)

1. (b) Massugu

2. (b) Tsugi no kōsaten o migi e

3. (b) Futatsu-me no shingō o hidari e

4. (b) Tsukiatari o hidari e

5. (b) Hodōkyō no tokoro o migi e

Drill 5 (p. 89)

1. e   2. c   3. b   4. a   5. d

Drill 6 (p. 90)

	A	B	C
Dialogue 1	b	a	c
Dialogue 2	a	d	a
Dialogue 3	d	b	b

Drill 7 （解答例） (p. 90)

1. Tōkyō-eki no chikaku made onegaishimasu.

2. Futatsu-me no shingō o migi e onegaishimasu.

3. Massugu itte kudasai.

4. Tsugi no kōsaten o hidari e onegaishimasu.

5. Kono hen de ii desu.

6. Kono densha wa Shinbashi ni tomarimasu ka.

7. Ginza ni ikitai n desu ga, basutei wa koko desu ka.

8. Shimoda-yuki no densha wa dore desu ka.

Drill 8 (p. 91)

1. d   2. b   3. a   4. c

Drill 9 (p. 91)

1. (a) → c → b → d → e

2. (d) → b → c → a

Lesson 7

Comprehension Drill
● **Dialogue 1** (p. 94)
1. 1. T 2.F 3. DK 4.T 5. F
2. d → e → a → c → (b)
● **Dialogue 2** (p. 95)
1. T 2. F 3. DK 4. T 5. F

Drill 1 （解答例） (p. 100)
1. (a) *Sumimasen. Kutsu-uriba wa doko desu ka.*
   (b) *Josei-yō desu.*
   (c) *Arigatō gozaimasu.*
2. (a) *Sumimasen. Kore to onaji pen wa arimasu ka.*
   (b) *Sō desu ka. 7-kai desu ne.*
3. (a) *Sumimasen. Yasui-san wa imasu ka.*
   (b) *A, hontō da. Dōmo.*
4. (a) *Kawashima-san wa doko desu ka.*
   (b) *Sō desu ka.*
5. (a) *ATM (ētīemu) wa doko desu ka.*
   (b) *Chika desu ne.*

Drill 2 （略）
Drill 3 (p. 101)
1. <u>*Hochikisu*</u> wa doko ni **arimasu** ka.
2. <u>*Jidō hanbaiki*</u> wa doko ni **arimasu** ka.
3. <u>*Shorui*</u> wa doko ni **arimasu** ka.
4. <u>*Takagi buchō*</u> wa doko ni **imasu** ka.
5. <u>*Yasui-san*</u> wa doko ni **imasu** ka.

Drill 4 (p. 102)
1. ④ 2. ⑥ 3. ③ 4. ② ⑤ 5. ①
Drill 5 (p. 102)
1. ④ 2. ⑥ 3. ⑤ 4. ② 5. ①
Drill 6 (p. 103)
1. ③ 2. ⑤ 3. ① 4. ② 5. ⑥
Drill 7 (p. 104)
R–(1) 5F–(3) 4F–(×) 3F–(5)
2F–(2) 1F–(×) B1F–(4)
Drill 8 （解答例） (p. 104)
1. *Pen wa doko desu ka.*
2. *Pen wa shiroi kyabinetto no ue desu.*
3. *Kawashima-san wa doko desu ka.*
4. *Kawashima-san wa kaigishitsu ni imasu.*
5. *Toire wa doko desu ka.*
6. *Toire wa erebētā no tonari desu.*
7. *Akagawa-san no tsukue wa doko desu ka.*
8. *Howaito-san wa seki ni imasen.*

Drill 9 (p. 105)
1. b 2. d 3. c 4. a
Drill 10 (p. 105)
1. c → b → a
2. (d) → c → e → a → b

Lesson 8

Comprehension Drill
● **Dialogue 1** (p. 109)
1. 1. T 2. DK 3. T 4. F 5. F
2. (c) → a → b → d → e
● **Dialogue 2** (p. 110)
1. F 2. T 3. F 4. DK 5. T

Drill 1 （解答例） (p. 114)
1. (a) *Giri no ryōshin ga Amerika kara kimasu. Issho ni Kyōto e ikimasu.*
   (b) *Iroiro shitai desu. Otera o mimasu. Kaimono o shimasu.*
2. (a) *Ē, nomimasu.*
   (b) *Wain o sukoshi nomimasu.*
   (c) *Iie. Tsuma/Otto wa nomimasen.*
3. (a) *Kazoku to kōen e ikimasu.*
   (b) *Hai, arimasu. Soko de hirugohan o tabemasu.*
   (c) *Ongaku o kikimasu. Hon ya zasshi o yomimasu.*
4. (a) *Yasui-san wa, asagohan wa nani o tabemasu ka.*
   (b) *Tōsuto to kōhī desu.*
5. (a) *Kamakura e ikimashita.*
   (b) *Tomodachi to ikimashita.*
   (c) *Iie. Mimasendeshita.*

Drill 2 (p. 116)

1. *tabemasu* — (*tabemasen*) — *tabemashita* — *tabemasendeshita*

2. *nomimasu* — *nomimasen* — (*nomimashita*) — *nomimasendeshita*

3. *mimasu* — *mimasen* — *mimashita* — (*mimasendeshita*)

4. *yomimasu* — (*yomimasen*) — *yomimashita* — *yomimasendeshita*

5. *kikimasu* — *kikimasen* — (*kikimashita*) — *kikimasendeshita*

Drill 3 (p. 116)

1. *Eiga <u>o mimasu</u>.*

2. *Shōchū <u>o nomimasu</u>.*

3. *Ongaku <u>o kikimasu</u>.*

4. *Shinbun <u>o yomimasu</u>.*

5. *Sushi o <u>tabemasu</u>.*

Drill 4 (p. 117)

1. <u>*Shūmatsu eigakan de*</u> *eiga o mimasu.*

2. <u>*Konban izakaya de*</u> *shōchū o nomimasu.*

3. <u>*Mainichi densha no naka de*</u> *ongaku o kikimasu.*

4. <u>*Maiasa uchi de*</u> *shinbun o yomimasu.*

5. <u>*Doyōbi ni resutoran de*</u> *sushi o tabemasu.*

Drill 5 （略）

Drill 6 (p. 118)

1. *Nichiyōbi <u>ni</u> yoku <u>×</u> kazoku <u>to</u> bōringu <u>o</u> shimasu.*

2. *Kawashima-san <u>wa</u> itsumo <u>×</u> kaisha <u>de</u> shinbun <u>o</u> yomimasu.*

3. *Watashi <u>wa</u> amari <u>×</u> uchi <u>de</u> bangohan <u>o</u> tabemasen.*

4. *Tsuma to watashi <u>wa</u> doyōbi <u>ni</u> uchi <u>de</u> sukoshi <u>×</u> wain <u>o</u> nomimasu.*

5. *Watashi <u>wa</u> zenzen <u>×</u> tegami <u>o</u> kakimasen.*

Drill 7 (p. 118)

Dialogue 1 — tomorrow / nearby park / play soccer / friends

Dialogue 2 — this weekend / Kamakura / do some shopping / girl friend

Dialogue 3 — Saturday / park in Shinjuku / see the blossoms / family

Dialogue 4 — next week / Hokkaido / eat crab / colleagues

Drill 8 （解答例） (p. 119)

1. 14th—Japanese lesson at 7 p.m.

2. 19th, 21st—Tennis

3. 6th—Movie in Ginza with Tsukada-san

4. 12th—Bought a TV at Bic Camera

5. 17th—Drinks in Shinjuku with Kacho

Drill 9 （解答例） (p. 119)

1. *Ashita wa nani o shimasu ka.*

2. *Uchi no chikaku no kōen e ikimasu.*

3. *Kōen de nani o shimasu ka.*

4. *Tomodachi to tenisu o shimasu.*

5. *Senshū no doyōbi wa nani o shimashita ka.*

6. *Asakusa e ikimashita.*

7. *Asakusa de nani o shimashita ka.*

8. *Nihon no omiyage o kaimashita.*

Drill 10 (p. 120)

1. d   2. a   3. b   4. c

Drill 11 (p. 120)

1. (d) → c → a → b

2. (c) → e → b → d → a

Lesson 9

Comprehension Drill

● **Dialogue 1** (p. 123)

1.   1. T   2. F   3. F   4. T   5. DK

2.   b → e → d → a → (c)

● **Dialogue 2** (p. 125)

1. F   2. T   3. F   4. DK   5. T

Drill 1 （解答例） (p. 129)

1. *Kinō no Tokyō no tenki wa dō deshita ka.*

2. (a) *Totemo ii ryokō deshita. Tanoshikatta desu.*

   (b) *Tatoeba Nara no daibutsu desu. Subarashikatta desu.*

3. *Ē, okagesama de, mainichi isogashii desu.*

4. (a) *A, kore? Dōzo.*

   (b) *Ē. Sore ni karui desu. Kono dezain mo suki desu.*

   (c) *Nikon no desu.*

5. (a) *Kono shiroi kappu wa dō desu ka.*

(b) *Ūn, sō desu ne. Demo chotto ōkii desu ne.*

(c) *Kono kuroi no wa chotto omoi desu ne.*

(d) *Yappari, shiroi no ga ii desu ne.*

Drill 2 (p. 131)

1. (*takai desu*) — *takakunai desu* — *takakatta desu* — *takakunakatta desu*

2. *oishii desu* — (*oishikunai desu*) — *oishikatta desu* — *oishikunakatta desu*

3. *isogashii desu* — *isogashikunai desu* — (*isogashikatta desu*) — *isogashikunakatta desu*

4. *samui desu* — *samukunai desu* — *samukatta desu* — (*samukunakatta desu*)

5. *omoshiroi desu* — (*omoshirokunai desu*) — *omoshirokatta desu* — *omoshirokunakatta desu*

6. *ii desu* — *yokunai desu* — (*yokatta desu*) — *yokunakatta desu*

7. (*benri desu*) — *benri ja arimasen* — *benri deshita* — *benri ja arimasendeshita*

8. *hima desu* — (*hima ja arimasen*) — *hima deshita* — *hima ja arimasendeshita*

9. *kirei desu* — *kirei ja arimasen* — (*kirei deshita*) — *kirei ja arimasendeshita*

10. *suki desu* — *suki ja arimasen* — *suki deshita* — (*suki ja arimasendeshita*)

Drill 3 （略）

Drill 4 (p. 132)

1. *Shinsen na sarada o tabemashita.*

2. *Shizuka na resutoran e ikimasu.*

3. *Furui tomodachi ga kimasu.*

4. *Suteki na hito desu.*

5. *Amai dezāto ga suki desu.*

Drill 5 (p. 132)

1. *dō* 2. *Nani* 3. *Donna* 4. *dō* 5. *donna*

Drill 6 (p. 133)

1. b 2. c. 3. a. 4. a. 5. c.

Drill 7 (p. 134)

1. a, d 2. b, c 3. a, d 4. a, c 5. b, c

Drill 8 （解答例）(p. 134)

1. *Natsuyasumi wa dō deshita ka.*

2. *Okagesama de, totemo tanoshikatta desu.*

3. *Tenki wa dō deshita ka.*

4. *Tenki wa amari yokunakatta desu.*

5. *Konshū no kin'yōbi wa isogashii desu ka.*

6. *Iie, isogashikunai desu.*

7. *Atarashii uchi wa dō desu ka.*

8. *Eki no chikaku desu kara, benri desu.*

Drill 9 (p. 134)

1. c 2. d 3. a 4. b

Drill 10 (p. 135)

1. (b) → a → d → c

2. (a) → d → b → c

Lesson 10

Comprehension Drill

● **Dialogue 1** (p. 138)

1. 1. F 2. F 3. T 4. DK 5. T

2. c → b → (e) → a → d

● **Dialogue 2** (p. 140)

1. F 2. T 3. DK 4. T 5. F

Drill 1 （解答例）(p. 144)

1. (a) *Doyōbi, issho ni eiga ni ikimasen ka.*

(b) *(Reddo Kurifu [Red Cliff]) wa dō desu ka.*

2. (a) *Ē, hima desu yo.*

(b) *Hai. Zehi ikitai desu.*

(c) *Doko de aimashō ka.*

3. (a) *Sumimasen. Chotto ii desu ka.*

(b) *Tōkyō no kankō wa doko ga ii desu ka.*

(c) *Omiyage o kaitai desu. Nani ga ii desu ka.*

(d) *Sore wa nan desu ka.*

4. (a) *Iie. Yotei wa arimasen.*

(b) *Ii desu ne. Ikitai desu.*

(c) *Hai. Wakarimashita.*

5. (a) *Hai. Nan deshō ka.*

(b) *Ōsutoraria no doko desu ka.*

(c) *Sō desu ne . . . Burū maunten wa dō desu ka.*

Drill 2 (p. 145)

1. (*ikimasen ka*) — *ikimashō* — *ikanai?* — *ikō*
2. *nomimasen ka* — *nomimashō* — *nomanai?* — (*nomō*)
3. *aimasen ka* — *aimashō* — (*awanai?*) — *aō*
4. *tabemasen ka* — (*tabemashō*) — *tabenai?* — *tabeyō*
5. (*shimasen ka*) — *shimashō* — *shinai?* — *shiyō*
6. *kimasen ka* — (*kimashō*) — *konai?* — *koyō*

Drill 3 (p. 146)

1. A: <u>*Ashita eiga o mimasen ka.*</u>
   B: *Hai,* <u>*mimashō.*</u>
2. A: <u>*Mō kaerimasen ka.*</u>
   B: *Sō desu ne,* <u>*kaerimashō.*</u>
3. A: <u>*Ato de kōhī o nomimasen ka.*</u>
   B: *Ii desu yo,* <u>*nomimashō.*</u>
4. A: <u>*Issho ni bangohan o tabemasen ka.*</u>
   B: *Hai,* <u>*tabemashō.*</u>
5. A: <u>*Raishū, Yokohama e ikimasen ka.*</u>
   B: *Hai,* <u>*ikimashō.*</u>

Drill 4 (p. 147)

1. *doko* 2. *itsu* 3. *nani* 4. *dare* 5. *doko*

Drill 5 （略）

Drill 6 (p. 147)

1. b 2. a 3. c 4. a 5. b

Drill 7 (p. 148)

1. b 2. c 3. b 4. c 5. a

Drill 8 （解答例） (p. 148)

1. *Sakura wa itsu ga ii desu ka.*
2. *3-gatsu no owari kara 4-gatsu made desu.*
3. *Kondo no shūmatsu, hima desu ka.*
4. *Issho ni resutoran e ikimasen ka / ikanai?*
5. *Hai, ikimashō. / Un, ikō.*
6. *(Gozen) 10-ji ni robī de aimashō ka / aō ka.*
7. *10-ji wa chotto. 11-ji wa dō desu ka.*
8. *(Jā), (gozen) 11-ji ni robī de.*

Drill 9 (p. 149)

1. b 2. d 3. a 4. c

Drill 10 (p. 149)

1. (b) → c → d → a
2. (c) → b → d → a

Index

Profile of OLG

Some of the co-authors of *Basic Japanese for Expats* formerly taught Japanese at Pegasus Language Services (PLS), which was an in-company language training program run by Mobil Sekiyu K.K. from 1971 to 1994. Due to corporate restructuring, PLS was closed at the end of 1994, and Otemachi Language Group, Ltd. (OLG; Representative Director: Keiko Kawai) was established to continue providing the same services to expatriates and their families.

While its mainstream business is to provide Japanese language training programs to company employees and their families, OLG has extensively diversified its activities. OLG launched a teacher training program in August 2002, as well as "Kids English" and "Club Japanese" programs at a fitness club in August and September 2002, respectively. These were followed by the establishment of an intensive Japanese language training program and curriculum consulting services for Chinese employees of a Japanese company in December 2002, and the inauguration of Japanese programs at a university in April 2003. Furthermore, OLG has written *Catchy Japanese Phrases* (2003) and *Catchy Japanese Phrases II* (2005), which were published by The Japan Times, Ltd.

　本書の著者の一部は、1971 年より 94 年まで、モービル石油（株）の社内語学研修機関ペガサス・ランゲージ・サービス（PLS）でビジネスピープルとその家族の日本語教育に従事。1994 年 12 月、リストラによる閉鎖を機に、有志と共に Otemachi Language Group (OLG)（有）（代表：川井恵子）を設立した。

　OLG は、企業の社員とその家族向けの日本語教育を主流業務とするが、その他の業務も展開している。2002 年 8 月、日本語教師養成講座を開設。同 8 月、フィットネスクラブに Kids English 及び Club Japanese を開設。同年 12 月より中国人社員の日本語研修及びカリキュラム・コンサルティングを担当。また、2003 年 4 月より大学の日本語教育にも参入した。さらに、『日本語丸暗記帳』(2003)、『日本語丸暗記帳 II』(2005) をジャパンタイムズから出版、今日にいたる。

Authors（著者）
　　Keiko Kawai（川井恵子）
　　Yukari Ikeda（池田ゆかり）
　　Akane Miyakawa（宮川あかね）
　　Chie Fujii（藤井知恵）